Warman's

Records

FIELD GUIDE

Edited by Tim Neely

©2004 Krause Publications

Published by

 **krause publications**
An F+W Publications Company

700 East State Street • Iola, WI 54990-0001
715-445-2214 • 888-457-2873
www.krause.com

Our toll-free number to place an order or obtain
a free catalog is (800) 258-0929.

Library of Congress Catalog Number: 2004100945

ISBN: 0-87349-863-1

Designed by Kim Schierl

Edited by Tracy Schmidt

Printed in the United States

Contents

W elcome to the Warman's® Records Field Guide.
Inside this book you'll find a cross-section of
both common and hard-to-find items, mostly
from the 1955-1989 era, but with a few earlier and later
items as well.

Rather than try to focus on any one genre or type of
record, we have chosen approximately 200 different
popular recording artists of the past 50 years. These artists,
who are in alphabetical order, encompass mostly the genres
of pop, rock, country, and rhythm & blues. For each of
them, we have illustrated a popular or interesting, or both,
album cover or 45 rpm picture sleeve from their catalog.
Underneath that photo, we say what it is, give other
identifying information, and add a range of values.

On the facing page for each artist, you'll see a list of 10
to 15 other records by that same performer, listed first by
type of record (usually 45 or LP, but sometimes seven-inch
extended play discs, abbreviated EP, and 12-inch singles),
then alphabetically by the record's title. Once again, each of
these is explained, with a range of prices given.

Finally, each artist has an "MVP," or "Most Valuable Platter."
Based on information in the Krause Publications records
database, the listed record is either the most valuable, or
one of the most valuable, records in the performer's
catalog. We thoroughly describe it, as many of these are rare

variations of otherwise common items. Some of the price ranges for these items may astound you.

After the alphabetical artist section, we continue with a series of "stand-alone" albums and 45 rpm sleeves. Some of these are by performers for whom two pages are hopelessly inadequate; some of these are by artists whose material, even if we listed all of it, would not fill two pages; others are by artists that otherwise are not in the main section of the book. Once again, each of the photos is identified and a range of prices follows.

Important! The value range is for examples in *excellent to near mint condition only.* In other words, to get a price in the range given, the record must show few signs of wear of any kind – they must be in at least *excellent* (or *very good plus*) condition, and preferably even better. The higher prices are reserved for those discs that look as if they just came from a retail shop. Records that do not meet this stringent standard are worth less than the values in the book, and sometimes are literally worthless for common titles.

Also, the values listed are specific for the labels and numbers listed, and for the type of record listed. If they don't match, they aren't worth these prices.

Finally, only *records* are listed, not compact discs or tapes. Some of the items in this book were released as recently as 2003; even those listings are vinyl records. Despite beliefs to the contrary, records are still being manufactured, and in some cases, they are quite rare and valuable.

We have made no attempt to be complete in this book. If this is your first glimpse into record collecting, and you want to learn more than what you see here, we recommend several titles, depending on your level of interest:

— *Goldmine Records & Prices*

— *Goldmine Record Album Price Guide*

— *Goldmine Price Guide to 45 RPM Records*

— *Goldmine Standard Catalog Of®*
  American Records, 1950-1975

— *Goldmine Standard Catalog Of®*
  American Records, 1976-Present

Other titles exist in the *Goldmine* series, but these are the most general.

We hope you enjoy this book and that it may spur you on to re-discovering, or discovering for the first time, some great music. Happy collecting!

Tim Neely

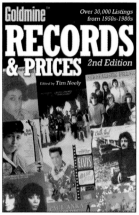

*Goldmine Records
& Prices*

*Goldmine Record
Album Price Guide*

*Goldmine Standard
Catalog Of®
American Records,
1950-1975*

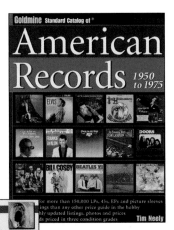

*Goldmine Standard
Catalog Of®
American Records,
1976-Present*

Record collecting's "holy grails"

Learn to know and love these records

by John Koenig

What excites you? Does the opportunity to find a nice copy of that long-desired and searched-for record take your breath away?

Many collectors always carry lists with them of records they are looking for. Sometimes it's the titles or variations they need for their collection. That obscure 45 rpm B-side may turn up at any time, and if you own a great many records (as if that's a problem!) it's often difficult to remember whether you own one particular record or not. Often the list is comprised of what they have, so if a record in their hands isn't on the list, it's needed.

Other lists are often of records they've read about or perhaps heard legendary stories of. Some music collectors are fortunate enough to live in an area with a college radio station, which turns them on to new sounds. Or they read the reviews in collecting publications such as *Discoveries* and *Goldmine*, which lead people to the best in both new recordings, reissues and compilations.

But the single most common list carried by dealers and collectors, whether on paper or in their heads, is the "holy grail" checklist. These are the records that are so valuable, so collectible, that everyone is on the lookout for them. Whether one likes the music or the artists on these records doesn't make a difference. Learn about these collectibles and keep the data stored somewhere, 'cause if you have the opportunity to pull one of these out of a dealer's stock at a show or from that dusty box of records under a table at a flea market, you want to recognize what you're seeing and buy it. (Price guides such as the *Goldmine Standard Catalog Of® American Records 1950-1975* is a good resource in order to look up the tiny variations that may make a difference in knowing if a record is the valuable edition.)

1. David Bowie — *Diamond Dogs*. Released in 1974 on RCA, the rare cover clearly features a dog's genitals. Almost all copies were destroyed prior to release, creating a collectible album worth several thousand dollars in near-mint condition. It's not clear whether copies actually ever made it to retail shelves; virtually all the known copies came from people inside the industry.

2. Nirvana — "Love Buzz"/"Big Cheese" was released in 1988 on Sub Pop Records (23). The very first Nirvana single, the label pressed only 1,000 copies in a hand-numbered edition, in a picture sleeve. Today it's worth a good $1,500. Considered the most important band of the 1990s, Nirvana has proven to be a collectible artist.

3. Bob Dylan — *The Freewheelin' Bob Dylan*. This 1963 Columbia release was initially shipped with four songs on it that created a ruckus, to the point that the album was recalled and reissued without them. The titles in question are "Let Me Die In My Footsteps," "Rocks And Gravel," "Talkin' John Birch Blues" and "Gamblin' Willie's Dead Man's Hand." Find a copy of the record with these songs on the album and listed on the cover, and you'll have a record worth $15,000 to $30,000.

4. The Beatles — *Butcher Cover*. Much has been written about this Capitol recording over the years, making it well known to more than just collectors. In 1966, when The Beatles released *Yesterday And Today*, they decided that a cover showing them wearing butcher's smocks, smeared with blood and with dismembered baby doll bodies scattered about, was a good idea. Capitol Records went along with them (it was The Beatles, after all), and the album was shipped. Immediately, there was a huge outcry of alarm from

The 1966 *Yesterday And Today* album by The Beatles was initially released with the above cover photograph. Pulled from the market and pasted over, these *Butcher Cover*s are highly collectible today. Even the *Butcher Cover*s that were pasted over with the trunk cover are collectible as well. How can you tell if you have a *Butcher Cover* underneath your copy? Look for Ringo Starr's turtleneck, which shows through the white cover fairly easily (at arrow, below). Today, collectors recommend *not* removing the top cover, not only because of the risk of damage, but because fewer "paste-over" jackets remain intact.

Courtesy of Bruce Spizer's The Beatles' Story On Capitol Records

the rack jobbers, distributors and stores, so Capitol immediately recalled all of them.

A small number of the *Butcher Cover*s made it to retail sale and into customers' hands. Others were kept by personnel at Capitol Records and elsewhere along the distribution chain. The new covers were literally pasted over the old and re-shipped. Close examination will reveal the old cover under the new.

Original *Butcher Cover* albums never pasted over are called "first state" and are the most desirable. They are worth thousands of dollars. *Butcher*s pasted over, even though they're far from rare, are highly collectible and desirable. The publicity afforded this record over the years has created constant, high demand for it from collectors and any Beatles fan. An excellent or very good–plus condition cover pasted over is still worth up to $500.

5. Jimi Hendrix — The original *Electric Ladyland* album, released in England on Track Records in 1968, features naked women on the cover and is worth several thousand dollars. Hendrix, by the way, was aghast at the cover. This cover was never released in the United States. Most copies that show up today are pretty beat and not worth too much, if they're on Track. Track was later absorbed by Polydor Records, who kept printing the naked cover version, so they're worth only $50 to $60 today.

An American Reprise label stock copy of *Axis: Bold As Love*, also from 1968, in mono, is worth several thousand dollars.

6. Elvis Presley Sun Records. The reason people search out Sun records is for Elvis Presley. These are basically the records that created rock 'n' roll. All five of Presley's singles on Sun are avidly sought after, ranging in value from $1,000-$6,000, depending upon condition. These records form the cornerstone of any solid rock 'n' roll collection.

The songs include: "That's All Right"/"Blue Moon Of Kentucky" (Sun 209), "Good Rockin' Tonight"/"I Don't Care If The Sun Don't Shine" (Sun 210), "You're A Heartbreaker"/"Milkcow Blues Boogie" (Sun 215), "Baby Let's Play House"/"I'm Left, You're Right, She's Gone" (Sun 217), "Mystery Train"/"I Forgot To Remember To Forget" (Sun 223).

Presley's Sun 45 were also released on 78 rpm records with the same catalog numbers. They are also highly collectible but only go for about half the price of a Presley Sun 45.

From a collectible perspective there are rare rockabilly singles that are valuable, though all are obscure. Other notable artists on Sun were Johnny Cash, Jerry Lee Lewis, and Roy Orbison, but generally speaking, their recordings

Above are the Side 1 and Side 2 labels of one of the two known stereo copies of *The Freewheelin' Bob Dylan* that include four songs quickly removed from the LP. On Side 1, songs 2 and 3 were replaced, and on Side 2, songs 2 and 5 were replaced. Adding to the strangeness, on these discs — both sides of which have the suffix "-1A" attached to the master numbers in the trail-off wax — song 3, "Let Me Die In My Footsteps," and song 6, " A Hard Rain's A-Gonna Fall," are in the wrong order. The last time a copy of this record was sold, in 2002, it went for about $30,000.

An obscure single and its flip side, featuring Jimi Hendrix on guitar, from 1966: Jimmy Norman's "You're Only Hurting Yourself"/"That Little Old Groovemaker" on Samar Records. The original mixes for these songs are available only on these 45s. Versions that appear on later compilations are drastically different.

Courtesy of Niko Bauer, www.earlyhendrix.com

aren't that valuable.

7. Prewar blues 78s. These old shellac records are the standard bearers for collectible pre–World War II music. The recordings produced by performers such as Robert Johnson and Charley Patton went on to heavily influence rock musicians from the 1960s onward. Several of their songs were covered and became hits, decades later, by white rock groups.

Manufactured in much lower quantities than those released after WWII, prewar blues 78s are generally much more valuable than their postwar counterparts. Look for the Paramount Records label or slogans such as "Vocalian race records" on a label.

8. The Rolling Stones — "Street Fighting Man" 45 rpm picture sleeve (1968). This is a normal production sleeve that was recalled, as it was deemed objectionable due to the cover. There are only about a dozen known copies. It was distributed, so chances are there are additional copies somewhere. This is worth $10,000.

9. The MC5 — "Looking At You"/ "Borderline" (1967). The record itself is worth $150 today and the sleeve an additional $350. This is a very rare record by an influential band. Often found without the sleeve, A2 Records seems to have pressed many more records than they did sleeves.

10. The Beatles — "My Bonnie." The Decca 45 issued in 1962 under the name Tony Sheridan & The Beat Brothers is the first record released by The Beatles, even though it doesn't have their name on it. The multicolored label stock copy is worth a lot, around $20,000, while a pink label promo copy is worth "only" $2,000.

11. Bruce Springsteen — "Blinded By The Light" (1972) on Columbia is a solid $500 record, and the picture sleeve alone sells for $500. The second single, "Spirit In The Night" sells for $1,500 (no picture sleeve for this exists). This is a straight Columbia single from 1973.

12. The Beach Boys — "Surfin'" on X Records, their first single from 1961. The Candix version is a reissue, though it's a matter of contention and they came out about the same time. The X single is much rarer. This is a good $1,000 record. No pic sleeve exists.

13. The Sex Pistols — "God Save The Queen" picture sleeve, U.K. A&M, 1977. The original sleeve is worth a solid $4,000 to $5,000 and is extremely rare. Only a few copies were in existence until someone found some in the London A&M offices a few years ago and they made it onto the secondary market. Counterfeits abound, and most copies for sale today are fake. This is the most important punk record of the era.

14. Frank Wilson — "Do I Love You, Indeed I Do"

Released in 1962, "My Bonnie" was the first record ever released with The Beatles performing, even though their names are not on the label. One of these records changed hands at *Goldmine*'s National Record Show™ at The Rock And Roll Hall Of Fame in Cleveland in the summer of 2003.

MY BONNIE
(Arr: Tony Sheridan)

DECCA

REG. U.S. PAT. OFF. MARCA REGISTRADA
MFD. BY DECCA RECORDS INC. NEW YORK - U.S.A.

RECORD NO.
31382
(40 66 833 A)
(2:58)

TONY SHERIDAN
AND THE BEAT BROTHERS
Vocal With Instrumental Accompaniment
RECORDED IN EUROPE BY DEUTSCHE
GRAMMOPHON/POLYDOR (R) SERIES

At left is dealer Rodney Branham, who purchased it from the walk-in seller — and who sold it later that day to another dealer for $3,500.

©2003 Goldmine/by Chuck Miller

— Soul 35019, 1966. Wilson wrote the song, the label pressed the 45 as a promo but didn't want to release it. As far as anyone knows, all copies out there are promo copies. This is the rarest and most collectible Northern Soul record and is worth $25,000.

15. Early sides featuring Jim Hendrix on guitar — "(My Girl) She's A Fox" b/w "(I Wonder) What It Takes" (Samar S111) by The Icemen. Released in 1966, this single features Hendrix playing guitar. Lonnie Youngblood arranged the recording.

"You're Only Hurting Yourself" b/w "That Little Old Groovemaker" (Samar S112) by Jimmy Norman. Johnny Bratley produced this single in 1966, also with Hendrix on guitar. Over the years these songs have been edited, overdubbed and mislabeled and are sometimes coupled with a fake, Hendrix-like guitar player. They have appeared on numerous releases without any clarification.

The original mixes for The Icemen and Norman singles are available only on the Samar 45s issued in 1966.

To read more about collectible records, and in-depth articles about all genres and eras of music, subscribe to Discoveries *and* Goldmine. *(www.collect.com/records.)*

Record collecting's "problem children"

by John Koenig

If you're like other collectors, you have a mental checklist of vinyl albums you are watching for. These are the top 10 records to keep your eyes open for... *and avoid*!

1. Dave Mason — *Alone Together* (1970). Originally released with "marble" vinyl, this was made in huge quantities. It's common and retails for around $7.

2. Lynyrd Skynyrd — *Street Survivors* (1977). The wall of flames behind the band members on the LP cover was taken off after the band's airplane crashed, killing several members. Sealed, this version will bring around $40; the revised version without flames is worth about $12.

3. Elvis — *Moody Blue* (1977). Any copies of this *not* on blue vinyl are actually collectible; the blue vinyl is common. There is a black vinyl original that is quite rare and sells for $100. The black-vinyl edition with the ASL1 prefix is the original one; any other prefix in the label number is common and virtually worthless.

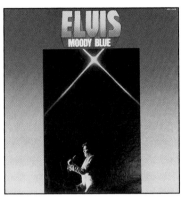

Right: The only valuable copies of Elvis' *Moody Blue* **are on black vinyl or some color** *other than* **blue.**

4. The Rolling Stones — *Their Satanic Majesties Request* (1967). The infamous 3-D cover isn't rare. Stereo copies with that cover bring $20.

5. The Who — *Live At Leeds* (1970). Many people find this album, stuffed with the reproductions of The Who's original contract from Woodstock and assorted other memorabilia, and somehow think that document showed up in a local yard sale. Not likely, is it? This is a $10 record, in "excellent" condition, with all the contents.

6. The Beatles — *White Album* (1968).

This album is valuable if the covers are really clean and are complete with the poster, four photos and a protective sheet. With everything there, in excellent condition, it's a $250 record. Otherwise, it's a $4 album.

7. *Introducing The Beatles* (1964). The most common version of this album is fake. This counterfeit has "Love Me Do" printed on the back cover, and "stereophonic" across the front. On the label, the band name and album title will be separated by the center hole of the record if it's fake. However, not all the copies with the words above the hole are genuine. If it doesn't say stereo anywhere on the label, it is fake and worthless.

8. The Rolling Stones — *Sticky Fingers* (1971). The first release has the working zipper on the front cover. Unfortunately for those who saved their copies, nearly every copy was saved, and there are huge quantities of them. Near-mint copies sell for $10.

9. Vaughn Meader — *First Family* LP (1962). Meader was once one of the best-selling celebrities in the world. This album sold millions of copies. Today, near-mint copies sell for only $1.

10. *JFK Memorial Album.* Released in 1963, this album is like old *Life* magazines; everyone seems to have kept theirs. near- mint copies sell for $3.

Thanks to Gary Johnson of Rockaway Records for his assistance.

John Koenig is the editor of Discoveries *magazine.*

Buying and selling tips

by Greg Loescher

I f you're thinking of quitting your day job because you think your record collection will carry you into retirement, stop right here. Few record dealers are rich. Many are part-timers and have other sources of income. All are certainly in it for the love of the music and the physical recordings. The money is secondary. That doesn't mean there isn't money to be made — and saved. Here are a few keys to successful buying and selling:

• **Condition is king** — Except in a few rare instances, unless a record is not in near-mint condition, collectors won't bite.

• **Become knowledgeable** — Read collector publications such as *Discoveries* and *Goldmine*. Attend record shows and record stores to talk with dealers and collectors. Look at online collectors sites. Purchase price guides. There are so many variations for the more valuable items that you need to make sure the copy you are buying or selling is indeed the rare one and not one of the commonly released pieces (the majority are the latter). Read the fine print for explanations as to what makes a particular recording valuable.

• **Curb your bidding enthusiasm online** — In the past decade the Internet has become a valuable tool for collectors. However, those in the know are amazed at how much some very common records go for online. Except for those recordings that are indeed extremely rare or one-of-a-kind pieces of memorabilia, with a little patience collectors should be able to pick up the same recordings for far less money at a used record store, show or through a mail-order dealer.

• **Price guides are just that, guides** — Demanding that a dealer or collector buy or sell a recording at a price listed in a guide just won't work. For one thing, dealers will only purchase an item at usually about a third of the price listed in the guides, and with more common vinyl, may not want the items at all. For another, regional and local collecting interests can dictate that certain artists and genres are worth more than elsewhere.

• **Buy because you like it** — "Investing" in records is worse than "guessing" at the stock market. Buy a record because you want to listen to it or enjoy the artwork and want to frame it. You'll be far happier *and* have more money to buy other recordings.

Definitions
to know

bootleg: something that was not put out by the artist's
record company.

counterfeit: produced to appear just like the original and is
meant to be sold as an original to an unsuspecting buyer.

cutout: an album that is sent back to the company unsold;
the company then sells the records to a mass merchandizer
at a great discount. These are marketed as cutouts with
notches or holes through a cover, for example.

DJ/promo copy: a promotional copy of an album sent to a
radio station. Often a promo record's catalog number, label
and/or cover will be different than the version of the album
sold in stores (and fewer copies pressed), thus making it
desirable to collectors.

rare/out of print: one problem is the overuse of the terms
"rare" and "out of print." Know what you're bidding on
before taking a seller's word that a piece is actually rare.
Just because something is out of print doesn't mean that it's
difficult to come by. Keep your eyes open; shop around.

reissue: a rerelease of an album a second time, often at a
much later date and not always by the same record
company as produced the first.

Caring for your records

by Tim Neely

Compared to many other collectibles, records are painless to maintain. But you can't merely stick them in a corner and do nothing, either.

If you want your records to stay in the same condition they were in when you bought them, here are a few pointers.

45s and 78s

If the records are no longer in any sleeves, the first thing you should do is to buy sleeves for them. Records that are not protected by sleeves are far more likely to get scuffed or scratched. Several mail-order companies sell generic white or various colored sleeves.

Always store the records on edge, never on top of each other.

Plastic sleeves, available from the same places where you buy paper sleeves, are a good way to protect picture sleeves. Store the records outside the sleeves. Keeping a record inside a picture sleeve can create ring wear on the sleeve, which will significantly decrease the value of the sleeve. If you want to keep them together, store the 45 in the same outer plastic sleeve as its picture sleeve, but *not* inside the picture sleeve. (See more tips on picture-sleeve care, p. 29.)

45s (and picture sleeves and albums) should be stored in protective sleeves.

Albums

As with other records, albums should always be stored on edge, *never* on top of one another.

Keeping the cover in top shape should be a priority. Plastic outer bags help protect the covers.

When storing records, whether in boxes or on shelves, don't pack them too tightly, as ring wear can result. Also, don't pack them too loosely, as cardboard covers can become misshapen over time.

You may wish to replace the inner sleeve that came with the album with a generic plastic-lined one, as often are found with classical or audiophile-oriented records. But don't throw out the original inner sleeve! Most of them from the 1970s forward have photos, song lyrics and other information, and saving the sleeve will enhance the value of the entire package.

Some collectors will even store the record and its inner sleeve outside the LP jacket but in the same outer plastic sleeve to keep them together. Some will consider this excessive, but it is a good way to prevent the bottom seam on the LP cover from splitting.

General

Make sure that your turntable is the best you can afford, and make sure that the stylus and tone arm are in good shape and properly aligned. (See p. 32 for suggestions on where to purchase a turntable.)

Always handle records gently by their edges and/or label area (in the case of a 45, using the large center hole and an edge is fine). Fingerprints can scuff a record, and they can be tough to remove.

After playing a record, return it to its sleeve as soon as possible.

Records are heavy! If you have a lot of them, consider investing in sturdy wooden shelves for storage.

Tim Neely is the author of many Goldmine *price guides.*

The care and feeding of picture sleeves

by Charles Szabla

If you're new to the hobby of assembling an impressive collection of 45 rpm sleeves, let's discuss their care and feeding. Storage and protection for your little darlings is a good place to start.

The first thing to do after returning home from a record show, second-hand store or flea market is to get that record out of the picture sleeve! You'll often see the phrase "ring wear" used to describe the condition of a sleeve. That's the result of keeping the record in the sleeve. Don't get me started on that nasty striated rib that Apple and Capitol put on their 45s. Whose vicious idea was that?

Stick the record into a plain white paper sleeve and gently slip the picture sleeve into a fresh 100-percent pure virgin polyethelyne clear-plastic sleeve. You can almost hear the sleeve breathe a sigh of comforted relief. In my case, I also add a piece of acid-free matboard behind the picture sleeve to decrease the risk of accidental bending or folding. Matboard can be purchased at any art supply store. Don't use cardboard as a cheap substitute. Cardboard is acidic and over time will yellow and deteriorate precious collectibles.

Once this is done, store the protected sleeve in a handy 45 record storage box. These are available in plastic or cardboard. Despite my rant on the evils of cardboard, I believe the cardboard storage boxes are satisfactory if one has already encased the picture sleeve in a polyethelyne sleeve. Paper sleeves, poly sleeves and storage boxes are available from a number of reputable mail- order sources. The cost will vary based on the type of sleeve chosen and quantity ordered. I use regular-weight white paper sleeves to store my records; ordered by the case (1-2,000) they average 4¢ a piece. The type of poly sleeve I like best are top-o'-the-line 6 mil thick. They're not cheap (between 9-14¢ depending on quantity), but man, it sure feels good sliding one of my most prized picture sleeves into one. Generally I find the 4 mil acceptable and the 2.5-3 mil adequate for storing sleeves you would like to upgrade eventually.

Finally I'd like to address the sticky issue of cleaning and repairing picture sleeves. My best advice is, "Don't bother." The risk of further damaging a sleeve by attempting to remove a sticker, taping together rips or tears, erasing pencil writing, rubbing away stains or any other well-meaning endeavor is too great.

However, I must admit to tackling the irritating issue of

sticker removal. I tried both rubber cement thinner and lighter fluid to dissolve the adhesive. It sounds slightly insane and definitely unsafe, but it occassionally worked. A few times it caused problems. A reaction between the solvent, adhesive and ink

Here you can see one of the dangers of attempting to remove tape from a picture sleeve. Ouch!

not only removed the sticky substance but also removed the ink, leaving a hideous faded splotch in the shape of the sticker. Luckily the only sleeves affected were ones by Debbie Gibson, Poison, and Journey. I reiterate, "Leave well enough alone." Now you see why sleeves in near-mint condition are so highly sought after; no muss, no fuss.

Charles Szabla writes Goldmine's *picture sleeve-collecting column,* Picture This!

Where to buy a turntable

Playing your records again doesn't cost much

by Greg Loescher

Despite the overwhelming dominance of CD sales over vinyl in the marketplace, vinyl is still being produced and turntables are still being manufactured, fueled in large part to the hip-hop and rap DJ explosion as well as collectors and those who just love the warmer sound of vinyl.

If you still have an old turntable that's been collecting dust over the years, it might just need a tuneup — a new belt or a new stylus — to get it running again. Take it down to a local electronics store and have it checked out before thinking about buying a new one, especially if your old turntable is a higher-priced model. With proper care turntables — as well as vinyl records — should last a lifetime or two.

If you don't already own a turntable or want to upgrade,

there are many options available both locally and through mail-order. Turntable prices can range from $100 for low-end models to $13,000 and higher for audiophile turntables produced by firms such as Basis (U.S.), Acoustic Signature (Germany), Clearaudio (Germany), Blue Note (Italy) and Kuzma (Slovenia).

National chain stores such as Best Buy or Circuit City stock basic turntables. Best Buy sells for just $149 an American Audio direct-drive turntable that plays 33 1/3 and 45 rpm records, while Circuit City carries Audio-Technica turntables for $99.

Deck systems with a turntable, CD player, cassette player and a radio are also available. Teac's DC-D2831 Mini System contains a three-speed turntable (33 1/3, 45, 78 rpm), a three-CD drawer-type changer, a dual-cassette deck and AM/FM stereo tuner. It retails for less than $200.

While Crosley Radio is better-known for its radios than any other product, it does carry a line of excellent turntables, including the CR49 suitcase-style turntable that retails for just $129. The CR49 is a self-contained unit with stereo speakers enclosed. The best part of the CR49 is that it plays 78, 45 and 33 1/3 rpm — and at a very reasonable price. The only drawback is that you can't hook up larger speakers to it — yet. (Crosley is working on it!) But it's perfect for casual listening or to bring to a record show to test records before buying them.

Professional DJs consider Technics the best turntable, with the SL-1200 MK2 quartz drive manual the turntable of choice, for under $400. Technics' popular SL-BD22 semi-automatic turntable retails for $210, although the company has a variety of turntables that sell for much more and a few for less. Technics' products are available at most major electronics stores and via mail order.

However, K-A-B USA's Kevin Barrett warns consumers they should steer clear of turntables with short, "straight" tonearms. Barrett said these are manufactured with "scratchers" in mind, as the arm stays in the record's grooves better and has limited distortion. Since they also cost a bit less than regular curved tonearms, struggling DJs buy them to also save some money. But Barrett said the straight tonearms will ruin records played in the conventional manner.

"The groove is asking the needle [on the short straight arm] to do something it can't do, thus turning [record] collections into nothing," he pointed out.

K-A-B USA is a mail-order firm that not only sells many varieties of turntables, but also stocks needles, turntable belts and mats, record-cleaning and record-care products and lots more. Its Web site's FAQ section contains a wealth of answers to turntable questions ranging from what types of needles should be used on a given turntable to connecting a turntable to a computer's soundcard. It also has a list of commonly used terms related to turntables.

Needle Doctor also sells turntables, including the high-end ones mentioned previously in this story, and it also has a close-out section on its Web site.

In addition to stocking needles, cartridges and belts, Needle Express has a database of technical information on more than 13,000 turntables.

With all of these options, there's no reason to leave your records unplayed any longer.

Greg Loescher is former editor of Goldmine *magazine and has a Technics turntable.*

TURNTABLES

CROSLEY RADIO
1-866-CROSLEY (1-866-276-7539)
www.crosleyradio.com/products/portable_turntables

KAB USA
908-754-1479   www.kabusa.com

PANASONIC/TECHNICS
www.panasonic.com
(Search site for "turntables"; also provides contact information for local stores that sell Technics turntables.)

REPLACEMENT NEEDLES

If you cannot locate a store locally that stocks needles and cartridges for turntables, these mail-order companies can help you. They also stock turntable belts.

K-A-B USA
908-754-1479   www.kabusa.com

NEEDLE DOCTOR
1-800-229-0644   www.needledoctor.com

NEEDLE EXPRESS
1-800-982-2620   www.needleexpress.com

NEEDLES UNLIMITED
1-800-662-8090

ABBA

LP, *Voulez-Vous*, Atlantic SD 16000, 1979...5.00 - 10.00

45, Dancing Queen/That's Me, Atlantic 3372, 1976 ....2.00 - 4.00
45, The Name of the Game/I Wonder (Departure), Atlantic 3449,
    1977...2.00 - 4.00
45, SOS/Man in the Middle, Atlantic 3265, 1975 ....2.50 - 5.00
45, Take a Chance on Me/I'm a Marionette, Atlantic 3457, 1978
    Record only...2.00 - 4.00
    Picture sleeve only..3.00 - 6.00
45, Waterloo/Watch Out, Atlantic 3035, 1974
    Record only...2.50 - 5.00
    Promotional picture sleeve only ....7.50 - 15.00
45, The Winner Takes It All/Elaine, Atlantic 3776, 1980
    ....2.00 - 4.00
LP, *Arrival*
    Atlantic SD 18207, 1977, original..6.00 - 12.00
    Atlantic SD 19115, 1977, reissue..5.00 - 10.00
    Nautilus NR-20, 1981, "Super Disc" on cover ....15.00 - 30.00
LP, *Greatest Hits*
    Atlantic SD 18189, 1976, original..6.00 - 12.00
    Atlantic SD 19114, 1977, reissue..5.00 - 10.00
LP, *Greatest Hits, Vol. 2*, Atlantic SD 16009, 1979 ....6.00 - 12.00
LP, *The Magic of Abba*, K-Tel NU 9510, 1978 ....7.50 - 15.00

MVP:

LP, *The Abba Special*, Atlantic PR 436 (2-record set), 1983, promotional
    issue only ....25.00 - 50.00

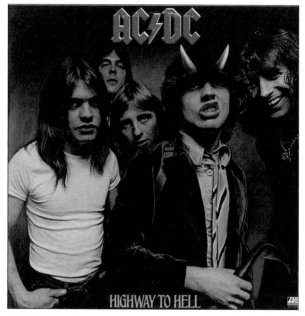

LP, *Highway to Hell*
    Atlantic SD 19244, 1979, original...5.00 - 10.00
    Epic E 80206, 2003, reissue...6.00 - 12.00

45, Back in Black/What Do You Do for Money Honey, Atlantic 3787,
   1980..2.50 - 5.00
45, Guns for Hire/Landslide, Atlantic 89774, 1983
   Record only..2.00 - 4.00
   Picture sleeve only..3.00 - 6.00
45, Highway to Hell/Night Prowler, Atlantic 3617, 1979 ....2.50 - 5.00
45, Let's Get It Up/Snowballed, Atlantic 3894, 1982
   Record only..2.00 - 4.00
   Picture sleeve only..3.00 - 6.00
45, You Shook Me All Night Long/Have a Drink on Me, Atlantic 3761,
   1980..2.50 - 5.00
LP, *Back in Black*
   Atlantic SD 16018, 1980, original...5.00 - 10.00
   Epic E 80207, 2003, reissue..6.00 - 12.00
LP, *Dirty Deeds Done Dirt Cheap*
   Atlantic SD 16033, 1981, original...5.00 - 10.00
   Epic E 80202, 2003, reissue..6.00 - 12.00
LP, *For Those About to Rock We Salute You*
   Atlantic SD 11111, 1981, original...5.00 - 10.00
   Epic E 80208, 2003, reissue..6.00 - 12.00
LP, *The Razors Edge*
   Atco 91413, 1990, original..7.50 - 15.00
   Epic E 80213, 2003, reissue..6.00 - 12.00

MVP:

LP, *AC/DC*, Epic 90643 (16-record set), 2003, box set with 15 albums on 16
   records in black slipcase..100.00 - 200.00

LP, *Aerosmith*
Columbia KC 32005, 1973, orange cover with correct title "Walking The Dog"
    on back cover..7.50 - 15.00
Columbia KC 32005, 1973, orange cover with back cover typo "Walking The Dig"
    on back cover...10.00 - 20.00
Columbia KC 32005, 1970s, light blue cover, most (if not all) of which say
    "Featuring 'Dream On' " on front..6.00 - 12.00

45, Dream On/Somebody
    Columbia 4-45894, 1973, with remixed edited version of "Dream On"
    ....3.00 - 6.00
    Columbia 3-10278, 1975, with album version of "Dream On"........2.50 - 5.00
45, Dude (Looks Like a Lady)/Simoriah, Geffen 7-28240, 1987
    Record only..1.50 - 3.00
    Picture sleeve only...1.50 - 3.00
45, Walk This Way/Round and Round, Columbia 3-10206, 1975 ....3.00 - 6.00
45, Walk This Way/Uncle Salty, Columbia 3-10449, 1976 ....2.50 - 5.00
LP, *Aerosmith's Greatest Hits*
    Columbia FC 36865, 1980...5.00 - 10.00
    Columbia PC 36865, 1984...4.00 - 8.00
LP, *Permanent Vacation*, Geffen GHS 24162, 1987 ....5.00 - 10.00
LP, *Rocks*
    Columbia JC 34165, 1976, early reissue, some copies have "Rocks" in quotes
    on the cover, others don't..5.00 - 10.00
    Columbia PC 34165, 1976, original, no bar code, some copies have "Rocks" in
    quotes on the cover, others don't ....6.00 - 12.00
    Columbia PC 34165, 1980s, with bar code....................................4.00 - 8.00
    Columbia PCQ 34165, 1976, quadraphonic ....12.50 - 25.00
LP, *Toys in the Attic*
    Columbia JC 33479, 1977, reissue with new prefix ....5.00 - 10.00
    Columbia PC 33479, 1975, original issue, no bar code on back...6.00 - 12.00
    Columbia PC 33479, 1980s, reissue, bar code on back ....4.00 - 8.00
    Columbia PCQ 33479, 1975, quadraphonic ....12.50 - 25.00

MVP:
LP, *Pure Gold from Rock 'n' Roll's Golden Boys*, Columbia A3S 187, 1976,
    promo-only compilation...25.00 - 50.00

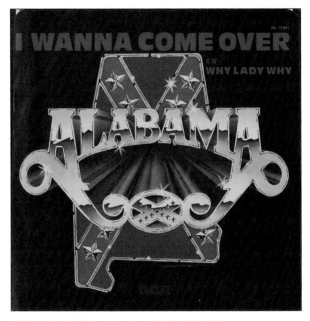

45, Why Lady Why/I Wanna Come Over, RCA PB-12091, 1980
  Record only..2.00 - 4.00
  Picture sleeve only..2.50 - 5.00

45, The Closer You Get/You Turn Me On, RCA PB-13524, 1983 ....2.00 - 4.00

45, Feels So Right/See the Embers, Feel the Flame , RCA PB-12236,
1981 ....2.00 - 4.00

45, Forever's As Far As I'll Go/Starting Tonight, RCA 2706-7-R, 1990...2.50 - 5.00

45, I'm In a Hurry (And Don't Know Why)/Sometimes Out of Touch,
RCA 62336, 1992 ....1.50 - 3.00

45, Love in the First Degree/Ride the Train, RCA PB-12288, 1981 ....2.00 - 4.00

45, Mountain Music/Never Be One, RCA PB-13019, 1981
Record only ....2.00 - 4.00
Picture sleeve only ....2.50 - 5.00

45, Take Me Down/Lovin' You Is Killin' Me, RCA PB-13210, 1982 ....2.00 - 4.00

LP, *Christmas*
RCA Victor ASL1-7014, 1985, original with gold embossed letters on
cover ....6.00 - 12.00
RCA Victor ASL1-7014, 1986, later copies with white non-embossed
letters on cover..5.00 - 10.00

LP, *The Alabama Band* , Alabama ALA-78-9-01, 1978.................200.00 - 400.00

LP, *The Closer You Get*, RCA Victor AHL1-4663, 1983..........................4.00 - 8.00

LP, *Feels So Right*, RCA Victor AHL1-3930, 1981 ....4.00 - 8.00

LP, *Greatest Hits*, RCA Victor AHL1-7170, 1986 ....4.00 - 8.00

LP, *Mountain Music*, RCA Victor AHL1-4229, 1982.............................4.00 - 8.00

MVP:
LP, *Wild Country*, LSI 0275, 1975, as "Wild Country," the band's original
name ....1,125.00 – 1,500.00

45, Straight from the Heart/Leavin', Arista 0618, 1981
    Record only...2.00 - 4.00
    Picture sleeve only ....2.00 - 4.00

45, Crazy Love/Just Ain't Easy, Capricorn 0320, 1979 ....2.00 - 4.00

45, Jessica/Come and Go Blues, Capricorn 0036, 1973........................2.50 - 5.00

45, Ramblin Man/Pony Boy, Capricorn 0027, 1973..............................2.50 - 5.00

45, Revival (Love Is Everywhere)/Leave My Blues at Home, Capricorn
8011, 1971..2.50 - 5.00

45, Whipping Post/Midnight Rider, Capricorn 8014, 1971 ....2.50 - 5.00

LP, *The Allman Brothers Band at Fillmore East,* 2-record set

    Capricorn 2CP 0131, stereo, 1974, reissue ....7.50 - 15.00

    Capricorn CX4 0131, quadraphonic, 1974 ....15.00 - 30.00

    Capricorn CPN2 0131, stereo, early 1980s, reissue......................6.00 - 12.00

    Capricorn 2-802, mono, 1971, sticker on front cover says "Promotional DJ
Copy Monaural Not for Sale" ....40.00 - 80.00

    Capricorn SD 2-802, stereo, 1971, original store edition............10.00 - 20.00

    Nautilus NR-30, 1982, "Super Disc" on cover ....50.00 - 100.00

    Polydor 823 273-1, 1984, reissue ....5.00 - 10.00

LP, *Brothers and Sisters*

    Capricorn CP 0111, 1973, original..6.00 - 12.00

    Capricorn CPN 0111, early 1980s, reissue ....4.00 - 8.00

    Mobile Fidelity 1-213, 1994, "Original Master Recording" at top of
cover ....15.00 - 30.00

    Polydor 825092-1, 1985, reissue ....4.00 - 8.00

MVP:

LP, *Eat a Peach*, Mobile Fidelity 1-157 (2-record set), 1984, "Original Master
Recording" at top of cover (other versions are much less) ....100.00 - 200.00

LP, *S.R.O.*
    A&M SP-119, mono, 1966..5.00 - 10.00
    A&M SP-4119, stereo, 1966 ....6.00 - 12.00

45, Taste of Honey/Third Man Theme, A&M 775, 1965 ....3.00 - 6.00
45, This Guy's in Love with You/A Quiet Tear, A&M 929, 1968
    Record only..2.50 - 5.00
    Picture sleeve only...4.00 - 8.00

45, What Now My Love/Spanish Flea, A&M 792, 1966
    Record only..3.00 - 6.00
    Picture sleeve only...5.00 - 10.00
45, Zorba the Greek/Tijuana Taxi , A&M 787, 1965 ....3.00 - 6.00
LP, *The Beat of the Brass*
    A&M SP-3266, 1984, reissue..4.00 - 8.00
    A&M SP-4146, 1968..5.00 - 10.00
LP, *What Now My Love*
    A&M LP-114, mono, 1966..5.00 - 10.00
    A&M SP-3265, 1984, reissue..4.00 - 8.00
    A&M SP-4114, stereo ....6.00 - 12.00
LP, *Whipped Cream & Other Delights*
    A&M LP-110, mono, 1965..5.00 - 10.00
    A&M SP-3157, 1980s, reissue ....4.00 - 8.00
    A&M SP-4110, stereo, 1965 ....6.00 - 12.00
    A&M ST-90387, stereo, 1965, Capitol Record Club edition ....7.50 - 15.00

MVP:
LP, *The Lonely Bull* , A&M SP-101, stereo, 1962, original issues with this number
    (later, common issues were SP-4101).......................................12.50 - 25.00

LP, *The Greatest Hits of Eric Burdon and the Animals*, MGM SE-4602, 1969...7.50 - 15.00

45, Bring It On Home to Me/For Miss Caulker, MGM K13339, 1965
Record only...6.00 - 12.00
Picture sleeve only...12.50 - 25.00
45, Don't Let Me Be Misunderstood/Club A-Go-Go, MGM K13311,
1964..7.50 - 15.00
45, House of the Rising Sun/Bring It On Home to Me, Abkco 4025, 1973,
reissue, full-length version of A-side..............................4.00 - 8.00
45, The House of the Rising Sun/I'm Crying, MGM KGC 179, 1960s, reissue,
despite the "2:58" on label, this has the full-length version of the
A-side ....5.00 - 10.00
45, The House of the Rising Sun/Talkin' About You, MGM K13264, 1964
Record only, edited version of A-side...........................7.50 - 15.00
Picture sleeve only ....15.00 - 30.00
45, We Gotta Get Out of This Place/I Can't Believe It, MGM K13382,
1965..6.00 - 12.00
45, When I Was Young/A Girl Called Sandoz, MGM 13721, 1967, as
"Eric Burdon and the Animals".....................................5.00 - 10.00
45, Sky Pilot (Part 1)/Sky Pilot (Part 2), MGM K13939, 1968, as
"Eric Burdon and the Animals"
Black label...5.00 - 10.00
Blue and gold label ....4.00 - 8.00
LP, *Animal Tracks*
MGM E-4305, mono, 1965...20.00 - 40.00
MGM SE-4305, rechanneled stereo, 1965 ....15.00 - 30.00
MGM T 90571, mono, 1965, Capitol Record Club edition...........25.00 - 50.00

MVP:
45 box set, *Celebrity Scene: The Animals*, MGM CS-11-5, 1967, with box, yellow-label singles numbered K13791, K13792, K13793, K13794 and K13795,
jukebox title strips and short biography; price is for entire set ...40.00 - 80.00

LP, *Paul Anka Sings His Big 15*

    ABC-Paramount ABC-323, mono, 1960 ....25.00 - 50.00

    ABC-Paramount ABCS-323, rechanneled stereo, 1960s ....15.00 - 30.00

45, Diana/Don't Gamble with Love, ABC-Paramount 45-9831,
    1957..10.00 - 20.00
45, I Confess/Blau-Wile Deveest Fontaine
    RPM 472, 1956 ....40.00 - 80.00
    RPM 499, 1957, reissue ....15.00 - 30.00
45, Lonely Boy/Your Love
    ABC-Paramount 45-10022, mono, 1959............................7.50 - 15.00
    ABC-Paramount 45-S-10022, stereo, 1959 ....25.00 - 50.00
45, Love Me Warm and Tender/I'd Like to Know
RCA Victor 37-7977, 1962, "Compact Single 33," small hole, plays at LP
    speed...12.50 - 25.00
    RCA Victor 47-7977, 1962, regular issue with large hole ....5.00 - 10.00
    RCA Victor 47-7977, 1962, picture sleeve only............................10.00 - 20.00
45, Put Your Head on My Shoulder/Don't Ever Leave Me
    ABC-Paramount 45-10040, mono, 1959............................7.50 - 15.00
    ABC-Paramount 45-S-10040, stereo, 1959 ....25.00 - 50.00
    ABC-Paramount 45-10040, 1959, picture sleeve only ....12.50 - 25.00
45, (You're) Having My Baby/Papa, United Artists XW-454, 1974........2.00 - 4.00
LP, *Anka*, United Artists UA-LA314-G, 1974....................................5.00 - 10.00
LP, *Paul Anka Swings for Young Lovers*
    ABC-Paramount ABC-347, mono, 1960 ....15.00 - 30.00
    ABC-Paramount ABCS-347, stereo, 1960 ....20.00 - 40.00

MVP:
LP, *Paul Anka and Others*, Riviera 0047, mono, 1959, with his two RPM single
    tracks plus songs by other artists ....75.00 - 150.00

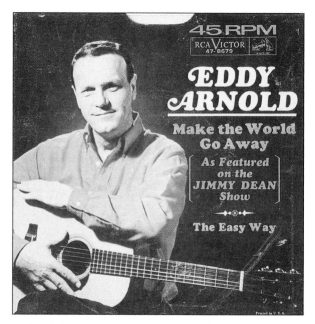

45, Make the World Go Away/The Easy Way, RCA Victor 47-8679, 1965
   Record only...4.00 - 8.00
   Picture sleeve only...7.50 - 15.00

45, Bouquet of Roses/Texarkana Baby
    RCA Victor 48-0001, 1949, green vinyl...25.00 - 50.00
    RCA Victor 48-0001, 1950s, green label, black vinyl..................12.50 - 25.00
    RCA Victor 48-0001, 1949, picture sleeve only, light brown with dark brown
    print ....40.00 - 80.00
RCA Victor 47-4597, 1952..10.00 - 20.00
45, The Cattle Call/The Kentuckian Song, RCA Victor 47-6139,
    1955..10.00 - 20.00
45, I Want to Go With You/Better Stop Tellin' Lies (About Me), RCA Victor
    47-8749, 1965
    Record only...4.00 - 8.00
    Picture sleeve only..7.50 - 15.00
45, I'll Hold You in My Heart (Till I Can Hold You in My Arms)/Don't Bother to Cry
    RCA Victor 48-0030, 1949, green vinyl...25.00 - 50.00
    RCA Victor 48-0030, 1950s, green label, black vinyl..................12.50 - 25.00
45, Then You Can Tell Me Goodbye/Apples, Raisins and Roses, RCA Victor 47-
    9606, 1968...3.00 - 6.00
LP, *The Best of Eddy Arnold*
    RCA Victor LPM-3565, mono, 1967...10.00 - 20.00
    RCA Victor LSP-3565, stereo, 1967...7.50 - 15.00
LP, *My World*
    RCA Victor LPM-3466, mono, 1965...6.00 - 12.00
    RCA Victor LSP-3466 , stereo, 1965...7.50 - 15.00
LP, *Wanderin' with Eddy Arnold* , RCA Victor LPM-1111, mono only,
    1955..25.00 - 50.00

MVP:
LP, *The Romantic World of Eddy Arnold* , RCA Victor LPM-4009, mono (the
    stereo version, LSP-4009, is worth only 10 percent of this) .....75.00 - 150.00

45, Ten Little Indians/County Fair, Capitol 4880, 1962
  Record only..15.00 - 30.00
  Picture sleeve only..100.00 - 200.00

45, I Get Around/Don't Worry Baby
   Capitol 5174, 1964, orange and yellow swirl label, original........12.50 - 25.00
   Capitol 5174, 1969, red and orange "target" label.......................6.00 - 12.00
   Capitol 5174, 1972, orange label with "Capitol" at bottom ....4.00 - 8.00
   Capitol 5174, 1978, purple label.......................................2.50 - 5.00
   Capitol 5174, 1982, black label with colorband...........................2.50 - 5.00
   Capitol 5174, 1964, picture sleeve only.....................................20.00 - 40.00
45, Good Vibrations/Let's Go Away for Awhile, Capitol 5676, 1966
   Record only...10.00 - 20.00
   Picture sleeve only...15.00 - 30.00
45, Kokomo/Tutti-Frutti, Elektra 69385, 1988, B-side by Little Richard1.50 - 3.00
45, Rock and Roll Music/The T M Song, Brother/Reprise 1354, 1976.2.00 - 4.00
45, Surfer Girl/Little Deuce Coupe, Capitol 5009, 1963...................12.50 - 25.00
LP, *Beach Boys Concert*
   Capitol SM-2198, 1970s, reissue ....5.00 - 10.00
   Capitol STAO 2198, stereo, 1964, with booklet...........................15.00 - 30.00
   Capitol STAO-8-2198, stereo, 1969, Capitol Record Club edition 40.00 - 80.00
   Capitol TAO 2198, mono, 1964, with booklet.............................15.00 - 30.00

MVP:
45, Surfin'/Luau, X 301, 1961, versions on Candix 301 and Candix 331 go for
   less, and on other labels, a lot less.....................................500.00 – 1,000.00

LP, *Rubber Soul*

    Capitol ST 2442, stereo, 1965, black label with colorband ....30.00 - 60.00

    Capitol ST 2442, stereo, 1968, black colorband label; border print adds
"A Subsidiary of Capitol Industries Inc." ....25.00 - 50.00

    Capitol ST 2442 , stereo, 1969, lime green label........................20.00 - 40.00

    LP, Capitol T 2442, mono, 1965 ....60.00 - 120.00

(Other label variations of ST 2442 exist, all of which go for less)

(NOTE: In order to list as many different records as possible, only originals are listed below. In some cases, reissues are worth more than the originals, in most cases, they sell for less. Consult a more detailed guide as mentioned in the Introduction for more details.)

45, Can't Buy Me Love/You Can't Do That, Capitol 5150, 1964
   Record only, orange and yellow swirl, without "A Subsidiary Of"... in perimeter
   label print..15.00 - 30.00
   Picture sleeve only ....400.00 - 800.00
—*Original:*
45, Let It Be/You Know My Name (Look Up My Number), Apple 2764, 1970
   Record only, with small Capitol logo on bottom of B-side label.....6.00 - 12.00
   Picture sleeve only ....50.00 - 100.00
45, Paperback Writer/Rain, Capitol 5651, 1966
   Record only, orange and yellow swirl, without "A Subsidiary Of"... in perimeter
   label print..12.50 - 25.00
   Picture sleeve only ....37.50 - 75.00
45, Penny Lane/Strawberry Fields Forever, Capitol 5810, 1967
   Record only, orange and yellow swirl, without "A Subsidiary Of"...
   in perimeter label print ....12.50 - 25.00
   Picture sleeve only...50.00 - 100.00
LP, *Sgt. Pepper's Lonely Hearts Club Band*
   Capitol MAS 2653, mono, 1967..150.00 - 300.00
   Capitol SMAS 2653, stereo, 1967, black label with colorband...50.00 - 100.00
   Add to above if cut-out inserts are included ....1.50 - 3.00
   Add to above if red-pink psychedelic inner sleeve is included ......7.50 - 15.00

MVP:
45, My Bonnie/The Saints, Decca 31382, 1962, credited to "Tony Sheridan and
   the Beat Brothers"; black label with color bars; promotional copy on a pink
   label goes for about 20 percent this amount ....11,250.00 – 15,000.00

LP, *Trafalgar*

    Atco SD 7003, 1971 ....6.00 - 12.00

    Mobile Fidelity 1-263, 1996, "Original Master Recording" on cover

    ....20.00 - 40.00

Bee Gees

45, Alone/How Deep Is Your Love, Polydor 31457 1006 7, 1997.........1.50 - 3.00
45, How Deep Is Your Love/Can't Keep a Good Man Down, RSO 882,
   1977..2.00 - 4.00
45, I Started a Joke/Kilburn Towers, Atco 6639, 1969........................4.00 - 8.00
45, I've Gotta Get a Message to You/Kitty Can, Atco 6603, 1968 ....4.00 - 8.00
45, Jive Talkin'/Wind of Change, RSO 510, 1975 ....2.00 - 4.00
45, Night Fever/Down the Road, RSO 889, 1978 ....2.00 - 4.00
45, One/Wing and a Prayer, Warner Bros. 7-22899, 1989
   Record only...1.50 - 3.00
   Picture sleeve only...1.50 - 3.00
45, Stayin' Alive/If I Can't Have You, RSO 885, 1977 ....2.00 - 4.00
LP, *Bee Gees' 1st*
   Atco 33-223, mono, 1967 ....15.00 - 30.00
   Atco SD 33-223, stereo, 1967, brown and purple label..............10.00 - 20.00
   Atco SD 33-223, stereo, 1969, yellow label ....5.00 - 10.00
LP, *Main Course*
   RSO RS-1-3024, 1977, reissue ....4.00 - 8.00
   RSO SO 4807, 1975, original..5.00 - 10.00
LP, *Spirits Having Flown*
   RSO RS-1-3041, 1979, with either cardboard or slick paper inner
   sleeve ....5.00 - 10.00
   RSO RS-1-3042, 1979, picture disc ....7.50 - 15.00

MVP:
12-inch single, You Should Be Dancing (B-side blank), RSO RS 853, 1976, white
   label promotional issue, pressed in the United States; a Canadian issue with
   the same catalog number goes for less....................................75.00 - 150.00

LP, *Jump Up Calypso*

    RCA Victor LPM-2388, mono, 1961..10.00 - 20.00

    RCA Victor LSP-2388, stereo, 1961..12.50 - 25.00

    DCC Compact Classics LPZ-2039, 1997, 180-gram virgin vinyl edition

    ....30.00 - 60.00

45, Banana Boat (Day-O)/Star-O, RCA Victor 47-6771, 1956
   Record only..6.00 - 12.00
   Picture sleeve only...12.50 - 25.00
45, Jamaica Farewell/Once Was, RCA Victor 47-6663, 1956
   Record only..6.00 - 12.00
   Picture sleeve only...12.50 - 25.00
45, Mama Look a Boo Boo (Shut Your Mouth - Go Away)/Don't Ever Love Me,
   RCA Victor 47-6830, 1957, alternate title for "Mama Look at Bubu"
   ....6.00 - 12.00
45, Mama Look at Bubu/Don't Ever Love Me, RCA Victor 47-6830, 1957
   Record only..6.00 - 12.00
   Picture sleeve only...12.50 - 25.00
45, Mary's Boy Child/Venezuela, RCA Victor 47-6735, 1956
   Record only..6.00 - 12.00
   Picture sleeve only...12.50 - 25.00
LP, *Calypso*
   RCA Victor LPM-1248, mono, 1956, original with "Long Play" on
   label..15.00 - 30.00
   RCA Victor LSP-1248(e), rechanneled stereo, 1960s ....6.00 - 12.00
   RCA Victor AFL1-1248(e), 1977, reissue with new prefix............5.00 - 10.00
   RCA Victor AYL1-3801(e), 1980, "Best Buy Series" reissue............4.00 - 8.00
LP, *The Midnight Special*
   RCA Victor LPM-2449, mono, 1962.......................................15.00 - 30.00
   RCA Victor LSP-2449, stereo, 1962..20.00 - 40.00

MVP:
LP, *Belafonte at Carnegie Hall* , RCA Victor LSO-6006 (2-record set), stereo,
   1959, large "Living Stereo" banner on top and "Living Stereo" on labels
   (other versions go for less) ....50.00 - 100.00

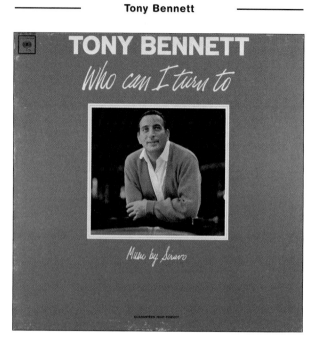

LP, *Who Can I Turn To*

    Columbia CL 2285, mono, 1964..7.50 - 15.00

    Columbia CS 9085, stereo, 1964 ....10.00 - 20.00

45, Because of You/I Won't Cry Anymore, Columbia 4-39362,
1951...6.00 - 12.00
45, Can You Find It in Your Heart/Forget Her, Columbia 40667,
1956...5.00 - 10.00
45, Cold, Cold Heart/While We're Young, Columbia 4-39449,
1951...6.00 - 12.00
45, The Good Life/Spring in Manhattan, Columbia 4-42779,
1963...4.00 - 8.00
45, I Left My Heart In San Francisco/Once Upon a Time, Columbia
4-42332, 1962
Record only...4.00 - 8.00
Picture sleeve only...7.50 - 15.00
45, In the Middle of An Island/I Am, Columbia 4-40965, 1957 ....5.00 - 10.00
45, Rags to Riches/Here Comes That Heartache Again, Columbia
4-40048, 1953 ....6.00 - 12.00
LP, *I Left My Heart in San Francisco*
Columbia CL 1869, mono, 1962...7.50 - 15.00
Columbia CS 8669, stereo, 1962 ....10.00 - 20.00
Columbia PC 8669, 1980s, reissue with new prefix.......................4.00 - 8.00
LP, *I Wanna Be Around*
Columbia CL 2000, mono, 1963...7.50 - 15.00
Columbia CS 8800, stereo, 1963 ....12.50 - 25.00
LP, *Love Story*, Columbia C 30558, 1971.....................................6.00 - 12.00
LP, *Tony's Greatest Hits*
Columbia CL 1229, mono, 1958, red and black label with six white
"eye" logos...15.00 - 30.00
Columbia CS 8652, rechanneled stereo, 1962 ....7.50 - 15.00

MVP:
LP, *Because of You*, Columbia CL 6221, mono, 1952, 10-inch record
....40.00 - 80.00

LP, *The London Chuck Berry Sessions*

Chess CH-9295, 1989, reissue..5.00 - 10.00

Chess CH-60020, 1972, original..10.00 - 20.00

45, Johnny B. Goode/Around and Around, Chess 1691, 1958 ....15.00 - 30.00
45, Maybellene/Wee Wee Hours, Chess 1604, 1955 ....25.00 - 50.00
45, My Ding-a-Ling/Johnny B. Goode, Chess 2131, 1972
    Fading blue label..3.00 - 6.00
    Orange and blue label..2.00 - 4.00
45, No Particular Place to Go/You Two, Chess 1898, 1964
    Record only...10.00 - 20.00
    Picture sleeve only..25.00 - 50.00
45, Rock & Roll Music/Blue Feeling, Chess 1671, 1957....................15.00 - 30.00
45, Sweet Little Sixteen/Reelin' and Rockin', Chess 1683, 1958 ....15.00 - 30.00
45, You Never Can Tell/Brenda Lee, Chess 1906, 1964
    Record only...10.00 - 20.00
    Picture sleeve only ....20.00 - 40.00
LP, *After School Session*
    Chess LP-1426, mono, 1958..100.00 - 200.00
    Chess LPS-1426, rechanneled stereo, 1960s...................................6.00 - 12.00
    Chess CH-9284, 1989, reissue..5.00 - 10.00
LP, *The Great Twenty-Eight*, Chess CH2-92500 (2-record set),
    1983...6.00 - 12.00
LP, *One Dozen Berrys*
    Chess LP-1432, mono, 1958..100.00 - 200.00
    Chess LPS-1432, rechanneled stereo, 1960s...................................6.00 - 12.00

MVP:
EP, *After School Session* [contents: School Day (Ring, Ring Goes the Bell)/
    Wee Wee Hours//Brown Eyed Handsome Man/Too Much Monkey
    Business], Chess CH-5118, 1957, record and cardboard sleeve
    together...160.00 - 320.00

LP, *Sabbath Bloody Sabbath*
Warner Bros. BS 2695, 1974, "Burbank" palm trees label ....7.50 - 15.00
Warner Bros. BS 2695, 1979, white or tan label ....4.00 - 8.00

45, Iron Man/Electric Funeral
    Warner Bros. 7530, 1971...4.00 - 8.00
    Warner Bros. 7802, 1974...4.00 - 8.00
45, Paranoid/Wizard, Warner Bros. 7437, 1970................................5.00 - 10.00
LP, *Black Sabbath*
    Warner Bros. WS 1871, 1970, green label ....7.50 - 15.00
    Warner Bros. WS 1871, 1973, "Burbank" palm trees label..........5.00 - 10.00
    Warner Bros. WS 1871, 1979, white or tan label ....4.00 - 8.00
LP, *The Eternal Idol* , Warner Bros. 25548, 1987 ....5.00 - 10.00
LP, *Master of Reality*
    Warner Bros. BS 2562, 1971, green label, no poster ....7.50 - 15.00
    Warner Bros. BS 2562, 1973, "Burbank" palm trees label ....5.00 - 10.00
    Warner Bros. BS 2562, 1979, white or tan label ....4.00 - 8.00
LP, *Paranoid*
    Warner Bros. WS 1887, 1971, green label ....7.50 - 15.00
    Warner Bros. WS 1887, 1973, "Burbank" palm trees label..........5.00 - 10.00
    Warner Bros. WS4 1887, quadraphonic, 1974, "Burbank" palm trees
    label ....15.00 - 30.00
    Warner Bros. BSK 3104, 1978, reissue; "Burbank" palm trees
    label ....5.00 - 10.00
    Warner Bros. BSK 3104, 1979, reissue; white or tan label ....4.00 - 8.00

MVP:

LP, *Master of Reality,* Warner Bros. BS 2562, 1971, green label, with
    poster ....20.00 - 40.00

LP, *Parallel Lines*

    Chrysalis CHR 1192, 1978, with 3:54 version of "Heart of Glass" .7.50 - 15.00

    Chrysalis CHR 1192, 1979, with 5:50 version of "Heart of Glass (Disco
Version)"..5.00 - 10.00

    Chrysalis CHP 5001, 1979, picture disc.....................................12.50 - 25.00

    Chrysalis FV 41192, 1983, reissue..4.00 - 8.00

    Mobile Fidelity 1-050, 1980, "Original Master Recording" on cover
....15.00 - 30.00

45, Call Me/(Instrumental), Chrysalis 2414, 1980
  Record only..1.50 - 3.00
  Picture sleeve only, photo of Richard Gere ....2.50 - 5.00
  Picture sleeve only, photo of Deborah Harry ....1.50 - 3.00
45, Heart of Glass/11:59, Chrysalis 2295, 1979
  Record only..2.00 - 4.00
  Picture sleeve only..2.00 - 4.00
45, One Way or Another/Just Go Away, Chrysalis 2336, 1979 ....2.00 - 4.00
45, Rapture/Walk Like Me, Chrysalis 2485, 1981
  Record only..1.50 - 3.00
  Picture sleeve only..1.50 - 3.00
45, The Tide Is High/Suzy and Jeffrey, Chrysalis 2465, 1980
  Record only..1.50 - 3.00
  Picture sleeve only..1.50 - 3.00
LP, *Autoamerican*
  Chrysalis CHE 1290, 1980, original ....5.00 - 10.00
  Chrysalis PV 41290, 1983, reissue...4.00 - 8.00
LP, *Blondie*
  Chrysalis CHR 1165, 1977, early reissue ....6.00 - 12.00
  Chrysalis PV 41165, 1983, later reissue ....4.00 - 8.00
  Private Stock PS-2023, 1976, original ....12.50 - 25.00
LP, *Eat to the Beat*
  Chrysalis CHE 1225, 1979 ....5.00 - 10.00
  Chrysalis PV 41225, 1983, reissue...4.00 - 8.00

MVP:
LP, *At Home with Debbie Harry and Chris Stein*, Chrysalis CHS 24 PDJ,
    1981, promotional only interview record, with script ....25.00 - 50.00

LP, *Pat Boone Sings*

    Dot DLP-3158, mono, 1959 ....10.00 - 20.00
    Dot DLP-25158, stereo, 1959..12.50 - 25.00

45, Ain't That a Shame/Tennessee Saturday Night, Dot 15377, 1955
....10.00 - 20.00
45, April Love/When the Swallows Come Back to Capistrano, Dot 15660,
1957...7.50 - 15.00
45, Don't Forbid Me/Anastasia, Dot 15521, 1956.............................7.50 - 15.00
45, Friendly Persuasion (Thee I Love)/Chains of Love, Dot 15490, 1956
   Maroon label...10.00 - 20.00
   Black label ....7.50 - 15.00
45, I Almost Lost My Mind/I'm in Love with You, Dot 15472, 1956
....10.00 - 20.00
45, Love Letters in the Sand/Bernardine, Dot 15570, 1957
   Record only..7.50 - 15.00
   Picture sleeve only...15.00 - 30.00
45, Moody River/A Thousand Years, Dot 16209, 1961 ....7.50 - 15.00
45, Speedy Gonzales/The Locket, Dot 16368, 1962.........................6.00 - 12.00
LP, *Hymns We Love*
   Dot DLP-3068, mono, 1957 ....12.50 - 25.00
   Dot DLP-25068, stereo, 1959...................................15.00 - 30.00
LP, *Pat Boone's Golden Hits*
   Dot DLP-3455, mono, 1962.......................................6.00 - 12.00
   Dot DLP-25455, stereo, 1962...................................7.50 - 15.00
LP, *Pat's Great Hits*
   Dot DLP-3071, mono, 1957 ....12.50 - 25.00
   Dot DLP-25071, stereo, 1959...................................15.00 - 30.00

MVP:
LP, *Pat Boone Sings Guess Who?,* Dot DLP-25501, stereo, 1963,
   mono version (DLP-3501) goes for less....................40.00 - 80.00

LP, *Diamond Dogs*

    RCA Victor CPL1-0576, 1974, standard issue, with dog's genital area on
lower right back cover airbrushed ....10.00 - 20.00

    RCA Victor AYL1-3889, 1980, reissue ....4.00 - 8.00

    Ryko Analogue RALP 0137, 1990, clear vinyl with "Limited Edition"
obi strip; genitals are restored...10.00 - 20.00

45, Blue Jean/Dancin' with the Big Boys, EMI America B-8231, 1984
　　Record only, blue vinyl ....3.00 - 6.00
　　Record only, black vinyl ....1.50 - 3.00
　　Picture sleeve only, same sleever for both versions.........................1.50 - 3.00
45, Fame/Right, RCA Victor PB-10320, 1975
　　Orangel label...3.00 - 6.00
　　Tan label ....3.00 - 6.00
45, Let's Dance/Cat People (Putting Out Fire), EMI America B-8158, 1983
　　Record only...1.50 - 3.00
　　Picture sleeve only ....1.50 - 3.00
45, Space Oddity/The Man Who Sold the World, RCA Victor 74-0876, 1973
　　Record only..3.00 - 6.00
　　Picture sleeve only..10.00 - 20.00
45, Space Oddity/Wild-Eyed Boy from Freecloud, Mercury 72949,
　　1969..25.00 - 50.00
LP, *Changesonebowie*
　　RCA Victor AFL1-1732, 1978, reissue ....5.00 - 10.00
　　RCA Victor AFL1-1732, 1976, original ....5.00 - 10.00
　　RCA Victor AQL1-1732, 1984, reissue ....5.00 - 10.00
LP, *Young Americans*
　　RCA Victor APL1-0998, 1975, orange or tan label ....6.00 - 12.00
　　RCA Victor APL1-0998, 1976, black label....................................5.00 - 10.00
　　RCA Victor AQL1-0998, 1984, reissue ....5.00 - 10.00

MVP:
LP, *Diamond Dogs*, RCA Victor CPL1-0576, 1974, dog's "human" penis
　　and genitals clearly visible on the lower back cover, almost all were
　　destroyed prior to release; not to be confused with the reissue of Ryko
　　Analogue with the genitals visible ....2,000.00 – 4,000.00

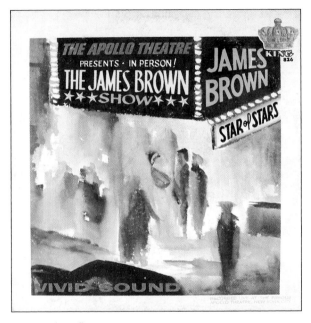

LP, *Live at the Apollo*

King 826, mono, 1963, custom back cover; "crownless" King label, original
....100.00 - 200.00

King KS-826, stereo, 1963, custom back cover; "crownless" King label, original
....150.00 - 300.00

(Other variations exist and sell for less.)

45, Call Me Super Bad (Part 1 & Part 2)/Call Me Super Bad (Part 3),
King 6329, 1970, original version with long title, orange and black
label ....10.00 - 20.00

45, Cold Sweat — Part 1/Cold Sweat — Part 2, King 6110, 1967......6.00 - 12.00

45, Get On the Good Foot Part 1/Get On the Good Foot Part 2, Polydor
14139, 1972..3.00 - 6.00

45, Get Up (I Feel Like Being A) Sex Machine (Part 1)/Get Up (I Feel Like
Being A) Sex Machine (Part 2), King 6318, 1970 ....4.00 - 8.00

45, I Got You (I Feel Good)/I Can't Help It (I Just Do, Do, Do), King
6015, 1965..7.50 - 15.00

45, Living in America/Farewell, Scotti Brothers ZS4-05682, 1985, B-side
by Vince Di Cola
Record only..1.50 - 3.00
Picture sleeve only ....1.50 - 3.00

45, Say It Loud — I'm Black and I'm Proud (Part 1)/Say It Loud —
I'm Black and I'm Proud (Part 2), King 6187, 1968, correct title on labels
....5.00 - 10.00

45, Say It Loud — I'm Black But I'm Proud (Part 1)/Say It Loud —
I'm Black But I'm Proud (Part 2), King 6187, 1968, incorrect title on labels
....12.50 - 25.00

45, Super Bad (Part 1 & Part 2)/Super Bad (Part 3), King 6329, 1970,
shorter title, all-black label ....4.00 - 8.00

LP, *It's a Man's Man's Man's World*
King 985, mono, 1966..25.00 - 50.00
King KS-985, stereo, 1966 ....35.00 - 70.00

LP, *Live at the Apollo, Volume II*, King LPS-1022 (2-record set), 1968
....35.00 - 70.00

MVP:
LP, *Please Please Please*, King 610, mono, 1958, "woman and man's legs"
cover, "King" on label is two inches wide, deduct 100.00-200.00 if
"King" on label is three inches wide..................................600.00 – 1,200.00

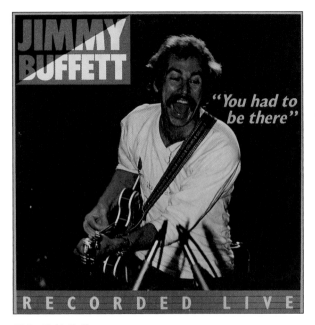

LP, *You Had to Be There*
   ABC AK-1008 (2-record set), 1978 ....7.50 - 15.00
   MCA 2-6005 (2-record set), 1981, reissue ....5.00 - 10.00

45, Changes in Latitudes, Changes in Attitudes/Landfall, ABC 12305, 1977
  Record only...2.00 - 4.00
  Picture sleeve only...3.00 - 6.00
45, Cheeseburger in Paradise/African Friend, ABC 12358, 1978..........2.00 - 4.00
45, Come Monday/The Wino and I Know
  ABC Dunhill 4385, 1974..2.50 - 5.00
  ABC Dunhill 15008, 1974..2.00 - 4.00
45, Fins/Dreamsicle, MCA 41109, 1979...2.00 - 4.00
45, Margaritaville/Miss You So Badly, ABC 12254, 1977.....................2.00 - 4.00
LP, *Changes in Latitudes, Changes in Attitudes*
  ABC AB-990, 1977...6.00 - 12.00
  MCA 37150, 1982..4.00 - 8.00
LP, *Son of a Son of a Sailor*
  ABC AA-1046, 1978..6.00 - 12.00
  MCA 37024, 1981..4.00 - 8.00
LP, *Volcano*
  MCA 5102, 1979...5.00 - 10.00
  MCA 37156, 1982..4.00 - 8.00
LP, *A White Sport Coat and a Pink Crustaceon*
  ABC Dunhill DSX-50150, 1974 ....7.50 - 15.00
  MCA 37026, 1981..4.00 - 8.00

MVP:
LP, *Down to Earth*, Barnaby Z 30093, 1970...................................50.00 - 100.00

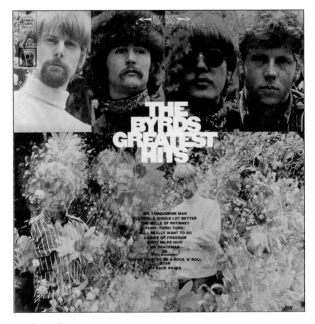

LP, *The Byrds' Greatest Hits*

    Columbia CL 2716, mono, 1967 .... 15.00 - 30.00
    Columbia CS 9516, stereo, 1967, red "360 Sound" label .... 10.00 - 20.00
    Columbia KCS 9516, stereo, 1971, orange label, new prefix .... 5.00 - 10.00
    Columbia PC 9516, stereo, 1970s, reissue with another new prefix 4.00 - 8.00

45, Eight Miles High/Why, Columbia 4-43578, 1966
> Record only .... 6.00 - 12.00
> Picture sleeve only .... 30.00 - 60.00

45, My Back Pages/Renaissance Fair, Columbia 4-44054, 1967 .... 6.00 - 12.00

45, So You Want to Be a Rock 'N' Roll Star/Everybody's Been Burned,
> Columbia 4-43987, 1967 .... 6.00 - 12.00

45, Turn! Turn! Turn! (To Everything There Is a Season)/She Don't Care
> About Time, Columbia 4-43424, 1965 .... 7.50 - 15.00

LP, *Mr. Tambourine Man*
> Columbia CL 2372, mono, 1965, "Guaranteed High Fidelity" on label
> .... 20.00 - 40.00
> Columbia CL 2372, mono, 1966, "360 Sound Mono" on label....15.00 - 30.00
> Columbia CS 9172, stereo, 1965, red label, "360 Sound" in black
> .... 20.00 - 40.00
> Columbia CS 9172, stereo, 1966, red label, "360 Sound" in white
> .... 12.50 - 25.00
> Columbia CS 9172, stereo, 1971, orange label .... 5.00 - 10.00
> Columbia PC 9172, stereo, 1980s, reissue with new prefix and bar
> code .... 4.00 - 8.00
> Sundazed LP 5057, stereo, 1999, reissue .... 7.50 - 15.00

LP, *Preflyte*
> Columbia C 32183, 1970s, second reissue .... 5.00 - 10.00
> Columbia KC 32183, 1973, first reissue .... 6.00 - 12.00
> Together ST-T-1001, 1969, original .... 12.50 - 25.00

MVP:

EP, *A Special Open-End Interview with the Byrds Talking About Their New LP
"Fifth Dimension"*, Columbia ZLP 116003 on one side, ZLP 116004 on the
other, 1966, promotional only, price includes both record and title sleeve
(record without sleeve is 60.00-120.00) .... 150.00 - 300.00

LP, *Mariah Carey*, Columbia C 45202, 1990 ....10.00 - 20.00

12-inch single, Always Be My Baby (Reggae Soul Dub Featuring Lil' Vicious) (Mr. Dupri Extended Mix Featuring Da Brat and Xscape) (Reggae Soul Acapella Featuring Lil' Vicious) (Album Version), Columbia 44-78277, 1996 ....5.00 - 10.00

12-inch single, Always Be My Baby (Always Club Mix) (Dub-a-Baby) (Groove-a-Pella) (St Dub), Columbia 44-78313, 1996 ....4.00 - 8.00

12-inch single, Make It Happen (Extended Version) (Dub Version) (C&C Classic Mix) (LP Version), Columbia 44-74189, 1992........................... 10.00 - 20.00

45, Always Be My Baby/Long Ago, Columbia 38-78276, 1996
Record only ....1.50 - 3.00
Picture sleeve only ....1.50 - 3.00

45, Emotions/Vanishing, Columbia 38-73977, 1991.............................1.50 - 3.00

45, Love Takes Time/Sent from Up Above, Columbia 38-73455, 1990..1.50 - 3.00

45, One Sweet Day/I Am Free, Columbia 38-78072, 1995, though it was the biggest hit in the history of the *Billboard* singles charts,the 45 was deleted on the day it was issued ....4.00 - 8.00

45, Someday (Album Version)/Alone in Love, Columbia 38-73561, 19902.50 - 5.00

45, Someday (New 7" Jackswing)/Alone in Love, Columbia 38-73561, 1991 ....1.50 - 3.00

45, Through the Rain (same on both sides), Monarc/Island 440 063 904-7, 2002 ....1.50 - 3.00

45, Vision of Love//Prisoner/All In Your Mind/Someday (album snippets), Columbia 38-73348, 1990..1.50 - 3.00

LP, *Emotions*, Columbia C 47980, 1991...7.50 - 15.00

LP, *Music Box*, Columbia C 53205, 1993 ....7.50 - 15.00

LP, *Rainbow*, Columbia C2 63800 (2-record set), 1999 ....7.50 - 15.00

MVP:
12-inch single, Joy to the World (Celebration Mix) (Flava Mix)/(Club Mix) (Crash Dub Crash) (LP Version), Columbia CAS 6646, 1994, promotional issue only on red vinyl ....12.50 - 25.00

LP, *Christmas Portrait*

    A&M SP-3210, 1980s, reissue ....4.00 - 8.00

    A&M SP-4726, 1978, original..7.50 - 15.00

45, Calling Occupants of Interplanetary Craft/Can't Smile Without You, A&M
1978, 1977

    Record only..2.00 - 4.00

    Picture sleeve only..3.00 - 6.00

45, Superstar/Bless the Beasts and Children, A&M 1289, 1971

    Record only..2.00 - 4.00

    Picture sleeve only..3.00 - 6.00

45, (They Long to Be) Close to You/IKept On Loving You, A&M 1183,
1970..2.50 - 5.00

45, Top of the World/Heather, A&M 1468, 1973

    Record only, brown label ....2.00 - 4.00

    Record only, silvery label ....1.50 - 3.00

    Picture sleeve only ....3.00 - 6.00

45, We've Only Just Begun/All of My Life, A&M 1217, 1970................2.50 - 5.00

LP, *Now & Then*

    A&M SP-3519, 1973, brown label ....6.00 - 12.00

    A&M SP-3519, 1974, silvery label..4.00 - 8.00

    A&M QU-53519, quadraphonic, 1974 ....10.00 - 20.00

LP, *The Singles 1969-1973*

    A&M SP-3601, 1973, with booklet..6.00 - 12.00

    A&M QU-53601, quadraphonic, 1974 ....10.00 - 20.00

LP, *A Song for You*

    A&M SP-3511, 1972, brown label ....6.00 - 12.00

    A&M SP-3511, 1974, silvery label..4.00 - 8.00

MVP:

45, I'll Be Yours/Looking for Love, Magic Lamp 704, 1967, as
    "Karen Carpenter"..1,000.00 – 2,000.00

LP, *Ring of Fire (The Best of Johnny Cash)*

 Columbia CL 2052, mono, 1963, "Guaranteed High Fidelity" on label

 ....10.00 - 20.00

 Columbia CL 2052, mono, 1965, "360 Sound Mono" on label ....6.00 - 12.00

 Columbia CS 8852, stereo, 1963, "360 Sound Stereo" in black on

 label ....12.50 - 25.00

 Columbia CS 8852, stereo, 1963, "360 Sound Stereo" in white on

 label ....7.50 - 15.00

45, Ballad of a Teenage Queen/Big River, Sun 283, 1958 ....12.50 - 25.00

45, A Boy Named Sue/San Quentin, Columbia 4-44944, 1969 ....3.00 - 6.00

45, Daddy Sang Bass/He Turned the Water Into Wine, Columbia 4-44689,
   1968...3.00 - 6.00

45, Folsom Prison Blues/The Folk Singer, Columbia 44513, 1968
   Record only..3.00 - 6.00
   Picture sleeve only ....5.00 - 10.00

45, Folsom Prison Blues/So Doggone Lonesome, Sun 232, 1956 .....15.00 - 30.00

45, Guess Things Happen That Way/Come In Stranger, Sun 295, 1958
   Record only..12.50 - 25.00
   Picture sleeve only ....20.00 - 40.00

45, I Walk the Line/Get Rhythm, Sun 241, 1956 ....20.00 - 40.00

45, One Piece at a Time/Go On Blues, Columbia 3-10321, 1976..........2.50 - 5.00

45, Ring of Fire/I'd Still Be There, Columbia 4-42788, 1963
   Record only..5.00 - 10.00
   Picture sleeve only ....15.00 - 30.00

LP, *Hello, I'm Johnny Cash*, Columbia KCS 9943, 1970.....................6.00 - 12.00

LP, *Johnny Cash at San Quentin*
   Columbia CS 9827, 1969, red label with "360 Sound Stereo" ....6.00 - 12.00
   Columbia CS 9827, 1970, orange label ....4.00 - 8.00
   Columbia CQ 30961, quadraphonic, 1971 ....10.00 - 20.00

MVP:

LP, *Johnny Cash with His Hot and Blue Guitar*, Sun SLP-1220, mono, 1956
   (reissues that claim to be "stereo" or "electronically enhanced for reproduc-
   tion on stereo phonographs" are a lot less) ....50.00 - 100.00

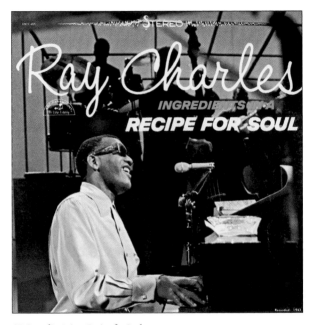

LP, *Ingredients in a Recipe for Soul*

ABC ABCS-465, stereo, 1967, reissue ....6.00 - 12.00

ABC-Paramount ABC-465, mono, 1963 ....10.00 - 20.00

ABC-Paramount ABCS-465, stereo, 1963 ....12.50 - 25.00

45, America the Beautiful/ Look What They've Done to My Song, Ma, ABC 11329, 1972 ....5.00 - 10.00

45, America the Beautiful/Sunshine, Crossover 985, 1976, new recording ....3.00 - 6.00

45, Busted/Making Believe, ABC-Paramount 10481, 1963 ....7.50 - 15.00

45, Georgia on My Mind/Carry Me Back to Old Virginny, ABC-Paramount 10135, 1960...7.50 - 15.00

45, Hit the Road Jack/The Danger Zone, ABC-Paramount 10244, 1961...7.50 - 15.00

45, I've Got a Woman/Come Back, Atlantic 1050, 1954, yellow label..25.00 - 50.00

45, I Can't Stop Loving You/Born to Lose, ABC-Paramount 10330, 1962...7.50 - 15.00

45, What'd I Say (Part I)/What'd I Say (Part II), Atlantic 2031, 1959...10.00 - 20.00

45, You Don't Know Me/Careless Love, ABC-Paramount 10345, 1962...7.50 - 15.00

LP, *The Great Hits of Ray Charles Recorded on 8-Track Stereo*, Atlantic SD 7101, stereo, 1966..12.50 - 25.00

LP, *Modern Sounds in Country and Western Music*

ABC ABCS-410, stereo, 1967, reissue..................................6.00 - 12.00

ABC-Paramount ABC-410, mono, 1962 ....12.50 - 25.00

ABC-Paramount ABCS-410, stereo, 1962 ....15.00 - 30.00

Rhino R1-70099, 1988, reissue...5.00 - 10.00

MVPs:

45, Baby, Let Me Hold Your Hand/Lonely Boy, Swing Time 250, 1951 (78 rpm versions are much less) ....250.00 - 500.00

45, Roll with Me Baby/The Midnight Hour, Atlantic 45-976, 1952 (78 rpm versions are much less) ....250.00 - 500.00

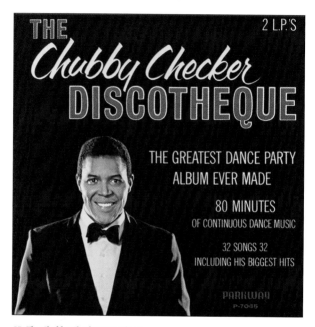

LP, *The Chubby Checker Discotheque*
   Parkway P 7045, (2-record set), mono, 1965............................15.00 - 30.00
   Parkway SP 7045 (2-record set), stereo, 1965 ....20.00 - 40.00

45, The Class/Schooldays, Oh Schooldays, Parkway 804, 1959 ....15.00 - 30.00
45, Let's Twist Again/Everything's Gonna Be Alright, Parkway 824, 1961
    Record only, black vinyl ....7.50 - 15.00
    Record only, orange vinyl ....100.00 - 200.00
    Picture sleeve only...12.50 - 25.00
45, Limbo Rock/Popeye The Hitch-Hiker, Parkway 849, 1962
    Record only..7.50 - 15.00
    Picture sleeve only...12.50 - 25.00
45, Pony Time/Oh, Susannah, Parkway 818, 1960............................7.50 - 15.00
45, The Twist/Toot, Parkway 811, 1960
    White label with blue print..15.00 - 30.00
    Orange label with black print...10.00 - 20.00
45, The Twist/Twistin' U.S.A., Parkway 811, 1961
    Record only..7.50 - 15.00
    Picture sleeve only ....12.50 - 25.00
LP, *Twist with Chubby Checker*, Parkway P 7001, mono, 1960
    All-orange label..20.00 - 40.00
    Orange and yellow label..15.00 - 30.00
LP, *Twistin' Round the World*
    Parkway P 7008, mono, 1962 ....15.00 - 30.00
    Parkway SP 7008, stereo, 1962 ....20.00 - 40.00

MVP:
45, You Just Don't Know/Two Hearts Make One Love, Parkway 965, 1965..200.00 - 400.00

LP, *Half-Breed* , MCA 2104, 1973, black label with rainbow ....6.00 - 12.00

45, All I Really Want to Do/I'm Gonna Love You, Imperial 66114,
1965...6.00 - 12.00

45, Bang Bang (My Baby Shot Me Down)/Needles and Pins, Imperial
66160, 1966...6.00 - 12.00

45, Bang Bang (My Baby Shot Me Down)/Our Day Will Come, Imperial
66160, 1966...6.00 - 12.00

45, Believe (Album Version)/(Xenomania Mix), Warner Bros. 7-17119,
1998...1.50 - 3.00

45, Dark Lady/Two People Clinging to a Thread, MCA 40161, 1973.....2.00 - 4.00

45, Gypsys, Tramps and Thieves/He'll Never Know, Kapp 2146, 1971
   Black label ....3.00 - 6.00
   Multi-color label; white Kapp logo in black box ....2.50 - 5.00
   Multi-color label; black Kapp logo stands alone...........................2.00 - 4.00

45, Half-Breed/Melody, MCA 40102, 1973 ....2.00 - 4.00

45, If I Could Turn Back Time/Some Guys, Geffen 7-22886, 1989
   Record only...1.50 - 3.00
   Picture sleeve only...2.50 - 5.00

45, Take Me Home/My Song (Too Far Gone), Casablanca 965, 1979...2.00 - 4.00

LP, *Heart of Stone*, Geffen GHS 24239, 1989
   Original cover with Cher in heart-shaped pose next to "skeleton rock"
   ....7.50 - 15.00
   Later cover with larger picture of Cher and no rock.....................5.00 - 10.00

LP, *The Sonny Side of Cher*
   Imperial LP-9301, mono, 1966 ....10.00 - 20.00
   Imperial LP-12301, stereo, 1966..12.50 - 25.00

MVP:
45, Ringo I Love You/Beatles Blues, Annette 1000, 1964, as "Bonnie Jo
   Mason"...350.00 - 700.00

LP, *Hot Streets*
    Columbia FC 35512, 1978, no bar code on back cover.................7.50 - 15.00
    Columbia FC 35512, 1980s, bar code on back cover ....4.00 - 8.00

45, Beginnings/Poem 58, Columbia 4-45011, 1969 ....3.00 - 6.00
45, Beginnings/Colour My World, Columbia 4-45417, 1971
    Record only..2.50 - 5.00
    Picture sleeve only ....4.00 - 8.00
45, Feelin' Stronger Every Day/Jenny, Columbia 4-45880, 1973 ....2.50 - 5.00
45, Hard to Say I'm Sorry/Sonny Think Twice, Full Moon 7-29979,
    1982..2.00 - 4.00
45, If You Leave Me Now/Together Again, Columbia 3-10390, 1976 ....2.50 - 5.00
45, Look Away/Come In from the Night, Reprise 7-27766, 1988
    Record only..1.50 - 3.00
    Picture sleeve only ....1.50 - 3.00
45, Make Me Smile/Colour My World, Columbia 4-45127, 1970
    Record only..2.50 - 5.00
    Picture sleeve only..4.00 - 8.00
    45, Saturday in the Park/Alma Mater, Columbia 4-45657, 1972 ......2.50 - 5.00
LP, *Chicago*, Columbia KGP 24 (2-record set), 1970, red labels with "360 Sound"
    at bottom; label and spine call the album "Chicago" ....20.00 - 40.00
LP, *Chicago II*
    Columbia KGP 24 (2-record set), 1970, red labels with "360 Sound" at bottom;
    label and spine call the album "Chicago II" ....12.50 - 25.00
    Columbia KGP 24 (2-record set), 1970, orange labels................10.00 - 20.00
    Columbia GQ 33258 (2-record set), quadraphonic, 1975 ....12.50 - 25.00
LP, *Chicago 16,* Full Moon 23689, 1982 ....5.00 - 10.00

MVP:
LP, *Chicago*, Columbia, no catalog number (17-record set), 1976, promotional-
    only set of the first 10 Chicago LPs with gold stamps on covers, box, side
    panel and wraparound ....125.00 - 250.00

EP, *Sing Again with the Chipmunks* (contents: Alvin's Orchestra/Swanee
River/Sing a Goofy Song/Witch Doctor), Liberty LSX-1008 .., 1961, record and
cardboard cover together, chipmunks look more "realistic" than the later
cartoon characters ....40.00 - 80.00

45, Alvin's Harmonica/Mediocre, Liberty 55179, 1959.....................10.00 - 20.00
45, The Chipmunk Song/Almost Good, Liberty 55168, 1958
    Blue-green label (standard) ....12.50 - 25.00
    Black label ....15.00 - 30.00
    Dark blue label ....15.00 - 30.00
45, The Chipmunk Song/Alvin's Harmonica
    Liberty 55250, 1959, blue-green label, no horizontal lines ....7.50 - 15.00
    Liberty 55250, 1961, blue-green label with horizontal lines..........6.00 - 12.00
    Liberty 55250, 1960s, black label with rainbow band at left ....4.00 - 8.00
    Liberty 55250, 1959, picture sleeve only, with "realistic" chipmunks
    ....20.00 - 40.00
    Liberty 55250, 1961, picture sleeve only, with "cartoon character"
    chipmunks ....15.00 - 30.00

LP, *Around the World with the Chipmunks*
    Liberty LRP-3170, mono, 1960, cover with "realistic" chipmunks on and
    near a plane ....20.00 - 40.00
    Liberty LRP-3170, mono, 1961, cover with "cartoon character" Chipmunks
    on and near a camel..10.00 - 20.00
    Liberty LST-7170, stereo, 1960, cover with "realistic" chipmunks on and
    near a plane ....25.00 - 50.00
    Liberty LST-7170, stereo, 1960, cover with "cartoon character" Chipmunks
    on and near a camel..12.50 - 25.00
LP, *The Chipmunks Sing the Beatles Hits*
    Liberty LRP-3388, mono, 1964..15.00 - 30.00
    Liberty LST-7388, stereo, 1964...20.00 - 40.00

MVP:
LP, *Let's All Sing with the Chipmunks*, Liberty LST-7132, stereo, 1959, red vinyl,
    mono version LRP-3132 on red vinyl is 30.00 – 60.00, black vinyl versions of
    either go for less ....40.00 - 80.00

LP, *Eric Clapton*

    Atco 33-329, mono, 1970, white label, promotional issue only

    ....50.00 - 100.00

    Atco SD 33-329, stereo, 1970, standard yellow label (also see next page)

    ....10.00 - 20.00

    Mobile Fidelity 1-220, 1995, "Original Master Recording" on cover

    ....12.50 - 25.00

    RSO RS-1-3008, 1977, reissue ....6.00 - 12.00

45, After Midnight/Easy Now, Atco 6784, 1970 ....3.00 - 6.00

45, I Shot the Sheriff/Give Me Strength

    RSO 409, 1974 ....2.50 - 5.00

    RSO 500, 1974, early reissue ....2.00 - 4.00

45, I've Got a Rock n' Roll Heart/Man in Love

    Duck 7-29780, 1983, silver label ....2.00 - 4.00

    Warner Bros. 7-29780, 1983, regular white WB label....................2.50 - 5.00

45, Lay Down Sally/Next Time You See Her, RSO 886, 1978 ....2.00 - 4.00

45, Let It Rain/Easy Now, Polydor 15049, 1972 ....3.00 - 6.00

45, Tears in Heaven/Tracks and Lines, Reprise 7-19038, 1992 ....2.50 - 5.00

LP, *461 Ocean Boulevard*

    RSO RS-1-3023, 1977, reissue ....6.00 - 12.00

    RSO QD 4801, quadraphonic, 1974 ....12.50 - 25.00

    RSO SO 4801, 1974, with "Give Me Strength" ....7.50 - 15.00

    RSO SO 4801, 1974, with "Better Make It Through the Day" ....6.00 - 12.00

    RSO 811 697-1, 1980s, reissue ....4.00 - 8.00

LP, *Slowhand*

    RSO RS-1-3030, 1977 ....6.00 - 12.00

    RSO 823 276-1, 1983, reissue ....4.00 - 8.00

    Mobile Fidelity 1-030, 1980, "Original Master Recording" on cover

    ....35.00 - 70.00

MVP:

LP, *Eric Clapton*, Atco SD 33-329, stereo, 1970, with alternate takes of "After Midnight" and "Blues Power" and remixes of other tracks, "CTH" appears in the trail-off area of the record; see previous page for other versions

....100.00 - 200.00

45, Glad All Over/I Know You, Epic 5-9656, 1964
  Record only...7.50 - 15.00
  Picture sleeve only ....10.00 - 20.00

45, Any Way You Want It/Crying Over You, Epic 5-9739, 1964 ....6.00 - 12.00
45, Because/Theme Without a Name, Epic 5-9704, 1964
    Record only...6.00 - 12.00
    Picture sleeve only...10.00 - 20.00
45, Bits and Pieces/All of the Time, Epic 5-9671, 1964 ....6.00 - 12.00
45, Catch Us If You Can/On the Move, Epic 5-9833, 1965
    Record only...6.00 - 12.00
    Picture sleeve only...10.00 - 20.00
45, Over and Over/I'll Be Yours (My Love), Epic 5-9863, 1965
    Record only...6.00 - 12.00
    Picture sleeve only...10.00 - 20.00
45, You Got What It Takes/Doctor Rhythm, Epic 5-10144, 1967
    Record only...6.00 - 12.00
    Picture sleeve only...10.00 - 20.00
LP, *The Dave Clark Five's Greatest Hits*
    Epic LN 24185, mono, 1966...12.50 - 25.00
    Epic BN 26185, rechanneled stereo, 1966, yellow label..............10.00 - 20.00
    Epic BN 26185, rechanneled stereo, 1973, orange label............20.00 - 40.00
LP, *Having a Wild Weekend*
    Epic LN 24162, mono, 1965...20.00 - 40.00
    Epic BN 26162, rechanneled stereo, 1965 ....15.00 - 30.00

MVP:
LP, *The Dave Clark Five Interview*, Epic XEM 77238 on one side, XEM 77239 on
    the other, promotional item only, 1964 ....300.00 - 600.00

LP, *In Love!*

    Laurie LLP-2032, mono, 1965 ....7.50 - 15.00

    Laurie SLP-2032, stereo, 1965 ....7.50 - 15.00

    Laurie ST-90497, stereo, 1965, Capitol Record Club edition ....10.00 - 20.00

45, Don't Sleep in the Subway/Here Comes the Morning, Warner Bros. 7049, 1967
....5.00 - 10.00
45, Downtown/You'd Better Love Me, Warner Bros. 5494, 1964
    Red label with arrows...7.50 - 15.00
    Orange label...5.00 - 10.00
45, I Know a Place/Jack and John, Warner Bros. 5612, 1965 ....5.00 - 10.00
45, Kiss Me Goodbye/I've Got Love Going for Me, Warner Bros. 7170, 1968
    Orange label...5.00 - 10.00
    Green label with "W7" logo..4.00 - 8.00
45, My Love/Where Am I Going, Warner Bros. 5684, 1965 ....5.00 - 10.00
45, A Sign of the Times/Time for Love, Warner Bros. 5802, 1966 ......5.00 - 10.00
45, This Is My Song/High, Warner Bros. 7002, 1967........................5.00 - 10.00
LP, *Downtown*
    Warner Bros. W 1590, mono, 1965, gray label ....7.50 - 15.00
    Warner Bros. W 1590, mono, 1966, gold label...........................6.00 - 12.00
    Warner Bros. WS 1590, stereo, 1965, gold label......................10.00 - 20.00
LP, *Greatest Hits, Volume I*
    Warner Bros. WS 1765, 1968, green label with "W7" logo ....5.00 - 10.00
    Warner Bros. ST-91598, 1968, Capitol Record Club edition..........7.50 - 15.00
LP, *I Couldn't Live Without Your Love*
    Warner Bros. W 1645, mono, 1966...5.00 - 10.00
    Warner Bros. WS 1645, stereo, 1966, gold label..........................6.00 - 12.00

MVP:
LP, *Petula Clark Swings the Jingle*, Coca-Cola 103, 1966, promotional-only col-
    lection of Coca-Cola jingles ....75.00 - 150.00

LP, *Golden Hits*

    Everest 1200, rechanneled stereo, 1962..6.00 - 12.00

    Everest 5200, mono, 1962 ....10.00 - 20.00

45, Crazy/Who Can I Count On, Decca 31317, 1961 ....6.00 - 12.00
45, I Fall to Pieces/Lovin' in Vain, Decca 31205, 1961 ....6.00 - 12.00
45, She's Got You/Strange, Decca 31354, 1962 ....6.00 - 12.00
45, Sweet Dreams (Of You)/Back in Baby's Arms, Decca 31483,
    1963...5.00 - 10.00
45, Walkin' After Midnight/A Poor Man's Roses (Or a Rich Man's Gold),
    Decca 9-30221, 1957
    Record only..10.00 - 20.00
    Picture sleeve only ....40.00 - 80.00
45, Walking After Midnight/That Wonderful Someone, Everest 2020,
    1963...6.00 - 12.00
LP, *The Patsy Cline Story*
    Decca DXB 176 (2-record set), mono, 1963 ....20.00 - 40.00
    Decca DXSB 7176 (2-record set), stereo, 1963 ....25.00 - 50.00
    MCA 4038 (2-record set), 1974, black labels with rainbow..........7.50 - 15.00
LP, *Patsy Cline's Greatest Hits*
    Decca DL 4854, mono, 1967...10.00 - 20.00
    Decca DL 74854, stereo, 1967..12.50 - 25.00
    MCA 12, 1973, black label with rainbow....................................6.00 - 12.00
    MCA 12, 1977, tan label...5.00 - 10.00
    MCA 12, 1980, blue label with rainbow......................................4.00 - 8.00

MVP:
LP, *Patsy Cline*, Decca DL 8611, mono, 1957, black label with silver print,
    editions with color bars on label go for less.............................50.00 - 100.00

LP, *Love Is the Thing*

    Capitol SW 824, stereo, 1959, black label with colorband, "Capitol" at

    left..15.00 - 30.00

    Capitol W 824, mono, 1957, gray label ....20.00 - 40.00

    DCC Compact Classics LPZ-2029, 1997, 180-gram virgin vinyl

    reissue..60.00 - 120.00

    (Other versions on Capitol exist and sell for less.)

45, A Blossom Fell/If I May, Capitol F3095, 1955 ....7.50 - 15.00

45, Darling Je Vous Aime Beaucoup/The Sand and the Sea, Capitol F3027,
1955..5.00 - 10.00

45, Mona Lisa/The Greatest Inventor (Of Them All), Capitol F1010,
1950..7.50 - 15.00

45, Ramblin' Rose/Good Times, Capitol 4804, 1962
Record only...6.00 - 12.00
Picture sleeve only..10.00 - 20.00

45, Those Lazy-Hazy-Crazy Days of Summer/In the Cool of Day, Capitol
4965, 1963
Record only...6.00 - 12.00
Picture sleeve only..10.00 - 20.00

45, Too Young/That's My Girl, Capitol F1449, 1951 ....6.00 - 12.00

LP, *Unforgettable*
Capitol DT 357, "duophonic," 1965 ....6.00 - 12.00
Capitol H 357, mono, 1952, 10-inch record ....30.00 - 60.00
Capitol SM-357, "duophonic," 1970s, reissue ....4.00 - 8.00
Capitol T 357, mono, 1955, turquoise label ....20.00 - 40.00
Capitol T 357, mono, 1958, black label with colorband, "Capitol" at
left..15.00 - 30.00
Capitol T 357, mono, 1962, black label with colorband, "Capitol" at
top...10.00 - 20.00
Capitol SN-16162, 1981, reissue ....4.00 - 8.00

MVP:

LP, *The Complete Capitol Recordings of the Nat King Cole Trio*, Mosaic
MR27-138 (27-record set), 1991 ....400.00 - 800.00

LP, *Hello, I Must Be Going!*, Atlantic 80035, 1982 ....4.00 - 8.00

45, Against All Odds (Take a Look at Me Now)/The Search, Atlantic
    7-89700, 1984, B-side by Larry Carlton
    Record only..1.50 - 3.00
    Picture sleeve only ....1.50 - 3.00
45, Another Day in Paradise/Heat on the Street, Atlantic 7-88774, 1989
    Record only..1.50 - 3.00
    Picture sleeve only ....1.50 - 3.00
45, I Missed Again/I'm Not Moving, Atlantic 3790, 1981
    Record only..1.50 - 3.00
    Picture sleeve only...3.00 - 6.00
45, In the Air Tonight/The Roof Is Leaking, Atlantic 3824, 1981
    Record only..1.50 - 3.00
    Picture sleeve only ....3.00 - 6.00
45, One More Night/The Man with the Horn, Atlantic 7-89588, 1985
    Record only..1.50 - 3.00
    Picture sleeve only ....1.50 - 3.00
45, Sussudio/I Like the Way, Atlantic 7-89560, 1985
    Record only..1.50 - 3.00
    Picture sleeve only ....1.50 - 3.00
LP, ... *But Seriously*, Atlantic 82050, 1989 ....6.00 - 12.00
LP, *Face Value*, Atlantic SD 16029, 1981 ....4.00 - 8.00
LP, *No Jacket Required*, Atlantic 81240, 1985.....................4.00 - 8.00

MVP:
LP, *Collins on Collins: Exclusive Candid Interview*, Atlantic PR 759, 1985, pro-
    motional-only interview album with cue sheets ....15.00 - 30.00

45, Nightshift/I Keep Running, Motown 1773, 1985
    Record only..1.50 - 3.00
    Picture sleeve only ....3.00 - 6.00

45, Brick House/Captain Quickdraw, Motown 1425, 1977 ....2.00 - 4.00
45, Easy/Can't Let You Tease Me, Motown 1418, 1977 ....2.00 - 4.00
45, Lady (You Bring Me Up)/Gettin' It, Motown 1514, 1981 ....2.00 - 4.00
45, Oh No/Lovin' You, Motown 1527, 1981 ....2.00 - 4.00
45, Sail On/Thumpin' Music, Motown 1466, 1979 ....2.00 - 4.00
45, Still/Such a Woman, Motown 1474, 1979 ....2.00 - 4.00
45, Sweet Love/Better Never Than Forever, Motown 1381, 1976 ....2.00 - 4.00
45, Three Times a Lady/Look What You've Done to Me, Motown 1443,
    1978 ....2.00 - 4.00
LP, *Commodores*
    Motown M5-222V1, 1982, reissue ....4.00 - 8.00
    Motown M7-884, 1977, original ....5.00 - 10.00
LP, *Heroes*, Motown M8-939, 1980 ....5.00 - 10.00
LP, *Hot on the Tracks*, Motown M6-867, 1976 ....5.00 - 10.00
LP, *Midnight Magic*, Motown M8-926, 1979 ....5.00 - 10.00
LP, *Natural High*, Motown M7-902, 1978..5.00 - 10.00
LP, *Nightshift*, Motown 6124 ML, 1985 ....5.00 - 10.00

MVP:
LP, *1978 Platinum Tour*, Motown PR 39, 1978, promotional-only
    compilation ....10.00 - 20.00

LP, *Saturday Night with Mr. C.*
    RCA Victor LOP-1004, mono, 1958, original with gatefold ....12.50 - 25.00
    RCA Victor LSO-1004, stereo, 1958, original with gatefold ....20.00 – 40.00
    RCA Victor LPM-1971, mono, 1959, reissue with no gatefold......10.00 - 20.00
    RCA Victor LSP-1971, stereo, 1959, reissue with no gatefold .....15.00 – 30.00

45, Catch a Falling Star/Magic Moments, RCA Victor 47-7128, 1957 ..6.00 - 12.00

45, Don't Let the Stars Get In Your Eyes/Lies, RCA Victor 47-5064,
1952...6.00 - 12.00

45, Hot Diggity (Dog Ziggity Boom)/Juke Box Baby, RCA Victor 47-6427, 1956
....5.00 - 10.00

45, If/Zing, Zing, Zoom, Zoom, RCA Victor 47-3997, 1950 ....6.00 - 12.00

45, It's Impossible/Long Life. Lots of Happiness, RCA Victor 74-0387,
1970...2.50 - 5.00

45, Ko Ko Mo (I Love You So)/You'll Always Be My Lifetime Sweetheart,
RCA Victor 47-5994, 1955...5.00 - 10.00

45, Round and Round/Mi Casa, Su Casa (My House Is Your House),
RCA Victor 47-6815, 1957..5.00 - 10.00

45, Tina Marie/Fooled, RCA Victor 47-6192, 1955 ....5.00 - 10.00

45, Wanted/Look Out the Window, RCA Victor 47-5647, 1954 ....6.00 - 12.00

LP, *Como's Golden Records*

RCA Victor LOP-1007, mono, 1958, with gatefold cover ....12.50 - 25.00

RCA Victor AFL1-1981, 1977, reissue with new prefix ....5.00 - 10.00

RCA Victor LPM-1981, mono, 1959, reissue with no gatefold......10.00 - 20.00

RCA Victor LSP-1981(e), rechanneled stereo, 1962 ....6.00 - 12.00

RCA Victor LPM-3224, mono, 1954, 10-inch record ....20.00 - 40.00

RCA Victor AYL1-3802, 1981, "Best Buy Series" reissue ....4.00 - 8.00

MVP:

EP box set, *Perry Como,* RCA Victor SPD-27, 1957, includes 10 extended play
singles plus box and booklet, value is for complete sets.............40.00 - 80.00

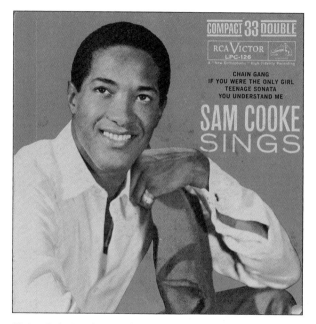

EP, *Sam Cooke Sings* (contents: Chain Gang/If You Were the Only Girl//Teenage
Sonata/You Understand Me), RCA Victor LPC-126, 1961, "Compact 33 Double,"
with both record and cardboard picture cover............................20.00 - 40.00

45, Another Saturday Night/Love Will Find a Way, RCA Victor 47-8164, 1963
    Record only..7.50 - 15.00
    Picture sleeve only...12.50 - 25.00
45, Chain Gang/I Fall in Love Every Day, RCA Victor 47-7783, 1960
    Record only..7.50 - 15.00
    Picture sleeve only...12.50 - 25.00
45, Cupid/Farewell, My Darling, RCA Victor 47-7883, 1961
    Record only..7.50 - 15.00
    Picture sleeve only...12.50 - 25.00
45, Shake/A Change Is Gonna Come, RCA Victor 47-8486, 1964........6.00 - 12.00
45, Twistin' the Night Away/One More Time, RCA Victor 47-7983,
    1962..7.50 - 15.00
45, You Send Me/Summertime
    Keen 3-4013, late 1950s, multicolor label, slightly different number than
    original edition...10.00 - 20.00
    Keen 34013, 1957, black label original....................12.50 - 25.00
LP, *The Best of Sam Cooke*
    RCA Victor AFL1-2625, 1977, reissue with new prefix................6.00 - 12.00
    RCA Victor LPM-2625, mono, 1962.........................15.00 - 30.00
    RCA Victor LSP-2625, rechanneled stereo, 1962.....10.00 - 20.00
    RCA Victor AYL1-3863, 1981, reissue.......................4.00 - 8.00
LP, *The Man and His Music*, RCA Victor CPL2-7127 (2-record set),
    1986..7.50 - 15.00

MVP:
LP, *I Thank God*, Keen 86103, mono, 1960 ....200.00 - 400.00

LP, *Killer*

 Warner Bros. BS 2567, 1971, with attached 1972 calendar/poster
 ....15.00 - 30.00
 Warner Bros. BS 2567, 1972, without attached poster, green label
 ....6.00 - 12.00
 Warner Bros. BS 2567, 1973, "Burbank" palm trees label ....5.00 - 10.00

45, How You Gonna See Me Now/No Tricks, Warner Bros. 8695, 1978.....2.50 - 5.00

45, I Never Cry/Go to Hell, Warner Bros. 8228, 1976 ....2.00 - 4.00

45, No More Mr. Nice Guy/Raped and Freezin', Warner Bros. 7691,
    1973...2.50 - 5.00

45, Only Women/Cold Ethyl, Atlantic 3254, 1975 ....2.50 - 5.00

45, Poison/Trash, Epic 34-68958, 1989 ....1.50 - 3.00

45, School's Out/Gutter Cat, Warner Bros. 7596, 1972
    Record only...2.50 - 5.00
    Picture sleeve only...5.00 - 10.00

45, You and Me/It's Hot Tonight, Warner Bros. 8349, 1977
    Record only...2.00 - 4.00
    Picture sleeve only...4.00 - 8.00

LP, *Alice Cooper Goes to Hell*, Warner Bros. BS 2896, 1976 ....5.00 - 10.00

LP, *Alice Cooper's Greatest Hits*
    Warner Bros. W 2803, 1974, "Burbank" palm trees label ....5.00 - 10.00
    Warner Bros. BSK 3107, 1977, reissue, "Burbank" palm trees
    label ....4.00 - 8.00
    Warner Bros. BSK 3107, 1979, reissue, white or tan label ....3.00 - 6.00

LP, *Welcome to My Nightmare*
    Atlantic SD 18130, 1975..5.00 - 10.00
    Atlantic SD 19157, 1978, reissue...4.00 - 8.00
    Mobile Fidelity 1-063, 1980, "Original Master Recording" on
    cover ....25.00 - 50.00

MVP:
45, Reflected/Living, Straight 101, 1969, regular stock copy, promotional copies
    go for 15.00 – 30.00..150.00 - 300.00

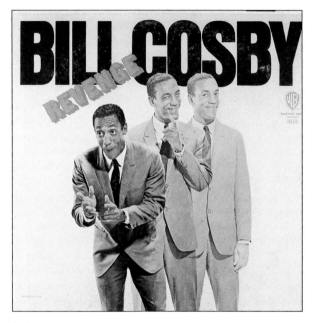

LP, *Revenge*

    Warner Bros. W 1691, mono, 1967...7.50 - 15.00

    Warner Bros. WS 1691, stereo, 1967, gold label.........................7.50 - 15.00

    Warner Bros. WS 1691, stereo, 1968, green "W7" label ....5.00 - 10.00

45, Little Ole Man (Uptight-Everything's Alright)/Don'cha Know, Warner Bros.
7072, 1967..4.00 - 8.00
45, Yes, Yes, Yes/Ben, Capitol 4258, 1976...2.00 - 4.00
LP, *The Best of Bill Cosby*
    Warner Bros. WS 1798, 1969, green "W7" box label...................6.00 - 12.00
    Warner Bros. WS 1798, 1970, green "WB" shield label ....5.00 - 10.00
LP, *Bill Cosby "Himself"*, Motown 6026 ML, 1982...........................5.00 - 10.00
LP, *Fat Albert*, MCA 333, 1973...5.00 - 10.00
LP, *For Adults Only*
    MCA 553, 1970s, reissue...4.00 - 8.00
    Uni 73112, 1971, original ....5.00 - 10.00
LP, *More of the Best of Bill Cosby*, Warner Bros. WS 1836, 1970, green
    label ....6.00 - 12.00
LP, *I Started Out as a Child*
    Warner Bros. W 1567, mono, 1964...7.50 - 15.00
    Warner Bros. WS 1567, stereo, 1964, gold label.......................10.00 - 20.00
    Warner Bros. WS 1567, stereo, 1968, green "W7" box label ....7.50 - 15.00
    Warner Bros. WS 1567, stereo, 1970, green "WB" shield label ...5.00 - 10.00
LP, *Those of You With or Without Children, You'll Understand*, Geffen
    GHS 24104, 1986 ....5.00 - 10.00
LP, *200 M.P.H.*, Warner Bros. WS 1757, 1968....................................6.00 - 12.00

MVP:
LP, *8:15 12:15*, Tetragrammaton T-5100 (2-record set), 1969.........10.00 - 20.00

LP, *Disraeli Gears*

    Atco 33-232, mono, 1967 ....25.00 - 50.00

    Atco SD 33-232, stereo, 1967, purple and brown label..............15.00 - 30.00

    Atco SD 33-232, stereo, 1969, yellow label ....7.50 - 15.00

    RSO RS-1-3010, 1977, reissue ....6.00 - 12.00

45, Badge/What a Bringdown, Atco 6668, 1969 ....4.00 - 8.00
45, Crossroads/Passing the Time, Atco 6646, 1969 ....4.00 - 8.00
45, Strange Brew/Tales of Brave Ulysses, Atco 6488, 1967 ....7.50 - 15.00
45, Sunshine of Your Love/SWLABR, Atco 6544, 1968.......................4.00 - 8.00
45, White Room/Those Were the Days, Atco 6617, 1968....................4.00 - 8.00

LP, *Fresh Cream*
    Atco 33-206, mono, 1967 ....25.00 - 50.00
    Atco SD 33-206, stereo, 1967, purple and brown label...............15.00 - 30.00
    Atco SD 33-206, stereo, 1969, yellow label ....7.50 - 15.00
    DCC Compact Classics LPZ-2015, 1996, 180-gram virgin vinyl
    issue...50.00 - 100.00
    RSO RS-1-3009, 1977, reissue ....6.00 - 12.00

LP, *Goodbye*
    Atco SD 7001, 1969, purple and brown label; deduct 33% if poster is
    missing..15.00 - 30.00
    Atco SD 7001, 1969, yellow label; deduct 33% if poster is
    missing..7.50 - 15.00
    RSO RS-1-3013, 1977, reissue ....6.00 - 12.00

LP, *Heavy Cream*, Polydor 24-3502 (2-record set), 1972.................7.50 - 15.00

LP, *Live Cream*
    Atco SD 33-328, 1970 ....12.50 - 25.00
    RSO RS-1-3014, 1977, reissue ....6.00 - 12.00

MVP:
LP, *Wheels of Fire*, Atco 2-700 (2-record set), mono, 1968, white label
    promotional copy only, stereo copies with an "SD" prefix go for much
    less...100.00 - 200.00

LP, *Cosmo's Factory*

    Analogue Productions AAPP-8402, 2002, audiophile reissue ......12.50 - 25.00

    Fantasy ORC-4516, 1981, reissue ....4.00 - 8.00

    Fantasy F-8402, 1970, dark blue label original ....7.50 - 15.00

    Fantasy F-8402, 1973, brown label..5.00 - 10.00

    Mobile Fidelity 1-037, 1979, "Original Master Recording" on cover

    ....35.00 - 70.00

45, Bad Moon Rising/Lodi, Fantasy 622, 1969 .... 3.00 - 6.00
45, Down on the Corner/Fortunate Son, Fantasy 634, 1969
    Record only .... 3.00 - 6.00
    Picture sleeve only .... 6.00 - 12.00
45, Green River/Commotion, Fantasy 625, 1969 .... 3.00 - 6.00
45, Lookin' Out My Back Door/Long As I Can See the Light, Fantasy 645, 1970
    Record only .... 3.00 - 6.00
    Picture sleeve only .... 6.00 - 12.00
45, Proud Mary/Born on the Bayou, Fantasy 619, 1969 .... 3.00 - 6.00
45, Suzie Q (Part One)/Suzie Q (Part Two), Fantasy 616, 1968 .... 3.00 - 6.00
45, Travelin' Band/Who'll Stop the Rain, Fantasy 637, 1970
    Record only .... 3.00 - 6.00
    Picture sleeve only .... 6.00 - 12.00
LP, *Creedence Clearwater Revival*
    Analogue Productions AAPP-8382, 2002, audiophile reissue ...... 12.50 - 25.00
    Fantasy ORC-4512, 1981, reissue .... 4.00 - 8.00
    Fantasy F-8382, 1968, dark blue label, no reference to "Susie Q" on the
    front cover .... 12.50 - 25.00
    Fantasy F-8382, 1968, dark blue label, with blurb advertising "Susie Q"
    on the front cover .... 7.50 - 15.00
    Fantasy F-8382, 1973, brown label .... 5.00 - 10.00

MVP:
45, Porterville/Call It Pretending, Scorpio 412, 1968 .... 40.00 - 80.00

45, White Christmas/God Rest Ye Merry Gentlemen

    Decca 9-23778, 1950, lines on either side of "Decca" on label; Sides 5 and
6 of "Album No. 9-65" ....6.00 - 12.00

    Decca 9-23778, 1955, star under "Decca" on label......................5.00 - 10.00

    Decca 23778, 1960, color bars on label ....4.00 - 8.00

    Decca 23778, 1960, picture sleeve only ....7.50 - 15.00

45, Around the World/Around the World, Decca 9-30262, 1957, B-side by
  Victor Young
  Record only...4.00 - 8.00
  Picture sleeve only ....7.50 - 15.00
45, Around the World/Mississippi Mud, Decca 9-38031, 1957, green label,
  promotional issue
  Record only...5.00 - 10.00
  Picture sleeve only..10.00 - 20.00
45, In a Little Spanish Town ('Twas On a Night Like This)/Ol' Man River,
  Decca 9-29850, 1956...4.00 - 8.00
45, Pistol Packin' Mama/Don't Fence Me In, with the Andrews Sisters
  Decca 9-23484, 1950, lines on either side of "Decca".................6.00 - 12.00
  Decca 9-23484, 1955, star under "Decca" ....5.00 - 10.00
LP, *The Best of Bing*
  Decca DXB 184 (2-record set), mono, 1965 ....12.50 - 25.00
  MCA 2-4045 (2-record set), 1970s, black labels with rainbow, gatefold
  cover ....6.00 - 12.00
  MCA 2-4045 (2-record set), 1980, blue labels with rainbow, regular
  cover ....5.00 - 10.00
LP, *Hey Jude/Hey Bing!*, Amos AAS-7001, 1969................................6.00 - 12.00
LP, *Some Fine Old Chestnuts*, Decca DL 8374, mono, 1957............20.00 - 40.00
LP, *Songs I Wish I Had Sung...The First Time Around*
  Decca DL 8352, mono, 1956, black label, silver print ....20.00 - 40.00
  Decca DL 78352, "enhanced for stereo," 1960s, black label with
  color bars..5.00 - 10.00

MVP:
LP, *High Tor*, Decca DL 8272, mono, 1956, soundtrack from television
  special ....200.00 - 400.00

LP, *Crosby, Stills & Nash*

    Atlantic SD 8229, 1969, original...10.00 - 20.00

    Atlantic SD 8229, 2000, "Manufactured and Distributed by Classic Records"

    on cover ....12.50 - 25.00

    Atlantic SD 19117, 1977, reissue...5.00 - 10.00

    Nautilus NR-48, 1982, "Super Disc" on cover .... 75.00 - 150.00

45, Just a Song Before I Go/Dark Star, Atlantic 3401, 1977
 Record only...2.00 - 4.00
 Picture sleeve only..2.50 - 5.00
45, Marrakesh Express/Helplessly Hoping, Atlantic 2652, 1969...........3.00 - 6.00
45, Ohio/Find the Cost of Freedom, Atlantic 2740, 1970
 Record only...3.00 - 6.00
 Picture sleeve only..6.00 - 12.00
45, Our House/Déjà Vu, Atlantic 2760, 1970.......................................3.00 - 6.00
45, Southern Cross/Into the Darkness, Atlantic 7-89969, 1982
 Record only...1.50 - 3.00
 Picture sleeve only..2.00 - 4.00
45, Suite: Judy Blue Eyes/Long Time Gone, Atlantic 2676, 1969...........3.00 - 6.00
45, Wasted on the Way/Delta, Atlantic 4058, 1982
 Record only...1.50 - 3.00
 Picture sleeve only..2.00 - 4.00
LP, *CSN*, Atlantic SD 19104, 1977 ....6.00 - 12.00
LP, *4 Way Street*, Atlantic SD 2-902 (2-record set), 1971 ....10.00 - 20.00
LP, *So Far*
 Atlantic SD 18100, 1974, original...6.00 - 12.00
 Atlantic SD 19119, 1977, reissue...5.00 - 10.00

MVP:
LP, *Déjà Vu*, Mobile Fidelity 1-088, 1980s, "Original Master Recording" at top of
 cover, other versions are much less...100.00 - 200.00

LP, *If I Were a Carpenter*

    Atlantic 8135, mono, 1967...7.50 - 15.00

    Atlantic SD 8135, stereo, 1967..25.00 - 50.00

45, Beyond the Sea/That's the Way Love Is, Atco 6158, 1960
  Record only..10.00 - 20.00
  Picture sleeve only...20.00 - 40.00
45, Dream Lover/Bullmoose, Atco 6140, 1959
  Record only..10.00 - 20.00
  Picture sleeve only...25.00 - 50.00
45, If I Were a Carpenter/Rainin', Atlantic 2350, 1966......................5.00 - 10.00
45, Mack the Knife/Was There a Call for Me, Atco 6147, 1959
  Record only..10.00 - 20.00
  Picture sleeve only...20.00 - 40.00
45, Splish Splash/Judy, Don't Be Moody, Atco 6117, 1958...............10.00 - 20.00
45, You're the Reason I'm Living/Now You're Gone, Capitol 4897, 1962
  Record only..5.00 - 10.00
  Picture sleeve only...7.50 - 15.00
LP, *The Best of Bobby Darin*
  Capitol ST 2571, stereo, 1966 ....7.50 - 15.00
  Capitol T 2571, mono, 1966...7.50 - 15.00
LP, *That's All*
  Atco 33-104, mono, 1959, yellow "harp" label ....20.00 - 40.00
  Atco 33-104, mono, 1962, gold and dark blue label..................10.00 - 20.00
  Atco SD 33-104, stereo, 1959, yellow "harp" label ....50.00 - 100.00
  Atco SD 33-104, stereo, 1962, purple and brown label.............12.50 - 25.00

MVP:
LP, *Finally,* Motown MS-739, 1972, officially unreleased, but some RCA test
  pressings exists; value is for one of those ....250.00 - 500.00

LP, *Sketches of Spain*

    Columbia CL 1480, mono, 1960, red and black label with six white "eye"
    logos ....25.00 - 50.00
    Columbia CS 8271, stereo, 1960, red and black label with six "eye"
    logos ....40.00 - 80.00
    (Other versions on Columbia exist and sell for less.)

45, Miles Runs the Voodoo Down/Spanish Key, Columbia 4-45171, 1970
....4.00 - 8.00

LP, *Birth of the Cool*
    Capitol T 762, mono, 1956...75.00 - 150.00
    Capitol DT 1974, "Duophonic" stereo, 1960s ....6.00 - 12.00
    Capitol T 1974, mono, 1963, reissue ....15.00 - 30.00
    Capitol N-16168, mono, 1980s, reissue..4.00 - 8.00

LP, *Bitches Brew*
    Columbia GP 26 (2-record set), 1970. "360 Sound Stereo" on red
    labels..20.00 - 40.00
    Columbia GP 26 (2-record set), 1970, orange labels...................7.50 - 15.00
    Columbia PG 26 (2-record set), 1977, orange labels, new prefix .6.00 - 12.00
    Columbia GQ 30997 (2-record set), quadraphonic, 1972 ....20.00 - 40.00

LP, *The Complete Birth of the Cool* , Capitol M-11026, mono, 1972
....6.00 - 12.00

LP, *Cookin' with the Miles Davis Quintet*
    Fantasy OJC-128, 1980s, reissue ....5.00 - 10.00
    Prestige PRLP-7094, mono, 1957, with W. 50th St. address on yellow
    label ....50.00 - 100.00
    Prestige PRLP-7094, mono, late 1950s, with Bergenfield, N.J. address on
    yellow label ....30.00 - 60.00
    Prestige PRLP-7094, mono, mid 1960s, with trident on blue
    label ....15.00 - 30.00

LP, *A Tribute to Jack Johnson*
    Columbia KC 30455, 1971..6.00 - 12.00
    Columbia PC 30455, 1977, reissue...4.00 - 8.00

MVP:
LP, *Miles Davis (Young Man with a Horn)*, Blue Note BLP-5013, mono, 10-inch
    album, 1952, not to be confused with a nearly identical reissue by Classic
    Records in 2002) ....150.00 - 300.00

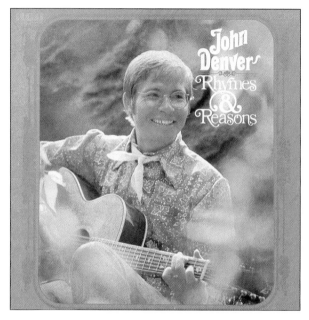

LP, *Rhymes & Reasons*, RCA Victor LSP-4207, 1969, orange label, sturdy
(non-flexible) vinyl...7.50 - 15.00

John Denver

45, Annie's Song/Cool An' Green An' Shady, RCA Victor APBO-0295, 1974, orange label ....2.00 - 4.00

45, I'm Sorry/Calypso, RCA Victor PB-10353, 1975, tan label ....2.00 - 4.00

45, Rocky Mountain High/Spring, RCA Victor 74-0829, 1972...............2.50 - 5.00

45, Sunshine on My Shoulders/Around and Around, RCA Victor APBO-0213, 1974..2.00 - 4.00

45, Take Me Home, Country Roads/Poems, Prayers and Promises, RCA Victor 74-0445, 1971 ....4.00 - 8.00

45, Thank God I'm a Country Boy/My Sweet Lady, RCA Victor PB-10239, 1975..2.00 - 4.00

LP, *John Denver's Greatest Hits*

RCA Victor APL1-0374, 1970s, reissue...4.00 - 8.00

RCA Victor AQL1-0374, late 1970s, reissue ....4.00 - 8.00

RCA Victor CPL1-0374, 1974, orange label, original ....5.00 - 10.00

RCA Victor CPL1-0374, 1975, tan label or black label, dog near top..4.00 - 8.00

LP, *Windsong*

RCA Victor AFL1-1183, 1970s, reissue..4.00 - 8.00

RCA Victor APL1-1183, 1975, tan label, original ....5.00 - 10.00

RCA Victor APL1-1183, 1976, black label, dog near top..................4.00 - 8.00

RCA Victor AQL1-1183, late 1970s, reissue ....4.00 - 8.00

RCA Victor AYL1-5191, 1980s, "Besy Buy Series" reissue...............3.00 - 6.00

MVP:

LP, *John Denver Sings*, HJD 66, 1966, private issue of 300 or so, made as Christmas gifts to friends ....250.00 - 500.00

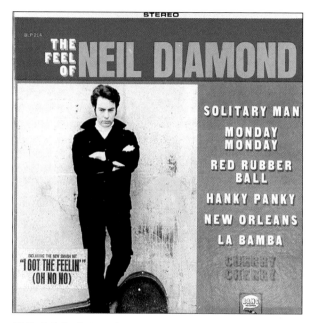

LP, *The Feel of Neil Diamond*

    Bang BLP 214, mono, 1966, all tracks play in mono as advertised
....30.00 - 60.00

    Bang BLP 214, mono, 1966, labeled mono but the record plays in stereo ....40.00 - 80.00

    Bang BLPS 214, stereo, 1966, red and yellow label.................50.00 - 100.00

    Bang BLPS 214, stereo, 1974, reissue on blue "clouds" label.......6.00 - 12.00

45, Cherry, Cherry/I'll Come Running, Bang 528, 1966 ....6.00 - 12.00
45, Cracklin' Rosie/Lordy, Uni 55250, 1970 ....3.00 - 6.00
45, Girl, You'll Be a Woman Soon/You'll Forget, Bang 542, 1967 ......6.00 - 12.00
45, Longfellow Serenade/Rosemary's Wine, Columbia 3-10043, 1974..2.50 - 5.00
45, Love on the Rocks/Acapulco, Capitol 4939, 1980
   Record only...2.00 - 4.00
   Picture sleeve only ....2.00 - 4.00
45, Song Sung Blue/Gitchy Goomy, Uni 55326, 1972...........................2.50 - 5.00
45, Sweet Caroline (Good Times Never Seemed So Good)/Dig In, Uni 55136,
   1969...3.00 - 6.00
LP, *I'm Glad You're Here with Me Tonight*, Columbia JC 34990, 1977
   ....6.00 - 12.00
LP, *On the Way to the Sky*, Columbia TC 37628, 1981 ....5.00 - 10.00
LP, *September Morn*, Columbia FC 36121, 1979 ....6.00 - 12.00
LP, *Tap Root Manuscript*
   MCA 2013, 1973, reissue, black label with rainbow.....................5.00 - 10.00
   MCA 37196, 1981, reissue, blue label with rainbow ....4.00 - 8.00
   Uni 73092, 1970, original ....10.00 - 20.00
   Uni ST-93501, 1970, Capitol Record Club issue ....12.50 - 25.00
LP, *You Don't Bring Me Flowers*, Columbia FC 35625, 1978 ....6.00 - 12.00

MVP:
12-inch single, We Wrote a Song Together/Beautiful Noise, Continuum II 001,
   1976, private pressing done for the grade school class of Jesse Diamond,
   Neil's son; all were autographed by Neil; the version of "Beautiful Noise"
   is an alternate take; supposedly, between 30 and 40 copies were made
   ....1,000.00 – 2,000.00

45, Ruby Baby/He'll Only Hurt You, Columbia 4-42662, 1962
  Record only..10.00 - 20.00
  Picture sleeve only...20.00 - 40.00

45, Abraham, Martin, and John/Daddy Rollin' (In Your Arms), Laurie
3464, 1968..6.00 - 12.00
45, Donna the Prima Donna/You're Mine, Columbia 4-42852,
1963..10.00 - 20.00
45, Runaround Sue/Runaway Girl
Laurie 3110, 1961, standard issue ....12.50 - 25.00
Laurie 3110, 1961, picture sleeve only ....20.00 - 40.00
Laurie 3110 , 1970s, "Stereo" in white area at right of label .....25.00 - 50.00
45, The Wanderer/The Majestic
Laurie 3115, 1961, standard Issue ....12.50 - 25.00
Laurie 3115, 1979, reissue on regular Laurie label with "From the Orion
Motion Picture 'The Wanderers'" on label....................5.00 - 10.00
Laurie 3115, 1961, picture sleeve only ....20.00 - 40.00
Laurie 3115 , 1970s, "Stereo" in white area at right of label.......25.00 - 50.00
LP, *Dion Sings His Greatest Hits*
Laurie LLP 2013, mono, 1962 ....35.00 - 70.00
Laurie SLP 2013, rechanneled stereo, 1960s.............25.00 - 50.00
Laurie DT-90386, rechanneled stereo, 1965, Capitol Record Club
edition ....60.00 - 120.00
Laurie T-90386, mono, 1965, Capitol Record Club edition........60.00 - 120.00
LP, *More of Dion's Greatest Hits*
Laurie LLP 2022, mono, 1964 ....25.00 - 50.00
Laurie SLP 2022, rechanneled stereo, 1960s.............15.00 - 30.00
Laurie DT-91128, rechanneled stereo, 1960s, Capitol Record Club
edition ....60.00 - 120.00
Laurie T-91128, mono, 1960s, Capitol Record Club edition ......60.00 - 120.00

MVP:
LP, *Runaround Sue*, Laurie LLP 2009, mono, 1961, gold, green or blue vinyl
(regular black vinyl versions are a lot less) ....400.00 - 800.00

LP, *This Is Fats*

    Imperial LP-9040, mono, 1957, maroon label ....75.00 - 150.00

    Imperial LP-9040, mono, 1958, black label with stars on top.....40.00 - 80.00

    Imperial LP-9040, mono, 1964, black and pink label................12.50 - 25.00

    Imperial LP-9040, mono, 1967, black and green label ....10.00 - 20.00

    Imperial LP-12391, rechanneled stereo, 1968 ....6.00 - 12.00

45, Ain't It a Shame/La La, Imperial X5348, 1955 ....20.00 - 40.00

45, Blue Monday/What's the Reason I'm Not Pleasing You, Imperial
X5417, 1957...12.50 - 25.00

45, Blueberry Hill/Honey Chile
Imperial X5407, 1956, red label, regular black vinyl ....12.50 - 25.00
Imperial X5407, 1956, red vinyl...75.00 - 150.00
Imperial X5407, 1957, black label, regular black vinyl................7.50 - 15.00

45, I Want to Walk You Home/I'm Gonna Be a Wheel Some Day, Imperial
5606, 1959..10.00 - 20.00

45, I'm in Love Again/My Blue Heaven, Imperial X5386, 1956.........12.50 - 25.00

45, I'm Walkin'/I'm in the Mood for Love, Imperial X5428, 1957
Record only, maroon or red label ....12.50 - 25.00
Picture sleeve only...25.00 - 50.00

45, Walking to New Orleans/Don't Come Knockin, Imperial 5675,
1960..10.00 - 20.00

LP, *Fats Is Back*, Reprise RS 6304, 1968..15.00 - 30.00

LP, *Here Stands Fats Domino*
Imperial LP-9038, mono, 1957, maroon label ....75.00 - 150.00
Imperial LP-9038, mono, 1958, black label with stars on top.....40.00 - 80.00
Imperial LP-9038, mono, 1964, black and pink label.................12.50 - 25.00
Imperial LP-9038, mono, 1967, black and green label ....10.00 - 20.00
Imperial LP-12390, rechanneled stereo, 1968 ....6.00 - 12.00

LP, *The Very Best of Fats Domino*, United Artists UA-LA233-G,
1974..6.00 - 12.00

MVP:
45, The Fat Man/Detroit City Blues, Imperial 45-5058, 1950, blue-label "script"
logo; pressed in 1952 or so; 78 rpm versions go for a lot less; counterfeits
exist...1,000.00 – 2,000.00

45, Mellow Yellow/Sunny South Kensington, Epic 5-10098, 1966

Record only..5.00 - 10.00

Picture sleeve only ....7.50 - 15.00

45, Atlantis/To Susan on the West Coast Waiting, Epic 5-10434, 1969
    Record only...4.00 - 8.00
    Picture sleeve only...6.00 - 12.00
45, Catch the Wind/Why Do You Treat Me Like You Do, Hickory 1309,
    1965..7.50 - 15.00
45, Hurdy Gurdy Man/Teen Angel, Epic 5-10345, 1968
    Record only...4.00 - 8.00
    Picture sleeve only...6.00 - 12.00
45, Sunshine Superman/The Trip, Epic 5-10045, 1966
    Record only...5.00 - 10.00
    Picture sleeve only...7.50 - 15.00
LP, *Catch the Wind*
    Hickory LPM-123, mono, 1965, cover has Donovan facing right, so it appears
    as if he's strumming his guitar with his left hand ....20.00 - 40.00
    Hickory LPM-123, mono, 1965, cover has Donovan facing left, so he is
    correctly strumming his guitar with his right hand.....................12.50 - 25.00
    Hickory LPS-123, rechanneled stereo, 1965 ....12.50 - 25.00
LP, *Donovan's Greatest Hits*
    Epic BXN 26439, 1969, yellow label ....6.00 - 12.00
    Epic BXN 26439, 1973, orange label ....5.00 - 10.00
    Epic PE 26439, 1979, dark blue label...4.00 - 8.00
LP, *Sunshine Superman*
    Epic LN 24217, mono, 1966...15.00 - 30.00
    Epic BN 26217, rechanneled stereo, 1966 ....7.50 - 15.00

MVP:
LP, *A Gift from a Flower to a Garden*, Epic L2N 6071 (2-record set), mono,
    1967, boxed set with portfolio of lyrics and drawings, stereo copies on B2N
    or E2 171 go for half this amount or less....................................25.00 - 50.00

45, Real Love/Thank You Love, Warner Bros. 49503, 1980
   Record only..2.00 - 4.00
   Picture sleeve only...2.50 - 5.00

45, Another Park, Another Sunday/Black Water, Warner Bros. 7795,
1974..2.50 - 5.00

45, Black Water/Song to See You Through, Warner Bros. 8062,
1974..2.00 - 4.00

45, China Grove/Evil Woman, Warner Bros. 7728, 1973 ....2.00 - 4.00

45, Listen to the Music/Toulouse Street, Warner Bros. 7619, 1972 ......2.50 - 5.00

45, Long Train Runnin'/Without You, Warner Bros. 7698, 1973 ....2.00 - 4.00

45, Take Me in Your Arms (Rock Me)/Slat Key Soquel Rag, Warner Bros.
8092, 1975..2.00 - 4.00

45, What a Fool Believes/Don't Stop to Watch the Wheels, Warner Bros. 8725, 1978
Record only..2.00 - 4.00
Picture sleeve only ....2.50 - 5.00

LP, *Best of the Doobies*
DCC Compact Classics LPZ-2053, 1998, reissue on 180-gram virgin
vinyl..20.00 - 40.00
Warner Bros. BS 2978, 1976, original............................6.00 - 12.00
Warner Bros. BSK 3112, 1978, reissue with new number, "Burbank" palm
trees label..5.00 - 10.00
Warner Bros. BSK 3112, 1979, tan or white label ....4.00 - 8.00

LP, *What Were Once Vices Are Now Habits*
Warner Bros. W 2750, 1974, "Burbank" palm trees label ....5.00 - 10.00
Warner Bros. W 2750, 1979, tan or white label, reissue ....4.00 - 8.00
Warner Bros. W4 2750, 1974, quadraphonic ....10.00 - 20.00

MVP:
LP, *The Captain and Me*, Nautilus NR-5, 1980, with "Super Disc" on
cover ....20.00 - 40.00

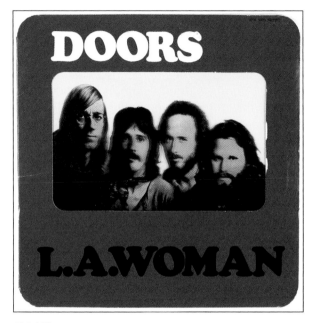

LP, *L.A. Woman*

DCC Compact Classics LPZ-2050, 1998, 180-gram virgin vinyl release
....75.00 - 150.00

LP, Elektra EKS-75011, 1971, butterfly label, with see-through window on cover and
  yellow innersleeeve with photo of Jim Morrison on a cross.........25.00 - 50.00
  (Other versions on Elektra exist and sell for less.)

45, Hello, I Love You/Love Street, Elektra 45635, 1968, red, black and white
label ....6.00 - 12.00

45, Hello, I Love You, Won't You Tell Me Your Name?/Love Street, Elektra
45635, 1968, original editions have long title ....10.00 - 20.00

45, Light My Fire/The Crystal Ship, Elektra 45615, 1967
Yellow and black label with "ELEKTRA" in all capital letters and a woman's
head above a white line at the top of the label............................15.00 - 30.00
Red, black and white label ....6.00 - 12.00
Red, black and pink label..7.50 - 15.00

45, Love Her Madly/(You Need Meat) Don't Go No Further, Elektra 45726,
1971...4.00 - 8.00

45, Riders on the Storm/Changeling, Elektra 45738, 1971 ....4.00 - 8.00

45, Tightrope Ride/Variety Is the Spice of Life, Elektra 45757, 1971 ....4.00 - 8.00

45, Touch Me/Wild Child, Elektra 45646, 1968.................................6.00 - 12.00

LP, *The Doors*
DCC Compact Classics LPZ-2046, 1997, 180-gram virgin vinyl reissue
....75.00 - 150.00
Elektra EKL-4007, mono, 1967 ....100.00 - 200.00
Elektra EKS-74007, stereo, 1967, brown labels.........................25.00 - 50.00
Elektra EKS-74007, stereo, 1969, red labels with large stylized
"E" ....7.50 - 15.00
Elektra EKS-74007, stereo, 1971, butterfly labels ....6.00 - 12.00
Elektra EKS-74007, stereo, 1980, red labels with Warner Communications
logo in lower right..5.00 - 10.00
Elektra EKS-74007, stereo, 1983, red and black labels ....4.00 - 8.00

MVP:
LP, *Waiting for the Sun*, Elektra EKL-4024, mono, 1968, stereo copies (74024)
sell for a lot less ....500.00 – 1,000.00

LP, *The Drifters' Golden Hits*

    Atlantic 8153, mono, 1968 ....15.00 - 30.00
    Atlantic SD 8153, stereo, 1968, green and blue label ....15.00 - 30.00
    Atlantic SD 8153, stereo, 1969, red and green label ....7.50 - 15.00

45, Dance with Me/(If You Cry) True Love, True Love, Atlantic 2040,
1959..10.00 - 20.00
45, Money Honey/The Way I Feel, Atlantic 1006, 1953, yellow label with
no "fan" logo under the "A"..40.00 - 80.00
45, On Broadway/Let the Music Play, Atlantic 2182, 1963.................7.50 - 15.00
45, Saturday Night at the Movies/Spanish Lace, Atlantic 2260, 1964
Record only...6.00 - 12.00
Picture sleeve only..20.00 - 40.00
45, Save the Last Dance for Me/Nobody But Me, Atlantic 2071,
1960..10.00 - 20.00
45, There Goes My Baby/Oh My Love, Atlantic 2025, 1959.............12.50 - 25.00
45, This Magic Moment/Baltimore, Atlantic 2050, 1960...................10.00 - 20.00
45, Under the Boardwalk/I Don't Want to Go On Without You, Atlantic
2237, 1964..7.50 - 15.00
45, Up On the Roof/Another Night with the Boys, Atlantic 2162,
1962..10.00 - 20.00
LP, *Save the Last Dance for Me*
Atlantic 8059, mono, 1962, red and purple label, white "fan" logo
at right..60.00 - 120.00
Atlantic 8059, mono, 1963, red and purple label, black "fan" logo
at right..30.00 - 60.00
Atlantic SD 8059, stereo, 1962, green and blue label, white "fan" logo
at right..100.00 - 200.00
Atlantic SD 8059, stereo, 1963, green and blue label, black "fan" logo
at right..50.00 - 100.00
Atlantic SD 8059, stereo, 1969, red and green label, white horizontal stripe
through center hole...12.50 - 25.00

MVP:
LP, *The Drifters' Greatest Hits*, Atlantic 8041, mono, 1960, black label with silver print (other label variations go for much less)..................300.00 - 600.00

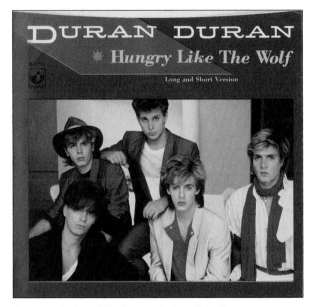

45, Hungry Like the Wolf (4:11)/Hungry Like the Wolf (5:14)
   Capitol B-5195, 1983, reissue on purple label, much scarcer than the
   Harvest edition ....2.50 - 5.00
   Harvest B-5195, 1982, record only ....1.50 - 3.00
   Harvest B-5195, 1982, picture sleeve only ....5.00 - 10.00

45, Ordinary World/Save a Prayer, Capitol S7-56945, 1993, "For Jukeboxes Only!"
   on label ....3.00 - 6.00
45, The Reflex/New Religion, Capitol B-5345, 1984
   Record only...2.00 - 4.00
   Fold-open poster sleeve...2.50 - 5.00
   Regular picture sleeve, much scarcer than the poster sleeve.........5.00 - 10.00
45, Union of the Snake/Secret Oktober, Capitol B-5290, 1983,
   Record only, custom label ....1.50 - 3.00
   Picture sleeve only ....1.50 - 3.00
LP, *Rio*
   Capitol ST-12211, 1983, Version 4: Capitol logo replaces Harvest logo on
   back cover, otherwise it's the same as Harvest Version 3, with the same
   trail-off markings...4.00 - 8.00
   Capitol R 163452, 1983, RCA Music Service edition, contains Harvest
   Version 1 of the album ....7.50 - 15.00
   Capitol ST-512211, 1983, Columbia House edition; contains Version 4 of
   the album ....5.00 - 10.00
   Harvest ST-12211, 1982, Version 1: Harvest logo on lower back cover,
   contains the same versions of the songs as the original UK release; trail-off
   wax number on Side 1 is "ST- 1-12211 Z1" ....10.00 - 20.00
   Harvest ST-12211, 1982, Version 2: Harvest logo on lower back cover, with
   five songs remixed by David Kershenbaum; Side 1 trail-off wax number is
   "ST-1-12211-Z13-RE1 #1" ....7.50 - 15.00
   Harvest ST-12211, 1982, Version 3: Harvest logo on lower back cover, with
   five songs remixed by David Kershenbaum, but with a different mix of
   "Hungry Like the Wolf" than Version 2; Side 1 trail-off wax number is
   "ST-1-12211-Z18" ....6.00 - 12.00

MVP:
LP, *Duran Goes Dutch*, Capitol SPRO-79097/8, 1987, promotional-only five-song
   EP, recorded live in Rotterdam ....40.00 - 80.00

LP, *Dylan*

    Columbia PC 32747, 1973, no bar code on cover ....7.50 - 15.00

    Columbia PC 32747, 1979, with bar code on back cover ....4.00 - 8.00

Bob Dylan

45, Knockin' on Heaven's Door/Turkey Chase, Columbia 4-45913, 1973
....2.50 - 5.00
45, Lay Lady Lay/Peggy Day, Columbia 4-44926, 1969........................4.00 - 8.00
45, Like a Rolling Stone/Gates of Eden, Columbia 4-43346, 1965....10.00 - 20.00

LP, *Blonde on Blonde*

Columbia C2L 41 (2-record set), mono, 1966, "female photos" inner
gatefold with two women pictured..50.00 - 100.00
Columbia C2L 41 (2-record set), mono, 1968, no photos of women inside
gatefold ....150.00 - 300.00
Columbia C2S 841 (2-record set), stereo, 1966, "female photos" inner
gatefold with two women pictured..30.00 - 60.00
Columbia C2S 841 (2-record set), stereo, 1968, no photos of women
inside gatefold; "360 Sound Stereo" on label ....15.00 - 30.00
Columbia C2S 841 (2-record set), stereo, 1970, orange labels.....7.50 - 15.00
Columbia CG 841 (2-record set), stereo, 1980s, reissue ....6.00 - 12.00
Sundazed LP 5110 (2-record set), mono, 2002, 180-gram reissue of the
original mono mix...12.50 - 25.00

LP, *Nashville Skyline*

Columbia JC 9825, 197?, reissue ....5.00 - 10.00
Columbia KCS 9825, 1969, "360 Sound Stereo" label ....15.00 - 30.00
Columbia KCS 9825, 1970, orange label ....6.00 - 12.00
Columbia PC 9825, 1980s, budget-line reissue ....4.00 - 8.00

MVP:

LP, *The Freewheelin' Bob Dylan*, Columbia CS 8786, stereo, 1963, "360
Sound Stereo" in black on label (no arrows); record plays, and label lists,
"Let Me Die in My Footsteps," "Rocks and Gravel," "Talkin' John Birch Blues"
and "Gamblin' Willie's Dead Man's Hand"; no known stereo copies play these
without listing them, but just in case, check the trail-off for the numbers
"XSM-58719-1A" and "XSM-58720-1A"; if the number after the dash is "2"
or higher, it's the standard version, which sells for a lot less
.... 22,500.00 – 30,000.00

LP, *Hotel California*

Asylum 6E-103, 1977, early reissue...4.00 - 8.00

Asylum 7E-1084, 1976, original ....5.00 - 10.00

Mobile Fidelity 1-126, 1984, "Original Master Recording" at top of

cover ....50.00 - 100.00

45, Best of My Love/Ol' 55, Asylum 45218, 1974 ....2.00 - 4.00
45, Heartache Tonight/Teenage Jail, Asylum 46545, 1979 ....2.00 - 4.00
45, Hotel California/Pretty Maids All in a Row, Asylum 45386, 1977 ....2.00 - 4.00
45, Lyin' Eyes/Too Many Hands, Asylum 45279, 1975 ....2.00 - 4.00
45, New Kid in Town/Victim of Love, Asylum 45373, 1976 ....2.00 - 4.00
45, One of These Nights/Visions, Asylum 45257, 1975 ....2.00 - 4.00
45, Please Come Home for Christmas/Funky New Year
    Asylum 45555, 1978, "clouds" label ....2.00 - 4.00
    Asylum 45555, 1984, black and yellow label...................................1.50 - 3.00
    Asylum 45555, 1978, picture sleeve only ....2.00 - 4.00
45, Take It Easy/Get You in the Mood, Asylum 11005, 1972................2.50 - 5.00
LP, *Eagles — Their Greatest Hits 1971-1975*
    Asylum 6E-105, 1977, early reissue..4.00 - 8.00
    Asylum 7E-1052, 1976, original ....5.00 - 10.00
    DCC Compact Classics LPZ-2051, 1998, 180-gram virgin vinyl
    reissue..50.00 - 100.00
LP, *The Long Run*, Asylum 5E-508, 1979 ....4.00 - 8.00
LP, *One of These Nights*
    Asylum 7E-1039, 1975 ....5.00 - 10.00
    Asylum EQ 1039, quadraphonic, 1975 ....10.00 - 20.00

MVP:
LP, *Hotel California*, DCC Compact Classics LPZ-2043, 1997, 180-gram virgin
    vinyl reissue...60.00 - 120.00

LP, *Spirit*

    Columbia PC 34241, 1976, no bar code......................................6.00 - 12.00

    Columbia PC 34241, 1980s, reissue with bar code ....4.00 - 8.00

    Columbia PCQ 34241, quadraphonic, 1976 ....12.50 - 25.00

45, After the Love Has Gone/Rock That!, ARC 3-11033, 1979 .... 2.50 - 5.00

45, Got to Get You Into My Life/I'll Write a Song for You, Columbia 3-
    10796, 1978 .... 2.50 - 5.00

45, September/Love's Holiday, ARC 3-10854, 1978 .... 2.50 - 5.00

45, Shining Star/Yearnin', Learnin', Columbia 3-10090, 1975
    Record only .... 2.50 - 5.00
    Picture sleeve only .... 5.00 - 10.00

45, Sing a Song/(Instrumental), Columbia 3-10251, 1975, with title as three
    words .... 2.50 - 5.00

45, Singasong/(Instrumental), Columbia 3-10251, 1975, with title as one
    word .... 3.00 - 6.00

LP, *The Best of Earth, Wind & Fire, Vol. 1,* ARC FC 35647, 1978 .... 5.00 - 10.00

LP, *Earth, Wind, and Fire,* Warner Bros. WS 1905, 1971, green
    label .... 10.00 - 20.00

LP, *I Am*
    ARC FC 35730, 1979, original .... 5.00 - 10.00
    ARC PC 35730, 1984, reissue .... 4.00 - 8.00

LP, *That's the Way of the World*
    Columbia PC 33280, 1975, original with no bar code .... 6.00 - 12.00
    Columbia PC 33280, 1980s, with bar code .... 4.00 - 8.00
    Mobile Fidelity 1-159, 1980s, "Original Master Recording" on top of
    front cover .... 15.00 - 30.00

MVP:

LP, *Powerlight* , Columbia HC 48367, with "Half-Speed Mastered" on cover
    (other editions go for less) 1983 .... 20.00 - 40.00

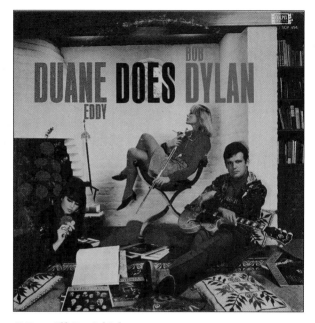

LP, *Duane Eddy Does Bob Dylan*
    Colpix CP-494, mono, 1965 ....15.00 - 30.00
    Colpix SCP-494, stereo, 1965 ....20.00 - 40.00

45, Because They're Young/Rebel Walk, Jamie 1156, 1960
    Record only..7.50 - 15.00
    Picture sleeve only...15.00 - 30.00
45, (Dance with the) Guitar Man/Stretchin' Out , RCA Victor 47-8087, 1962
    Record only..7.50 - 15.00
    Picture sleeve only...15.00 - 30.00
45, Forty Miles of Bad Road/The Quiet Three
    Jamie 1126, mono, 1959..10.00 - 20.00
    Jamie 1126, stereo, 1959, will be labeled "stereo" on record.....25.00 - 50.00
    Jamie 1126, 1959, picture sleeve only.......................25.00 - 50.00
45, Rebel-'Rouser/Stalkin, Jamie 1104, 1958...................12.50 - 25.00
LP, *The Best of Duane Eddy*
    RCA Victor LPM-3477, mono, 1965............................10.00 - 20.00
    RCA Victor LSP-3477, stereo, 1965, black label, dog at top........12.50 - 25.00
    RCA Victor LSP-3477, stereo, 1969, orange label ....7.50 - 15.00
LP, *$1,000,000.00 Worth of Twang*
    Jamie JLPS-3014, mono, 1960 ....20.00 - 40.00
    Jamie JLPS-3014, stereo, 1960 ....35.00 - 70.00
LP, *The "Twangs" The "Thang"*
    Jamie JLPM-3009, mono, 1959 ....20.00 - 40.00
    Jamie JLPS-3009, stereo, 1959 ....30.00 - 60.00
    Jamie ST-91301, stereo, 1966, Capitol Record Club edition ....30.00 - 60.00
    Jamie T-91301, mono, 1966, Capitol Record Club edition...........30.00 - 60.00

MVP:
45, Ramrod/Caravan, Ford 500, 1957, by "Duane Eddy and His Rock-A-Billies"
....1,000.00 – 1,500.00

LP, *Out of the Blue*

    Jet JT-LA823-L2 (2-record set), 1977, black vinyl, with poster and die-cut
cardboard "spaceship"..7.50 - 15.00
    Jet JT-LA823-L2 (2-record set), 1977, blue vinyl, promotional issue
only ....12.50 - 25.00
    Jet KZ2 35530 (2-record set), 1978, reissue................................6.00 - 12.00

45, Can't Get It Out of My Head/Illusions in G Major, United Artists UA-XW 573, 1974
    Record only...2.00 - 4.00
    Picture sleeve only...3.00 - 6.00
45, Don't Bring Me Down/Dreaming of 4000, Jet ZS9 5060, 1979.......2.00 - 4.00
45, Sweet Talkin' Woman/Fire on High Jet JT-XW 1145, 1978
    Black vinyl...2.00 - 4.00
    Purple vinyl ....2.50 - 5.00
    Picture sleeve only...2.50 - 5.00
45, Telephone Line/Poorboy (The Greenwood), United Artists UA-XW 1000, 1977
    Black vinyl...2.00 - 4.00
    Green vinyl...2.50 - 5.00
    Picture sleeve only...2.50 - 5.00
LP, *A New World Record*
    Jet JZ 35529, 1978, second issue ....5.00 - 10.00
    Jet PZ 35529, 1981, third issue ....4.00 - 8.00
    United Artists UA-LA679-G, 1976, original ....6.00 - 12.00
LP, *ELO's Greatest Hits*
    Jet FZ 36310, 1979, original..5.00 - 10.00
    Jet HZ 36310, 1981, "Half Speed Mastered" on cover.................20.00 - 40.00
    Jet PZ 36310, 1987, reissue ....4.00 - 8.00

MVP:
LP, *Ole Elo*, United Artists SP-123, 1976, gold vinyl, cover that says only "Ole Elo" on the front with no "Electric Light Orchestra" underneath, prtomotional release only (promo copies with other colors of vinyl and regular releases are less) ....50.00 - 100.00

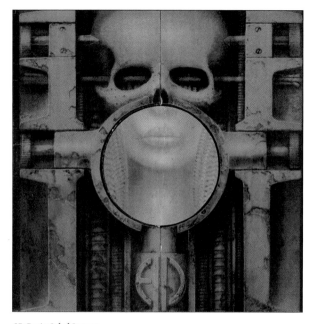

LP, *Brain Salad Surgery*

    Atlantic SD 19124, 1977, reissue...4.00 - 8.00

    Manticore ELP 66669. 1973, with booklet ....6.00 - 12.00

45, From the Beginning/Living Sin, Cotillion 44158, 1972....................2.50 - 5.00
45, Lucky Man/Knife's Edge, Cotillion 44106, 1971.............................3.00 - 6.00
45, Still...You Turn Me On/Brain Salad Surgery, Manticore 2003, 1973
    Record only..2.50 - 5.00
    Picture sleeve only ....5.00 - 10.00
LP, *Emerson, Lake and Palmer*
    Atlantic SD 19120, 1977, reissue...4.00 - 8.00
    Cotillion SD 9040, 1971, original ....6.00 - 12.00
LP, *Tarkus*
    Atlantic SD 19121, 1977, reissue...4.00 - 8.00
    Cotillion SD 9900, 1971, original ....6.00 - 12.00
    Mobile Fidelity 1-203, 1994, "Original Master Recording" at top of front
    cover ....12.50 - 25.00
LP, *Trilogy*
    Atlantic SD 19123, 1977, reissue...4.00 - 8.00
    Cotillion SD 9903, 1972, original ....6.00 - 12.00
    Cotillion SMAS-94773, 1972, Capitol Record Club edition ....7.50 - 15.00
    Mobile Fidelity 1-218,1994, "Original Master Recording" at top of front
    cover ....20.00 - 40.00
LP, *Works Volume 1*
    Atlantic PR 277, 1977, single disc sampler, promotional item only7.50 - 15.00
    Atlantic SD 7000 (2-record set), 1977...7.50 - 15.00
LP, *Works Volume 2*, Atlantic SD 19147, 1977 ....5.00 - 10.00

MVP:
LP, *On Tour with Emerson, Lake and Palmer*, Atlantic PR 281, 1977, promo-
    tional release only ....20.00 - 40.00

IP, *The Fabulous Style of the Everly Brothers*

Cadence CLP-3040, mono, 1960, maroon label with metronome

logo ....40.00 - 80.00

Cadence CLP-3040, mono, 1962, red label with black border ....25.00 - 50.00

Cadence CLP-25040, stereo, 1960, maroon label with metronome

logo ....60.00 - 120.00

Cadence CLP-25040, stereo, 1962, red label with black border .30.00 - 60.00

45, Bird Dog/Devoted to You
    Barnaby 510, 1970s, reissue ....2.50 - 5.00
    Cadence 1350, 1958, original ....12.50 - 25.00
45, Bye, Bye Love/I Wonder If I Care As Much
    Barnaby 502, 1970s, reissue ....2.50 - 5.00
    Cadence 1315, 1957, original ....12.50 - 25.00
45, Cathy's Clown/Always It's You
    Warner Bros. 5151, 1960, pink label..10.00 - 20.00
    Warner Bros. 5151, 1960, red label with arrows ....7.50 - 15.00
    Warner Bros. 5151, 1960, gold label, gold vinyl, promotional
    only ....50.00 - 100.00
    Warner Bros. 5151, 1960, picture sleeve only..........................25.00 - 50.00
    Warner Bros. S-5151, 1960, stereo ....25.00 - 50.00
LP, *The Very Best of the Everly Brothers*
    Warner Bros. W 1554, mono, 1964, yelllow letters on cover ......15.00 - 30.00
    Warner Bros. W 1554, mono, 1965, white letters on cover.........10.00 - 20.00
    Warner Bros. WS 1554, stereo, 1964, yellow letters on cover ....20.00 - 40.00
    Warner Bros. WS 1554, stereo, 1965, white letters on cover, gold
    label ....12.50 - 25.00
    Warner Bros. WS 1554, stereo, 1967, green "W7" label ....10.00 - 20.00
    Warner Bros. WS 1554, stereo, 1970, green "WB" label ....7.50 - 15.00
    Warner Bros. WS 1554, stereo, 1973, "Burbank" palm tree
    label ....6.00 - 12.00
    Warner Bros. WS 1554, stereo, 1979, white or tan label..............5.00 - 10.00
    Warner Bros. ST-91343, stereo, 1967, Capitol Record Club
    edition ....20.00 - 40.00

MVP:
45, Keep A Lovin' Me/The Sun Keeps Shining, Columbia 4-21496, 1956, maroon
    label (white label promo is about 40 percent of this) ....300.00 - 600.00

LP, *Music of Christmas*

    Columbia CL 588, mono, 1955, maroon label, gold print ....12.50 - 25.00

    Columbia CL 588, mono, 1956, red and black label with six white "eye"

    logos ....10.00 - 20.00

    (Versions with other catalog numbers go for less.)

45, Delicado/Festival, Columbia 4-39708, 1952 ....6.00 - 12.00

45, The Song from Moulin Rouge (Where Is Your Heart)/Swedish Rhapsody,
   Columbia 4-39944, 1953..5.00 - 10.00

45, Theme for Young Lovers/Bimini Goombay, Columbia 4-41655,
   1960...4.00 - 8.00

45, Theme from "A Summer Place"/Go-Go-Po-Go, Columbia 4-41490, 1959
   Record only..4.00 - 8.00
   Picture sleeve only ....7.50 - 15.00

LP, *Bouquet*
   Columbia CL 1322, mono, 1959, red and black label with six white "eye"
   logos ....7.50 - 15.00
   Columbia CS 8124, stereo, 1959, red and black label with six white "eye"
   logos ....7.50 - 15.00
   Columbia Limited Edition LE 10042, 1970s, reissue.....................5.00 - 10.00

LP, *Percy Faith's Greatest Hits*
   Columbia CL 1493, mono, 1960, red and black label with six white "eye"
   logos ....7.50 - 15.00
   Columbia CS 8637, rechanneled stereo, 1963, red "360 Sound Stereo"
   label ....5.00 - 10.00
   Columbia PC 8637, rechanneled stereo, 1980s, reissue ....4.00 - 8.00

LP, *Music of Christmas, Volume 2*
   Columbia CL 2405, mono, 1965..6.00 - 12.00
   Columbia CS 9205, stereo, 1965, red "360 Sound Stereo"
   label ....6.00 - 12.00
   Columbia Limited Edition LE 10088, 1970s, reissue.....................5.00 - 10.00

MVP:

LP, *The Columbia Album of Christmas Music*, Columbia C2L 15 (2-record set),
   mono, 1958, combines *Music of Christmas* and *Hallelujah!* into one gate-
   fold package...15.00 - 30.00

LP, *Portrait*, Bell 6045, 1970 ....6.00 - 12.00

45, Aquarius/Let the Sunshine In (The Flesh Failures)//Don'tcha Hear Me Callin'
To Ya, Soul City 772, 1969
   Record only..4.00 - 8.00
   Picture sleeve only ....7.50 - 15.00
45, Go Where You Wanna Go/Too Poor to Die, Soul City 753, 1967
   Record only..4.00 - 8.00
   Picture sleeve only..10.00 - 20.00
45, (Last Night) I Didn't Get to Sleep at All/The River Witch, Bell 45,195,
   1972...2.50 - 5.00
45, One Less Bell to Answer/Feelin' Alright?, Bell 940, 1970.................2.50 - 5.00
45, Stoned Soul Picnic/The Sailboat Song, Soul City 766, 1968
   Record only..4.00 - 8.00
   Picture sleeve only..7.50 - 15.00
45, Up-Up and Away/Which Way to Nowhere, Soul City 756, 1967 ....4.00 - 8.00
45, Wedding Bell Blues/Lovin' Stew, Soul City 779, 1969.....................4.00 - 8.00
LP, *The Age of Aquarius*, Soul City SCS-92005, 1969..........................7.50 - 15.00
LP, *Greatest Hits on Earth*, Bell 1106, 1972 ....5.00 - 10.00
LP, *Individually & Collectively*, Bell 6073, 1972 ....5.00 - 10.00
LP, *Up, Up and Away*
   Soul City SCM-91000, mono, 1967 ....10.00 - 20.00
   Soul City SCS-92000, stereo, 1967 ....7.50 - 15.00

MVP:
45, I'll Be Loving You Forever/Train, Keep On Moving, Soul City 752,
   1966..30.00 - 60.00

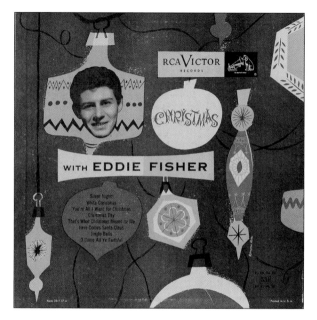

LP, *Christmas with Eddie Fisher*, RCA Victor LPM-3065, mono, 10-inch record, 1952..25.00 - 50.00

45, Any Time/Never Before, RCA Victor 47-4359, 1951 ....7.50 - 15.00

45, Cindy, Oh Cindy/Around the World, RCA Victor 47-6677, 1956 ....5.00 - 10.00

45, Count Your Blessings/Fanny, RCA Victor 47-5871, 1954, no subtitle on A-
side label ....7.50 - 15.00

45, Count Your Blessings (Instead of Sheep)/Fanny, RCA Victor 47-5871,
1954...7.50 - 15.00

45, I Need You Now/Heaven Was Never Like This, RCA Victor 47-5830,
1954...6.00 - 12.00

45, I'm Walking Behind You/Just Another Polka, RCA Victor 47-5293,
1953...6.00 - 12.00

45, Oh My Papa (O Mein Papa)/Until You Said Goodbye, RCA Victor 47-5552,
1953
Record only, with unpunctuated A-side title....................................6.00 - 12.00
Record only, with A-side as "Oh! My Pa-Pa (O Mein Papa)" ....6.00 - 12.00
Picture sleeve only ....12.50 - 25.00

45, Turn Back the Hands of Time/I Can't Go On Without You, RCA Victor
47-4257, 1951 ....7.50 - 15.00

EP, Wish You Were Here/I'll Hold You in My Heart (Till I Can Hold You in
My Arms)/Lady of Spain//I'm Walking Behind You/Downhearted/Outside
of Heaven, RCA Victor CEP-6144X, 1956, record only, with Coca-Cola
logo ....6.00 - 12.00

EP, *Souvenir Record from Coke Time with Eddie Fisher*, RCA Victor
CEP-6144X, 1956, paper picture sleeve only ....10.00 - 20.00

LP, *Eddie Fisher's Greatest Hits*
RCA Victor ANL1-1138, 1975, reissue...4.00 - 8.00
RCA Victor LPM-2504, mono, 1962..7.50 - 15.00
RCA Victor LSP-2504, stereo, 1962...10.00 - 20.00

MVP:

LP, *As Long As There's Music*, RCA Victor LSP-1647, stereo, 1958 (mono version,
LPM-1647, goes for less) ....25.00 - 50.00

LP, *Future Games*

    Reprise RS 6465, 1971, original edition with a pale yellow
cover ....12.50 - 25.00

    Reprise RS 6465, 1972, later edition with a pale green cover ....7.50 - 15.00

45, Don't Stop/Never Going Back Again, Warner Bros. 8413, 1977
 Record only...2.00 - 4.00
 Picture sleeve only...2.50 - 5.00
45, Dreams/Songbird, Warner Bros. 8371, 1977 ....2.00 - 4.00
45, Go Your Own Way/Silver Springs, Warner Bros. 8304, 1976 ....4.00 - 8.00
45, Oh Well, Part 1/Part 2, Reprise 0883, 1970 ....10.00 - 20.00
45, Rhiannon (Will You Ever Win)/Sugar Daddy, Reprise 1345,
 1976...2.50 - 5.00
LP, *Bare Trees*
 Reprise MS 2080, 1972, with brown line near all four edges of the front
 cover...6.00 - 12.00
 Reprise MS 2080, mid 1970s, without brown line on front cover; uncommon
 with the MS 2080 number ....7.50 - 15.00
 Reprise MSK 2278, 1977, reissue; no brown line on front cover ....4.00 - 8.00
LP, *Mirage*
 Mobile Fidelity 1-119, 1984, "Original Master Recording" at top of front
 cover ....20.00 - 40.00
 Warner Bros. 23607, 1982...5.00 - 10.00
LP, *Rumours*
 Nautilus NR-8, 1980, "Super Disc" on front cover ....20.00 - 40.00
 Warner Bros. BSK 3010, 1977, "Burbank" palm trees label, with short
 version (2:02) of "Never Going Back Again".................................5.00 - 10.00
 Warner Bros. BSK 3010, 1977, "Burbank" palm trees label, with long
 version (2:16) of "Never Going Back Again".................................4.00 - 8.00
 Warner Bros. BSK 3010, 1979, white label................................3.00 - 6.00
LP, *Tusk*, Warner Bros. 2HS 3350 (2-record set), 1979...................7.50 - 15.00

MVP:
LP, *Fleetwood Mac*, Epic LN 24402, mono, 1968, white label promotional copy
 (all yellow label versions are stereo and go for less) ....50.00 - 100.00

LP, *Foreigner*
    Atlantic SD 18215, 1977, original...5.00 - 10.00
    Atlantic SD 19109, 1977, reissue...4.00 - 8.00

45, Cold As Ice/I Need You, Atlantic 3410, 1977 ....2.00 - 4.00
45, Double Vision/Lonely Children, Atlantic 3514, 1978
    Record only..2.00 - 4.00
    Picture sleeve only ....2.50 - 5.00
45, Feels Like the First Time/Woman, Oh Woman, Atlantic 3394,
    1977..2.00 - 4.00
45, Hot Blooded/Tramontane, Atlantic 3488, 1978 ....2.00 - 4.00
45, I Want to Know What Love Is/Street Thunder, Atlantic 7-89596, 1984
    Record only, custom black and colorblocked label ....1.50 - 3.00
    Record only, regular red and black Atlantic label.........................2.00 - 4.00
    Picture sleeve only ....2.00 - 4.00
45, Waiting for a Girl Like You/I'm Gonna Win, Atlantic 3868, 1981
    Record only..2.00 - 4.00
    Picture sleeve only...2.50 - 5.00
LP, *Agent Provocateur*, Atlantic 81999, 1984....................................5.00 - 10.00
LP, *Double Vision*
    Atlantic SD 19999, 1978, first cover is mostly sepia-tone with the words
    "Double Vision" barely visible along the bottom ....6.00 - 12.00
    Atlantic SD 19999, 1978, second cover has a blue tint with the words
    "Double Vision" right under the band name ....5.00 - 10.00
    Atlantic SD 19999, 1979, third cover is the same as the second cover, but
    has a red tint ....4.00 - 8.00
LP, *Head Games*, Atlantic SD 29999, 1979 ....5.00 - 10.00

MVP:
LP, *Double Vision*, Mobile Fidelity 1-052, 1981, "Original Master Recording" on
    front cover (see above for other versions) ....15.00 - 30.00

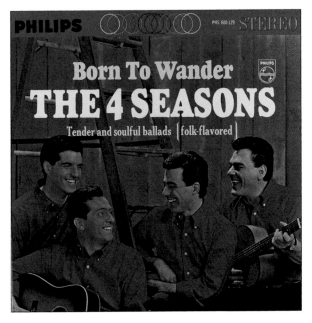

LP, *Born to Wander*

    Philips PHM 200-129, mono, 1964 ....10.00 - 20.00

    Philips PHS 600-129, stereo, 1964 ....12.50 - 25.00

45, Big Girls Don't Cry/Connie-O
    Vee Jay 465, 1962, black rainbow label with oval logo .... 10.00 - 20.00
    Vee Jay 465, 1963, all-black label .... 12.50 - 25.00
45, December, 1963 (Oh, What a Night)/Slip Away, Warner Bros. 8168,
    1975 .... 2.50 - 5.00
45, Let's Hang On!/On Broadway Tonight
    Philips 40317, 1965, black label .... 5.00 - 10.00
    Philips 40317, 1967, light blue label with "S" stamp .... 4.00 - 8.00
45, Rag Doll/Silence Is Golden
    Philips 40211, 1964, record only, black label .... 7.50 - 15.00
    Philips 40211, 1967, record only, light blue label with "S" stamp ... 4.00 - 8.00
    Philips 40211, 1964, picture sleeve only, green .... 15.00 - 30.00
    Philips 40211, 1964, picture sleeve only, yellow .... 15.00 - 30.00
45, Sherry/I've Cried Before
    Vee Jay 456, 1962, black rainbow label with oval logo .... 12.50 - 25.00
    Vee Jay 456, 1963, all-black label .... 12.50 - 25.00
LP, *Big Hits by Burt Bacharach...Hal David...Bob Dylan*
    Philips PHM 200-193, mono, 1965, "open book" cover .... 10.00 - 20.00
    Philips PHM 200-193, mono, 1966, group photos on cover ...... 15.00 - 30.00
    Philips PHS 600-193, stereo, 1965, "open book" cover .... 12.50 - 25.00
    Philips PHS 600-193, stereo, 1966, group photos on cover .... 20.00 - 40.00
LP, *2nd Vault of Golden Hits*
    Philips PHM 200-221, mono, 1966 .... 7.50 - 15.00
    Philips PHS 600-221, stereo, 1966 .... 10.00 - 20.00

MVP:
45, Lost Lullaby/Trance , Topix 6008, 1961, as "Billy Dixon and the Topics"
    .... 100.00 - 200.00

LP, *Four Tops Reach Out*

Motown M5-149V1, 1981, reissue..4.00 - 8.00
Motown MT-660, mono, 1967 ....15.00 - 30.00
Motown MS-660, stereo, 1967 ....12.50 - 25.00

45, Ain't No Woman (Like the One I've Got)/The Good Lord Knows, ABC
   Dunhill 4339, 1973 ....2.50 - 5.00
45, Baby I Need Your Loving/Call On Me, Motown 1062, 1964 ....7.50 - 15.00
45, Bernadette/I Got a Feeling, Motown 1104, 1967 ....6.00 - 12.00
45, I Can't Help Myself/Sad Souvenirs, Motown 1076, 1965 ....7.50 - 15.00
45, It's the Same Old Song/Your Love Is Amazing, Motown 1081,
   1965...7.50 - 15.00
45, Keeper of the Castle/Jubilee with Soul, ABC Dunhill 4330,
   1972...2.50 - 5.00
45, Reach Out I'll Be There/Until You Love Someone, Motown 1098, 1966
   Record only...7.50 - 15.00
   Picture sleeve only ....40.00 - 80.00
45, Standing in the Shadows of Love/Since You've Been Gone, Motown
   1102, 1966..7.50 - 15.00
45, When She Was My Girl/Something to Remember, Casablanca 2338,
   1981...2.00 - 4.00
LP, *The Four Tops Greatest Hits*
   Motown MT-662, mono, 1967 ....15.00 - 30.00
   Motown MS-662, stereo, 1967 ....10.00 - 20.00
LP, *Four Tops Second Album*
   Motown MT-634, mono, 1965 ....12.50 - 25.00
   Motown MS-634, stereo, 1965 ....15.00 - 30.00
LP, *Keeper of the Castle*, ABC Dunhill DSX-50129, 1972....................6.00 - 12.00

MVP:
45, If Only I Had Known/(B-side unknown), Grady 012, 1956, as "The Four
   Aims" ....300.00 - 600.00

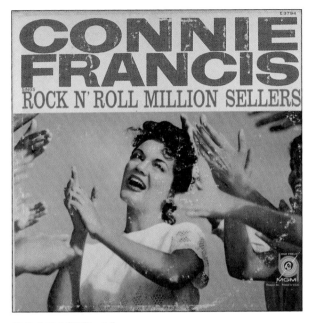

LP, *Rock 'N' Roll Million Sellers*

    MGM E-3794, mono, 1960 .... 15.00 - 30.00

    MGM SE-3794, stereo, 1960 .... 20.00 - 40.00

45, Don't Break the Heart That Loves You/Drop It, Joe, MGM K13059, 1962
    Record only...7.50 - 15.00
    Picture sleeve only..10.00 - 20.00
45, Everybody's Somebody's Fool/Jealous of You, MGM K12899, 1960
    Record only...7.50 - 15.00
    Picture sleeve only..10.00 - 20.00
45, Among My Souvenirs/God Bless America
    MGM K12841, mono, 1959, yellow label.....................15.00 - 30.00
    MGM K12841, mono, 1959, black label.......................10.00 - 20.00
    MGM SK-50133, stereo..25.00 - 50.00
45, My Heart Has a Mind of Its Own/Malaguena, MGM K12923, 1960
    Record only...7.50 - 15.00
    Picture sleeve only..10.00 - 20.00
45, Who's Sorry Now?/You Were Only Fooling, MGM K12588,
    1958...10.00 - 20.00
LP, *Connie's Greatest Hits*, MGM E-3793, mono, 1960 ....15.00 - 30.00
LP, *Italian Favorites*
    MGM E-3791, mono, 1959..15.00 - 30.00
    MGM SE-3791, stereo, 1959.......................................20.00 - 40.00
LP, *More Italian Favorites*
    MGM E-3871, mono, 1960..15.00 - 30.00
    MGM SE-3871, stereo, 1960.......................................20.00 - 40.00

MVP:
LP, *Who's Sorry Now?*, MGM E-3686, mono, 1958, yellow label (black label
    goes for less than half this amount) ....50.00 - 100.00

LP, *Aretha: Lady Soul*

    Atlantic 8176, mono, 1968..15.00 - 30.00

    Atlantic SD 8176, stereo, 1968, green and blue label.................10.00 - 20.00

    Atlantic SD 8176, stereo, 1969, green and red label ....6.00 - 12.00

45, Bridge Over Troubled Water/Brand New Me, Atlantic 2796,
1971..3.00 - 6.00
45, Chain of Fools/Prove It, Atlantic 2464, 1967 ....5.00 - 10.00
45, Freeway of Love/Until You Say You Love Me, Arista 9354, 1985
    Record only..1.50 - 3.00
    Picture sleeve only..1.50 - 3.00
45, I Knew You Were Waiting (For Me)/(Instrumental), Arista 9559, 1987,
    with George Michael
    Record only..1.50 - 3.00
    Picture sleeve only ....1.50 - 3.00
45, Respect/Dr. Feelgood, Atlantic 2403, 1967 ....5.00 - 10.00
45, Spanish Harlem/Lean On Me, Atlantic 2817, 1971 ....3.00 - 6.00
45, Until You Come Back to Me (That's What I'm Gonna Do)/If You Don't Think,
    Atlantic 2995, 1973 ....3.00 - 6.00
45, (You Make Me Feel Like) A Natural Woman/Baby, Baby, Baby, Atlantic
    2441, 1967 ....5.00 - 10.00
LP, *I Never Loved a Man the Way I Love You*
    Atlantic 8139, mono, 1967 ....12.50 - 25.00
    Atlantic SD 8139, stereo, green and blue label ....10.00 - 20.00
    Atlantic SD 8139, stereo, green and red label ....6.00 - 12.00
LP, *Who's Zoomin' Who*, Arista AL8-8286, 1985 ....5.00 - 10.00
LP, *Young, Gifted & Black*, Atlantic SD 7213, 1972 ....7.50 - 15.00

MVP:
LP, *Songs of Faith*, Checker 10009, mono, 1965, original cover has Aretha sitting
    at a piano (reissues are much less) ....250.00 - 500.00

LP, *What's Going On*

    Motown 5339 ML, 1980s, reissue ....5.00 - 10.00

    Tamla TS-310, 1971, original ....7.50 - 15.00

45, Got to Give It Up — Pt. 1/Got to Give It Up — Pt. 2, Tamla 54280, 1977
Record only..2.00 - 4.00
Picture sleeve only ....5.00 - 10.00
45, How Sweet It Is To Be Loved By You/Forever, Tamla 54107,
1964...7.50 - 15.00
45, I Heard It Through the Grapevine/You're What's Happening (In the World
Today), Tamla 54176, 1968 ....5.00 - 10.00
45, Mercy Mercy Me (The Ecology)/Sad Tomorrows, Tamla 54207,
1971...3.00 - 6.00
45, Pride and Joy/One of These Days, Tamla 54079, 1963 ....10.00 - 20.00
45, Sexual Healing/(Instrumental), Columbia 38-03302, 1982 ....2.00 - 4.00
45, Sexual Healing/(B-side blank), Columbia CNR-03344, 1982, special
"One Sided Single" with small hole ....3.00 - 6.00
45, Too Busy Thinking About My Baby/Wherever I Lay My Hat (That's My Home),
Tamla 54181, 1969 ....4.00 - 8.00
45, What's Going On/God Is Love, Tamla 54201, 1971 ....3.00 - 6.00
LP, *I Heard It Through the Grapevine*, Tamla TS 285, stereo, 1969, retitled
version of *In the Groove* ....10.00 - 20.00
LP, *In the Groove*
Tamla T 285, mono, 1968...25.00 - 50.00
Tamla TS 285, stereo, 1968..12.50 - 25.00
LP, *Let's Get It On*
Motown M5-192V1, 1981, reissue..5.00 - 10.00
Tamla T6-329, 1973, original..7.50 - 15.00

MVP:
LP, *The Soulful Moods of Marvin Gaye*, Tamla TM 221, mono, 1961, "twin
globes" label (reissues are much less) ....500.00 – 1,000.00

LP, *Nursery Cryme*

    Atlantic 80030, 1982, reissue...4.00 - 8.00

    Charisma CAS-1052, 1971, original..7.50 - 15.00

    Charisma CAS-1052, 2000, Classic Records reissue ....12.50 - 25.00

45, Invisible Touch/The Last Domino, Atlantic 7-89407, 1986
  Record only..1.50 - 3.00
  Picture sleeve only ....1.50 - 3.00
45, Land of Confusion/Feeding the Fire, Atlantic 7-89336, 1986
  Record only, red and black label..1.50 - 3.00
  Record only, black label with different Atlantic logo....................5.00 - 10.00
  Picture sleeve only ....5.00 - 10.00
45, Misunderstanding/Behind the Lines, Atlantic 3662, 1980
  Record only..2.00 - 4.00
  Picture sleeve only...2.50 - 5.00
LP, *Abacab*, Atlantic SD 19313, 1981, released with four different covers,
  lettered "A" through "D" on spine; no difference in value.............5.00 - 10.00
LP, *...And Then There Were Three*, Atlantic SD 19173, 1978 ....5.00 - 10.00
LP, *The Lamb Lies Down on Broadway*, Atco SD 2-401 (2-record set),
  1974, original with yellow labels...7.50 - 15.00
LP, *Trespass*
  ABC ABCX-816, 1971, early reissue ....6.00 - 12.00
  ABC Impulse! ASD-9205, 1971, original ....15.00 - 30.00
  MCA 816, 1979, reissue ....5.00 - 10.00
  MCA 37151, 1980s, later reissue..4.00 - 8.00
LP, *A Trick of the Tail*
  Atco SD 38-101, 1978, reissue ....5.00 - 10.00
  Atco SD 36-129, 1976, original ....6.00 - 12.00
  Mobile Fidelity 1-062, 1981, "Original Master Recording" on front
  cover ....25.00 - 50.00

MVP:
45, Silent Sun/That's Me, Parrot 3018, 1968, stock copy on black label (promos
  on orange labels are 50.00 – 100.00) ....200.00 - 400.00

LP, *Beauty and the Beat*

    I.R.S. SP 70021, 1981, original, peach-colored cover and light
label ....6.00 - 12.00
    I.R.S. SP 70021, 1981, second edition, dark blue cover and darker
label ....4.00 - 8.00

12-inch single, Cool Jerk (6 versions), I.R.S. 75021 7480 1, promotional issue only, 1990 ....4.00 - 8.00

45, Head Over Heels/Good for Gone, I.R.S. 9926, 1984
    Record only...1.50 - 3.00
    Picture sleeve only ....1.50 - 3.00

45, Our Lips Are Sealed/Surfing and Spying, I.R.S. 9901, 1981
    Record only...1.50 - 3.00
    Picture sleeve only ....3.00 - 6.00

45, Our Lips Are Sealed/We Got the Beat, I.R.S. 8690, 1980s, "Amnesia Series" reissue..1.50 - 3.00

45, Vacation/Beatnik Beach, I.R.S. 9907, 1982
    Record only...1.50 - 3.00
    Picture sleeve only..1.50 - 3.00

45, Vacation/Cool Jerk, I.R.S. 8691, 1980s, "Amnesia Series" reissue..1.50 - 3.00

45, We Got the Beat/Can't Stop the World, I.R.S. 9903, 1982
    Record only...1.50 - 3.00
    Picture sleeve only ....1.50 - 3.00

45, We Got the Beat/Our Lips Are Sealed, I.R.S. 8001, 1982, 7-inch picture disc in plastic sleeve ....5.00 - 10.00

LP, *Vacation*, I.R.S. SP 70031, 1982..4.00 - 8.00

LP, *Talk Show*, I.R.S. SP 70041, 1984...4.00 - 8.00

MVP:

12-inch single, Our Lips Are Sealed/Tonight/We Got the Beat, I.R.S. 70956, promotional release only, 1981 ....6.00 – 12.00

LP, *Grand Funk Hits*
  Capitol ST-11579, 1976, original ....5.00 - 10.00
  Capitol SN-16138, 1981, reissue ....4.00 - 8.00

45, The Loco-Motion/Destitute and Losin', Capitol 3840, 1974
    Record only (custom label) ....2.00 - 4.00
    Picture sleeve only ....2.50 - 5.00
45, Time Machine/High on a Horse, Capitol 2567, 1969.....................3.00 - 6.00
45, We're An American Band/Creepin', Capitol 3660, 1973
    Record only, custom label, gold vinyl ....3.00 - 6.00
    Record only, custom label, black vinyl............................2.00 - 4.00
    Picture sleeve only..2.50 - 5.00
LP, *Closer to Home*
    Capitol SKAO-471, 1970, lime green label original (orange label and purple
    label are less) ....7.50 - 15.00
    Capitol SN-16176, 1981, reissue ....4.00 - 8.00
LP, *E Pluribus Funk*, Capitol SW-853, 1971, round cover designed to look like a
    coin ....7.50 - 15.00
LP, *Good Singin' Good Playin'*, MCA 2216, 1976 ....6.00 - 12.00
LP, *On Time*
    Capitol ST-307, 1969, lime green label (orange label and purple label are less)
    ....7.50 - 15.00
    Capitol SN-16178, 1981, reissue ....4.00 - 8.00
LP, *We're An American Band*
    Capitol SMAS-11207, 1973, gold vinyl without sheet of four stickers
    ....10.00 - 20.00
    Capitol SMAS-11207, 1973, black vinyl ....5.00 - 10.00
    Capitol 21692, 1999, limited-edition reissue on 180-gram gold vinyl with origi-
    nal 1973 packaging..12.50 - 25.00

MVP:
LP, *We're An American Band* , Capitol SMAS-11207, 1973, gold vinyl with sheet
    of four stickers (see above for other versions) ....15.00 - 30.00

LP, *Age to Age*

    A&M SP-5056, 1985, reissue ....4.00 - 8.00

    Myrrh MSB-6697, 1982, original ....6.00 - 12.00

45, Baby Baby (2 mixes), A&M 75021 1549 7, 1991 ....2.00 - 4.00
45, Every Heartbeat (2 mixes), A&M 75021 1557 7, 1991..................2.00 - 4.00
45, Stay for Awhile/Love of Another Kind, A&M 2864, 1986
    Record only..1.50 - 3.00
    Picture sleeve only ....2.00 - 4.00
45, Tennessee Christmas/Little Town, A&M 2777, 1985
    Record only..2.00 - 4.00
    Picture sleeve only ....2.50 - 5.00
LP, *Amy Grant*
    A&M SP-5051, 1985, reissue, same as second Myrrh cover ....4.00 - 8.00
    Myrrh MSB-6586, 1977, with colorized "ugly cover" of Amy's head and
    shoulders; "Amy Grant" at upper left..7.50 - 15.00
    Myrrh MSB-6586, 1980s, with new cover of Amy in natural color;
    "Amy Grant" at upper right..5.00 - 10.00
LP, *The Collection*
    A&M SP-3900, 1986 ....4.00 - 8.00
    Myrrh 701-684306-8, 1986..5.00 - 10.00
LP, *Heart in Motion*, A&M 75021 5321 1, 1991 ....7.50 - 15.00
LP, *Straight Ahead*
    A&M SP-5058, 1985, reissue..4.00 - 8.00
    Myrrh 701-675706-4, 1984, original ....5.00 - 10.00
LP, *Unguarded*
    A&M SP-5060, 1985, four different covers exist, with "W," "O," "R" and "D"
    on the spine, each of equal value ....4.00 - 8.00
    Myrrh 701-680606-5, 1985, four different covers exist, with "W," "O," "R"
    and "D" on the spine, each of equal value ....5.00 - 10.00

MVP:
LP, *A Christmas Album*, Myrrh MSB-6768, 1983, picture disc, promotional item
    only (regular versions are much less)...40.00 - 80.00

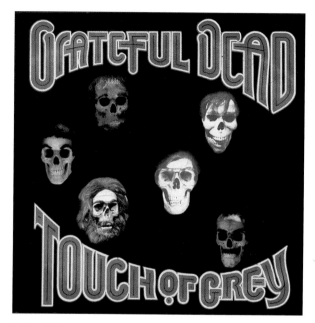

45, Touch of Grey/My Brother Esau, Arista 9606, 1987
   Record only, black vinyl ....1.50 - 3.00
   Record only, grey vinyl ....2.50 - 5.00
   Picture sleeve only, folds open into a poster ....2.50 - 5.00
   Record and picture sleeve together, still sealed in original shrink wrap,
   with custom sticker ....7.50 – 15.00

45, Truckin'/Ripple, Warner Bros. 7464, 1971 ....7.50 - 15.00
45, Uncle John's Band/New Speedway Boogie, Warner Bros. 7410, 1970..7.50 - 15.00
LP, *In the Dark*, Arista AL 8452, 1987 ....5.00 - 10.00
LP, *Terrapin Station*
    Arista AL 7001, 1977, regular copies ....7.50 - 15.00
    Arista AL 7001, 1977, promotional copies, banded for airplay....25.00 - 50.00
    Arista AL 8329, 1980s, reissue ....4.00 - 8.00
LP, *Wake of the Flood*
    Grateful Dead GD-01, 1973, with no contributing artists mentioned on back cover..10.00 - 20.00
    Grateful Dead GD-01, 1973, green vinyl fan club edition; ironically, most copies were damaged in a flood before distribution................200.00 - 400.00
    Grateful Dead GD-01, 1975, with contributing artists on back cover and United Artists distribution ....7.50 - 15.00
LP, *What a Long Strange Trip It's Been: The Best of the Grateful Dead*
    Warner Bros. 2WS 3091 (2-record set), 1977, "Burbank" palm-trees labels...10.00 - 20.00
    Warner Bros. 2WS 3091 (2-record set), 1979, white or tan labels....5.00 - 10.00
LP, *Workingman's Dead*
    Rhino R1 74396, 2003, reissue on 180-gram vinyl ....7.50 – 15.00
    Warner Bros. WS 1869, 1970, green label with "WB" logo, textured cover with back cover slick upside down...12.50 - 25.00
    Warner Bros. WS 1869, 1973, "Burbank" palm-trees label, standard cover with back cover right side up ....6.00 - 12.00
    Warner Bros. WS 1869, 1979, white or tan label ....4.00 - 8.00

MVP:
45, Stealin'/Don't Ease Me In, Scorpio 201, 1966 ....500.00 – 1,000.00

LP, *Al Green Explores Your Mind*, Hi SHL-32087, 1974.....................7.50 - 15.00

45, Call Me (Come Back Home)/What a Wonderful Thing Love Is, Hi 2235, 1973..2.50 - 5.00

45, Here I Am (Come and Take Me)/I'm Glad You're Mine, Hi 2247, 1973..2.50 - 5.00

45, I'm Still in Love with You/Old Time Lovin, Hi 2216, 1972 ....2.50 - 5.00

45, L-O-V-E (Love)/I Wish You Were Here, Hi 2282, 1975...................2.50 - 5.00

45, Let's Stay Together/Tomorrow's Dream, Hi 2202, 1971 ....2.50 - 5.00

45, Look What You Done for Me/La La for You, Hi 2211, 1972............2.50 - 5.00

45, Sha-La-La (Make Me Happy)/School Days, Hi 2274, 1974.............2.50 - 5.00

45, Tired of Being Alone/Get Back Baby, Hi 2194, 1971......................2.50 - 5.00

45, You Ought to Be with Me/What Is This Feeling, Hi 2227, 1972 ......2.50 - 5.00

LP, *I'm Still in Love with You*

Hi SHL-32074, 1972, original..7.50 - 15.00

Motown 5284 ML, 1980s, reissue..5.00 - 10.00

The Right Stuff T1-27627, 1995, reissue, green vinyl ....7.50 - 15.00

LP, *Let's Stay Together*

Hi SHL-32070, 1972, original..7.50 - 15.00

Motown 5290 ML,1980s, reissue...5.00 - 10.00

The Right Stuff T1-27121, 1995, reissue, green vinyl ....7.50 - 15.00

MVP:

LP, *Back Up Train,* Hot Line S-1500, stereo, 1967, as "Al Greene," mono version goes for less..40.00 - 80.00

LP, *Canned Wheat Packed By the Guess Who*
    RCA Victor ANL1-0983, 1975, reissue..5.00 - 10.00
    RCA Victor LSP-4157, 1969, orange label, non-flexible vinyl.......10.00 - 20.00
    RCA Victor LSP-4157, 1971, orange label, flexible vinyl ....6.00 - 12.00

45, American Woman/No Sugar Tonight, RCA Victor 74-0325, 1970 ....2.50 - 5.00
45, Clap for the Wolfman/Road Food, RCA Victor APBO-0324, 1974....2.50 - 5.00
45, Laughing/Undun, RCA Victor 74-0195, 1969 ....3.00 - 6.00
45, No Time/Proper Stranger, RCA Victor 74-0300, 1969 ....3.00 - 6.00
45, Shakin' All Over/Till We Kissed, Scepter 1295, 1965 ....7.50 - 15.00
45, Shakin' All Over/Monkey in a Cage, Scepter 1295, 1965, B-side by the
    Discotays ....15.00 - 30.00
45, Share the Land/Bus Rider, RCA Victor 74-0388, 1970
    Record only..2.50 - 5.00
    Picture sleeve only..5.00 - 10.00
45, These Eyes/Lightfoot, RCA Victor 74-0102, 1969 ....3.00 - 6.00
LP, *American Woman*
    RCA Victor AYL1-3673, 1979, reissue ....4.00 - 8.00
    RCA Victor AFL1-4266, 1977, reissue with new prefix ....5.00 - 10.00
    RCA Victor LSP-4266, 1970, orange label, non-flexible vinyl ....10.00 - 20.00
    RCA Victor LSP-4266, 1971, orange label, flexible vinyl ....6.00 - 12.00
LP, *The Best of the Guess Who*
    RCA Victor LSPX-1004, 1971 ....7.50 - 15.00
    RCA Victor AFL1-2594, 1978, reissue ....5.00 - 10.00
    RCA Victor AYL1-3662, 1979, reissue ....4.00 - 8.00

MVP:
LP, *Shakin' All Over*, Scepter SP-533, mono, 1966, credited to "The Guess Who's
    Chad Allan & The Expressions" on the cover (stereo version goes for less)
    ....20.00 - 40.00

LP, *Appetite for Destruction*

    Geffen GHS 24148, 1988, standard cover ....5.00 - 10.00

    Geffen XXXG 24148, 1988, original "rape cover"; the XXXG prefix is on the
    cover only; all copies of the record use the GHS prefix ....25.00 - 50.00

45, Don't Cry/Don't Cry (Alt. Lyrics), Geffen 19027, 1991 ....2.00 - 4.00
45, November Rain/Sweet Child O' Mine, Geffen 19067, 1992 ....2.00 - 4.00
45, Paradise City/Move to the City, Geffen 7-27570, 1989
    Record only...2.00 - 4.00
    Picture sleeve only ....2.00 - 4.00
45, Patience/Rocket Queen, Geffen 7-22996, 1989
    Record only...2.00 - 4.00
    Picture sleeve only...2.00 - 4.00
45, Sweet Child O' Mine/It's So Easy, Geffen 7-27963, 1988
    Record only...2.00 - 4.00
    Picture sleeve only...2.00 - 4.00
45, Sweet Child O' Mine/Welcome to the Jungle, Geffen 7-21901, 1989,
    reissue...1.50 - 3.00
45, Welcome to the Jungle/Mr. Brownstone, Geffen 7-27759, 1988
    Record only...2.00 - 4.00
    Picture sleeve only...2.00 - 4.00
LP, *G N' R Lies*, Geffen GHS 24198, 1988 ....5.00 - 10.00
LP, *Live Era '87-'93*, Geffen 490514-1 (4-record set), 1999............12.50 - 25.00
LP, *The Spaghetti Incident?*, Geffen GEF 24617, 1993, orange
    vinyl..7.50 - 15.00
LP, *Use Your Illusion I*, Geffen GEF 24415 (2-record set), 1991 .....10.00 - 20.00
LP, *Use Your Illusion II*, Geffen GEF 24420 (2-record set), 1991 ....10.00 - 20.00

MVP:
LP, *Live ?!*@ Like a Suicide*, Uzi Suicide USR 001, LP-sized EP, 1986
    ....60.00 - 120.00

LP, *Okie from Muskogee*
  Capitol ST-384, 1970, lime green label..10.00 - 20.00
  Capitol SN-16277, 1982, reissue ....4.00 - 8.00

45, From Graceland to the Promised Land/Are You Lonesome Tonight, MCA
40804, 1977 ....3.00 - 6.00

45, The Fugitive/Someone Told My Story Capitol 5803, 1966, original A-side
title ....6.00 - 12.00

45, I'm a Lonesome Fugitive/Someone Told My Story, Capitol 5803, 1967,
revised A-side title ....4.00 - 8.00

45, Mama Tried/You'll Never Love Me Now, Capitol 2219, 1968
Record only ....4.00 - 8.00
Picture sleeve only ....4.00 - 8.00

45, (My Friends Are Gonna Be) Strangers/Please Mr. D.J.,Tally 179,
1964 ....7.50 - 15.00

45, Okie from Muskogee/If I Had Left It Up to You, Capitol 2626, 1969
Record only ....4.00 - 8.00
Picture sleeve only ....4.00 - 8.00

LP, *The Best of Merle Haggard*
Capitol SKAO 2951, 1968, black label with rainbow ring ....12.50 - 25.00
Capitol SN-16054, 1979, reissue ....4.00 - 8.00

LP, *I'm a Lonesome Fugitive*
Capitol SM-2702, stereo, 1970s, reissue with new prefix ....5.00 - 10.00
Capitol ST 2702 , stereo, 1967 ....15.00 - 30.00
Capitol T 2702, mono, 1967 ....12.50 - 25.00

LP, *A Tribute to the Best Damn Fiddle Player in the World (Or, My Salute
to Bob Wills)*
Capitol ST-638, 1970 ....12.50 - 25.00
Capitol SN-16279, 1982, reiissue ....4.00 - 8.00

MVP:
LP, *The Land of Many Churches*, Capitol SWBO-803 (2-record set),
1971 ....30.00 - 60.00

EP, *Shake, Rattle and Roll* [contents: Shake, Rattle and Roll/A.B.C.
Boogie//(We're Gonna) Rock Around the Clock/Thirteen Women (And Only
One Man in Town)], Decca ED 2168, 1954, record and cardboard picture
cover together ....60.00 – 120.00

45, Crazy Man, Crazy/Whatcha Gonna Do, Essex 321, 1953 ....30.00 - 60.00

45, See You Later, Alligator/The Paper Boy (On Main Street, U.S.A.),
Decca 9-29791, 1956..12.50 - 25.00

45, Shake, Rattle and Roll/A.B.C. Boogie, Decca 9-29204, 1954
With lines on either side of "Decca"...20.00 - 40.00
With star under "Decca" ....10.00 - 20.00

45, Skinny Minnie/Sway with Me, Decca 9-30592, 1958 ....15.00 - 30.00

45, (We're Gonna) Rock Around the Clock/Thirteen Women (And Only One
Man in Town)
Decca 9-29124, 1954, with lines on either side of "Decca"........30.00 - 60.00
Decca 9-29124, 1955, with star under "Decca"...........................10.00 - 20.00
Decca 29124, 1960s, black label with color bars ....5.00 - 10.00
MCA 60025, 1973, reissue on black label with rainbow; made the Top
40 in 1974...2.50 - 5.00

LP, *Bill Haley's Golden Hits*
Decca DXSE-7211 (2-record set), 1972................................7.50 - 15.00
MCA 4010 (2-record set), 1973, reissue.....................................6.00 - 12.00

LP, *Rock 'N' Roll Revival*
Warner Bros. WS 1831, 1970...7.50 - 15.00
Warner Bros. ST-93103, 1970, Capitol Record Club edition........12.50 - 25.00

LP, *Shake, Rattle and Roll* , Decca DL 5560, mono, 1955, 10-inch LP
....400.00 - 800.00

MVP:

45, Rock the Joint/Icy Heart, Essex 303, 1952, as "Bill Haley and His
Saddlemen," red vinyl (black vinyl goes for much less) ...1,350.00 – 1,800.00

LP, *Bigger Than Both of Us*

    RCA Victor APL1-1467, 1976, original ....5.00 - 10.00

    RCA Victor AYL1-3866, 1980, reissue ....4.00 - 8.00

45, I Can't Go for That (No Can Do)/Unguarded Minute, RCA PB-12357, 1981
....2.00 - 4.00
45, Kiss on My List/Africa, RCA PB-12142, 1981 ....2.00 - 4.00
45, Maneater/Delayed Reaction, RCA PB-13354, 1982 ....1.50 - 3.00
45, Out of Touch/Cold, Dark, and Yesterday, RCA PB-13916, 1984
    Record only..1.50 - 3.00
    Picture sleeve only ....1.50 - 3.00
45, Private Eyes/Tell Me What You Want, RCA PB-12296, 1981 ....2.00 - 4.00
45, Rich Girl/London Luck, & Love, RCA PB-10860, 1976
    Record only..2.00 - 4.00
    Picture sleeve only..4.00 - 8.00
45, She's Gone/I'm Just a Kid (Don't Make Me Feel Like a Man)
    Atlantic 2993, 1973...4.00 - 8.00
    Atlantic 3332, 1976...2.00 - 4.00
LP, *Abandoned Luncheonette*
    Atlantic SD 7269, 1973, original...6.00 - 12.00
    Atlantic SD 19139, 1977, reissue...4.00 - 8.00
LP, *Daryl Hall & John Oates*
    RCA Victor APL1-1144, 1976, original, tan label ....5.00 - 10.00
    RCA Victor APL1-1144, 1976, early reissue, black label, dog near top
    ....4.00 - 8.00
    RCA Victor ANL1-3463, 1979, reissue...4.00 - 8.00
    RCA Victor AYL1-3836, 1980, reissue ....4.00 - 8.00
LP, *Private Eyes*, RCA Victor AFL1-4028, 1981 ....5.00 - 10.00

MVP:
12-inch single, Hold On to Yourself (eight mixes), Push 90405-1 (2-record set),
    1998, promotional release only ....20.00 - 40.00

LP, *Thirty Three and 1/3,* Dark Horse DH 3005, 1976,
   With no "cut-out" slice through one of the sides of the album ......5.00 - 10.00
   With "cut-out" slice through one of the sides of the album ....3.50 - 7.00

45, Got My Mind Set on You/Lay His Head, Dark Horse 7-28178, 1987
    Record only..2.00 - 4.00
    Picture sleeve only ....2.00 - 4.00
45, My Sweet Lord/Isn't It a Pity
    Apple 2995, 1970, with "Mfd. by Apple" on label (hit version) ......4.00 - 8.00
    Apple 2995, 1970, with black star on label ....20.00 - 40.00
    Apple 2995, 1970, picture sleeve only ....20.00 - 40.00
    Apple 2995, 1975, with "All Rights Reserved" disclaimer on
    label ....12.50 - 25.00
    Capitol 2995, 1976, orange label with "Capitol" at bottom ....10.00 - 20.00
    Capitol 2995, 1978, purple label; label has reeded edge.................3.00 - 6.00
    Capitol 2995, 1983, black label with colorband............................3.00 - 6.00
    Capitol 2995, 1988, purple label; label has smooth edge...............2.50 - 5.00
LP, *The Best of George Harrison*
    Capitol ST-11578, 1976, custom label, no bar code on back
    (original) ....7.50 - 15.00
    Capitol ST-11578, 1976, orange label ....90.00 - 180.00
    Capitol ST-11578, 1978, purple label, large Capitol logo..............5.00 - 10.00
    Capitol ST-11578, 1983, black label, print in colorband ....12.50 - 25.00
    Capitol ST-11578, 1988 , odd reissue with custom label; large stand-
    alone "S" in trail-off area; bar code on cover............................12.50 - 25.00
    Capitol ST-11578, 1989, purple label, small Capitol logo ....40.00 - 80.00
LP, *Cloud Nine*, Dark Horse 25643, 1987 ....5.00 - 10.00

MVP:
45, Love Comes to Everyone/Soft Touch, Dark Horse 8844, 1979, picture sleeve
    only (record by itself is 5.00 - 10.00) ....500.00 - 750.00

LP, *Dreamboat Annie*

Capitol SQ-12500, 1986, reissue ....4.00 - 8.00

Capitol 21184, 1999, 180-gram reissue ....12.50 – 25.00

Mushroom MRS-2-SP, 1978, picture disc in numbered cardboard
cover ....12.50 - 25.00

Mushroom MRS-5005, 1976, original ....5.00 - 10.00

Nautilus NR-3, 1980, "Super Disc" on cover ....20.00 - 40.00

45, Alone/Barracuda (Live), Capitol B-44002, 1987
    Record only..1.50 - 3.00
    Picture sleeve only ....1.50 - 3.00
45, Barracuda/Cry to Me, Portrait 6-70004, 1977................................2.00 - 4.00
45, Magic Man/How Deep It Goes, Mushroom 7011, 1976................2.50 - 5.00
45, Never (Remix)/Shell Shock, Capitol B-5512, 1985
    Record only..1.50 - 3.00
    Picture sleeve only ....1.50 - 3.00
45, These Dreams/Shell Shock, Capitol B-5541, 1985
    Record only..1.50 - 3.00
    Picture sleeve only..1.50 - 3.00
LP, *Bad Animals*, Capitol PJ-12546, 1987 ....5.00 - 10.00
LP, *Dog and Butterfly*
    Portrait FR 35555, 1978, original, no bar code ....5.00 - 10.00
    Portrait PR 35555, 1981, reissue, with bar code...........4.00 - 8.00
LP, *Heart* , Capitol ST-12410, 1985
    With original mix of "Never" ....7.50 - 15.00
    With remix of "Never"; side one trail-off wax has an "RE-1" ....5.00 - 10.00
LP, *Little Queen*
    Portrait JR 34799, 1977, original ....5.00 - 10.00
    Portrait PR 34799, 1984, reissue ....4.00 - 8.00
    Portrait HR 44799, 1981, "Half Speed Mastered" on cover........25.00 - 50.00

MVP:
LP, Magazine, Mushroom MRS-5008, 1977, original recalled edition; Side 2, Track 3 is "Blues Medley (Mother Earth) (You Shook Me Babe)." Also, at the bottom of the back cover is a lengthy statement beginning "Mushroom Records regrets that a contractural dispute..." ....30.00 - 60.00

LP, *Are You Experienced?*

    Reprise R 6261, mono, 1967 ....100.00 - 200.00

    Reprise RS 6261, stereo,1967, pink, gold and green label

    (original) ....25.00 - 50.00

    (Other versions on RS 6261 go for less.)

45, All Along the Watchtower/Burning of the Midnight Lamp, Reprise 0767,
1968..15.00 - 30.00
45, Foxey Lady/Hey Joe, Reprise 0641, 1967.....................................12.50 - 25.00
45, Purple Haze/The Wind Cries Mary, Reprise 0597, 1967 ....12.50 - 25.00
LP, *Axis: Bold As Love,*
    Reprise RS 6281, stereo, 1968, pink, gold and green label (original)
    ....40.00 - 80.00
    Reprise RS 6281, stereo, 1968, with "W7" and "r:" logos on two-tone orange
    label ....12.50 - 25.00
    Reprise RS 6281, stereo, 1970, with only "r:" logo on all-orange (tan)
    label ....6.00 - 12.00
    Reprise RS 6281, stereo, 1980s, red and black label or gold and light
    blue label ....4.00 - 8.00
    Experience Hendrix/MCA 11601, stereo, 1997, reissue on "heavy vinyl"
    with booklet ....25.00 - 50.00
    Track 612003, mono, 2000, distributed by Classic Records........12.50 - 25.00
LP, *Smash Hits*
    Reprise MS 2025, 1969, with "W7" and "r:" logos on two-tone orange
    label (original)...20.00 - 40.00
    Reprise MS 2025, 1969, add this amount if bonus poster is included
    ....20.00 - 40.00
    Reprise MS 2025,1970, with only "r:" logo on all-orange (tan) label
    ....6.00 - 12.00
    Reprise MSK 2276, 1977, reissue with new number ....5.00 - 10.00
    Experience Hendrix/MCA 112984, 2002, reissue on 180-gram
    vinyl ....7.50 - 15.00

MVP:
LP, *Axis: Bold As Love,* Reprise R 6281, mono , 1968 (see listings above for
    stereo versions)..1,250.00 – 2,500.00

LP, *The Best of Herman's Hermits, Volume 2*
    MGM E-4416, mono, 1966, without bonus photo (add 50% if it is there)
    ....6.00 - 12.00
    MGM SE-4416, stereo, 1966, without bonus photo (add 50% if it is there)
    ....5.00 - 10.00

45, Can't You Hear My Heartbeat/I Know Why, MGM K13310, 1964
Record only..5.00 - 10.00
Picture sleeve only ....7.50 - 15.00
45, I'm Henry VIII, I Am/The End of the World, MGM K13367, 1965
Record only..5.00 - 10.00
Picture sleeve only ....10.00 - 20.00
45, I'm Into Something Good/Your Hand in Mine, MGM K13280,
1964..5.00 - 10.00
45, Mrs. Brown You've Got a Lovely Daughter/I Gotta Dream On,
MGM K13341, 1965
Record only..5.00 - 10.00
Picture sleeve only ....7.50 - 15.00
45, There's a Kind of Hush (All Over the World)/No Milk Today,
MGM K13681, 1967
Record only, with title listed as "There's a Kind of Hush" ....4.00 - 8.00
Record only, with title listed as "There's a Kind of Hush (All Over the World)"
....5.00 - 10.00
Picture sleeve only...7.50 - 15.00
LP, *Introducing Herman's Hermits,* 1965
MGM E-4282, mono, with "Including Their Hit Single "I'm Into Something
Good" on front cover ....12.50 - 25.00
MGM SE-4282, rechanneled stereo, with "Including Their Hit Single
'I'm Into Something Good' " on front cover ....10.00 - 20.00
(Other versions go for less.)

MVP:
45, Hold On, MGM (no #), promotional-only picture sleeve similar to the LP
cover of the same name; rear of sleeve has "The Mod Shirts Are Here"
advertisement; this may have come with some promos of "Leaning on the
Lamp Post" (MGM 13500) ....125.00 - 250.00

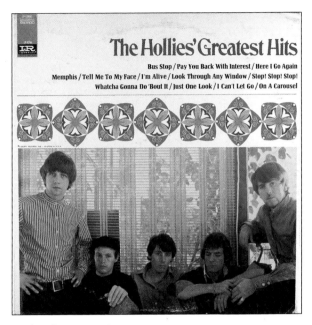

LP, *The Hollies' Greatest Hits*

    Imperial LP-9350, mono, 1967 ....10.00 - 20.00

    Imperial LP-12350, stereo, 1967..12.50 - 25.00

    (NOTE: This is a different album than the album of the same title on Epic)

45, The Air That I Breathe/No More Riders, Epic 5-11100, 1974.........2.50 - 5.00

45, Bus Stop/Don't Run and Hide, Imperial 66186, 1966 ....6.00 - 12.00

45, Carrie-Anne/Signs That Will Never Change, Epic 5-10180, 1967
    Record only..4.00 - 8.00
    Picture sleeve only ....7.50 - 15.00

45, He Ain't Heavy, He's My Brother/Cos You Like to Love Me, Epic 5-10532,
    1969...3.00 - 6.00

45, Long Cool Woman (In a Black Dress)/Look What We've Got, Epic
    5-10871, 1972 ....2.50 - 5.00

45, On a Carousel/All the World Is Love, Imperial 66231, 1967
    Record only..6.00 - 12.00
    Picture sleeve only ....15.00 - 30.00

45, Stop in the Name of Love/Musical Pictures, Atlantic 7-89819, 1983
    Record only..1.50 - 3.00
    Picture sleeve only..2.50 - 5.00

45, Stop Stop Stop/It's You, Imperial 66214, 1966 ....6.00 - 12.00

LP, *Distant Light*
    Epic KE 30958, 1972, yellow label ....7.50 - 15.00
    Epic KE 30958, 1974, orange label ....5.00 - 10.00
    Epic PE 30958, 1986, dark blue label...4.00 - 8.00

LP, *The Hollies' Greatest Hits* (not the same album as on Imperial)
    Epic KE 32061, 1973, yellow label ....6.00 - 12.00
    Epic KE 32061, 1974, orange label ....5.00 - 10.00
    Epic PE 32061, 1979, dark blue label...4.00 - 8.00

MVP:

LP, *Here I Go Again*, Imperial LP-9265, mono, 1964, black label with stars
    (other versions go for much less) ....75.00 - 150.00

LP, *The Best of Buddy Holly*

    Coral CXB 8 (2-record set), mono, 1966 ....40.00 - 80.00

    Coral CXSB 8 [(2-record set), "enhanced for stereo," 1966 ....25.00 - 50.00

45, Early in the Morning/Now We're One, Coral 62006, 1958.........25.00 - 50.00
45, It Doesn't Matter Anymore/Raining in My Heart, Coral 62074,
  1959...20.00 - 40.00
45, It Doesn't Matter Anymore/Peggy Sue, MCA 40905, 1978
  Record only...2.50 - 5.00
  Picture sleeve only..2.50 - 5.00
45, Peggy Sue/Everyday
  Coral 61885, 1957, orange label...25.00 - 50.00
  Coral 61885, 1960s, black label with color bars.......................12.50 - 25.00
45, Rave On/Take Your Time, Coral 61985, 1958.............................25.00 - 50.00
45, Heartbeat/Well...All Right, Coral 62051, 1958 ....25.00 - 50.00
LP, *Buddy Holly/The Crickets 20 Golden Greats*
  MCA 1484, 1980s, reissue ....4.00 - 8.00
  MCA 3040, 1978, original, tan label..7.50 - 15.00
LP, *The Buddy Holly Story*
  Coral CRL 57279, mono, 1959, maroon label, back color print in black
  and red...150.00 - 300.00
  Coral CRL 57279, mono, 1959, maroon label, back color print in all
  black..75.00 - 150.00
  Coral CRL 57279 , mono, 1963, black label with color bars.......40.00 - 80.00
  Coral CRL 757279, "enhanced for stereo," 1963 ....20.00 - 40.00
LP, *The Complete Buddy Holly*, MCA 80000 (6-record set), 1981, with box,
  booklet and custom innersleeves...25.00 - 50.00

MVP:
EP, *That'll Be the Day*, Decca ED 2575, 1958, record plus cover with liner notes
  (record plus cover with ads for other EPs is 600.00-1,200.00; record by itself
  is 300.00-600.00) ....1,300.00 – 2,600.00

LP, *Release Me*

    Parrot PA 61012, mono, 1967...10.00 - 20.00

    Parrot PAS 71012, stereo, 1967 ....7.50 - 15.00

45, Am I That Easy to Forget/Pretty Ribbons, Parrot 40023, 1967

    Record only...4.00 - 8.00

    Picture sleeve only ....6.00 - 12.00

45, After the Lovin'/Let's Remember the Good Times, Epic 8-50270,

    1976...2.50 - 5.00

45, The Last Waltz/That Promise, Parrot 40019, 1967

    Record only...4.00 - 8.00

    Picture sleeve only ....6.00 - 12.00

45, Release Me (And Let Me Love Again)/Ten Guitars, Parrot 40011, 1967

    Mono record; ''DR'' in trail-off wax on both sides before the master

    numbers ....4.00 - 8.00

    Stereo record, though not labeled as such; ''XDR'' stamped in trail-off wax

    on both sides before the master number ....10.00 - 20.00

45, There Goes My Everything/You Love, Parrot 40015, 1967 ....4.00 - 8.00

LP, *After the Lovin'*,

    Epic PE 34381, 1976, orange label ....5.00 - 10.00

    Epic PE 34381, 1979, dark blue label, no bar code on back

    cover ....4.00 - 8.00

    Epic PE 34381, 1980s, dark blue label, back cover has bar

    code ....3.00 - 6.00

LP, *Engelbert*, Parrot PAS 71026, 1969.................................7.50 - 15.00

LP, *The Last Waltz*

    Parrot PA 61015, mono, 1967..................................10.00 - 20.00

    Parrot PAS 71015, stereo, 1967 ....7.50 - 15.00

LP, *A Man Without Love*, Parrot PAS 71022, 1968 ....7.50 - 15.00

MVP:

LP, *Last of the Romantics*, Epic (no #), 1978. picture disc, promotional item

    only (regular versions go for much less) ....12.50 - 25.00

LP, *Keep On Pushing*

ABC-Paramount ABC-493, mono, 1964 ....15.00 - 30.00

ABC-Paramount ABCS-493, stereo, 1964 ....20.00 - 40.00

ABC-Paramount ST-90106, stereo, 1965, Capitol Record Club
edition ....25.00 - 50.00

45, Choice of Colors/Mighty Mighty Spade and Whitey, Curtom 1943, 1969..3.00 - 6.00
45, Finally Got Myself Together (I'm a Changed Man)/I'll Always Be Here, Curtom 1997, 1974 ....3.00 - 6.00
45, Gypsy Woman/As Long As You Love Me, ABC-Paramount 10241, 1961..7.50 - 15.00
45, I'm So Proud/I Made a Mistake, ABC-Paramount 10544, 1964 ....7.50 - 15.00
45, It's All Right/You'll Want Me Back, ABC-Paramount 10487, 1963..7.50 - 15.00
45, Keep On Pushing/I Love You (Yeah), ABC-Paramount 10554, 1964..7.50 - 15.00
45, People Get Ready/I've Been Trying, ABC-Paramount 10622, 1965..7.50 - 15.00
45, Talking About My Baby/Never Too Much Love, ABC-Paramount 10511, 1963..7.50 - 15.00
45, We're a Winner/It's All Over, ABC 11022, 1967 ....4.00 - 8.00
LP, *The Impressions' Greatest Hits*
ABC-Paramount ABC-515, mono, 1965 ....10.00 - 20.00
ABC-Paramount ABCS-515, stereo, 1965 ....12.50 - 25.00
LP, *People Get Ready*
ABC-Paramount ABC-505, mono, 1965 ....15.00 - 30.00
ABC-Paramount ABCS-505, stereo, 1965 ....20.00 - 40.00
LP, *16 Greatest Hits*, ABC ABCS-727, 1971 ....6.00 - 12.00
LP, *The Vintage Years*, Sire SASH-3717 [2-record set], 1977, includes solo hits by Jerry Butler and Curtis Mayfield ....7.50 - 15.00

MVP:
45, For Your Precious Love/Sweet Was the Wine, Vee Jay 280, 1958, by "Jerry Butler and the Impressions" (versions on Abner, Falcon, Lost-Nite and other labels sell for no more than 1/150th of this price and usually even less) ....6,000.00 – 8,000.00

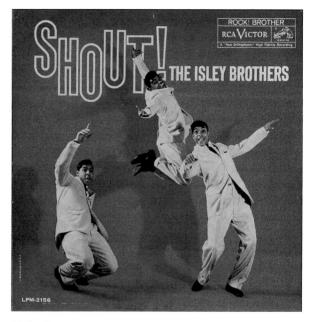

LP, *Shout!*

    RCA Victor LPM-2156, mono, 1959, "Long Play" label ....60.00 - 120.00
    RCA Victor LSP-2156, stereo, 1959, "Living Stereo" label ......100.00 - 200.00

45, Fight the Power Part 1/Fight the Power Part 2, T-Neck ZS8 2256,
1975...2.50 - 5.00

45, It's Your Thing/Don't Give It Away, T-Neck 901, 1969 ....3.00 - 6.00

45, Shout (Part 1)/Shout (Part 2)

    RCA Victor 47-7588, mono, 1959...15.00 - 30.00

    RCA Victor 61-7588, stereo, "Living Stereo" on label ....30.00 - 60.00

    RCA Victor 447-0589, 1962, black label, dog on top ....6.00 - 12.00

    RCA Victor 447-0589, 1965, black label, dog on side ....4.00 - 8.00

    RCA Victor 447-0589, 1969, red label..2.50 - 5.00

    RCA 447-0589, 1976, black label, dog near top ....2.00 - 4.00

45, That Lady (Part 1)/That Lady (Part 2), T-Neck ZS7 2251, 1973 .....2.50 - 5.00

45, This Old Heart of Mine (Is Weak for You)/There's No Love Left,
Tamla 54128, 1966 ....7.50 - 15.00

45, Twist and Shout/Spanish Twist, Wand 124, 1962 ....10.00 - 20.00

LP, *The Heat Is On*

    T-Neck PZ 33536, 1975, no bar code on cover ....6.00 - 12.00

    T-Neck PZ 33536, 1980s, with bar code..4.00 - 8.00

LP, *3 + 3*

    T-Neck KZ 32453, 1973, original...6.00 - 12.00

    T-Neck PZ 32453, 1970s, reissue with new prefix ....4.00 - 8.00

    T-Neck ZQ 32453, quadraphonic, 1974 ....10.00 - 20.00

LP, *The Very Best of the Isley Brothers*, United Artists UA-LA500-E,
1975..5.00 - 10.00

MVP:

45, Angels Cried/The Cow Jumped Over the Moon, Teenage 1004,
1957...400.00 - 800.00

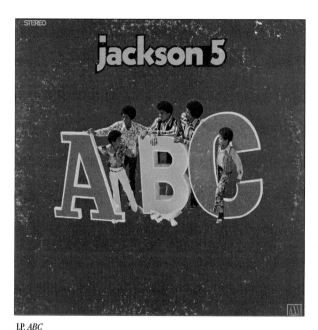

LP, *ABC*

    Motown M5-152V1, 1981, reissue..4.00 - 8.00

    Motown MS 709, 1970, original ....12.50 - 25.00

45, ABC/The Young Folks, Motown 1163, 1970..........................4.00 - 8.00

45, Enjoy Yourself/Style of Life, Epic/Philadelphia Int'l. 8-50289, 1976, first record as "The Jacksons" ....2.50 - 5.00

45, I Want You Back/Who's Lovin' You, Motown 1157, 1969 ....4.00 - 8.00

45, I'll Be There/One More Chance, Motown 1171, 1970 ....4.00 - 8.00

45, The Love You Save/I Found That Girl, Motown 1166, 1970 ....4.00 - 8.00

45, Mama's Pearl/Darling Dear, Motown 1177, 1971

    Record only...3.00 - 6.00

    Picture sleeve only..7.50 - 15.00

45, State of Shock/Your Ways, Epic 34-04503, 1984, A-side with Mick Jagger

    Record only...2.00 - 4.00

    Picture sleeve only..2.00 - 4.00

LP, *Diana Ross Presents the Jackson 5*

    Motown M5-129V1, 1981, reissue ....4.00 - 8.00

    Motown MS 700, 1969, original ....12.50 - 25.00

LP, *Jackson 5 Greatest Hits*

    Motown M5-201V1, 1981, reissue ....4.00 - 8.00

    Motown M-741, 1971, original ....7.50 - 15.00

LP, *Victory*

    Epic QE 38946, 1984, regular issue ....4.00 - 8.00

    Epic 8E8 39576, 1984, picture disc in plastic sleeve with sticker

    ....7.50 - 15.00

MVP:
45, Big Boy/You've Changed, Steeltown 681, 1968 ....50.00 - 100.00

LP, *Control*

    A&M SP-3905, 1986, second issue; most have a black label ....4.00 - 8.00

    A&M SP-5106, 1986, original issue; silver label with fading

    A&M logo ....5.00 - 10.00

12-inch single, Nasty (Extended Version 6:00) (Instrumental 4:00)
    (A Cappella 2:55), A&M SP-12178, 1986.......................................4.00 - 8.00
12-inch single, When I Think of You (Dance Remix) (Instrumental)
    (Extra Beats) (Dub A Cappella), A&M SP-12193, 1986 ....4.00 - 8.00
45, Control/Fast Girls, A&M 2877, 1986
    Record only...1.50 - 3.00
    Picture sleeve only..1.50 - 3.00
45, Let's Wait Awhile/Pretty Boy, A&M 2906, 1987
    Record only...1.50 - 3.00
    Picture sleeve only..1.50 - 3.00
45, Miss You Much/You Need Me, A&M 1445, 1989 ....3.00 - 6.00
45, Nasty/You'll Never Find (A Love Like Mine), A&M 2830, 1986
    Record only...1.50 - 3.00
    Picture sleeve only..2.50 - 5.00
45, That's the Way Love Goes/(Instrumental), Virgin S7-17332, 1993, "For
    Jukeboxes Only!" on label
    Original pressing on red vinyl..3.00 - 6.00
    Reissue on black vinyl...2.00 - 4.00
45, What Have You Done for Me Lately/He Doesn't Know I'm Alive, A&M 2812,
    1986
    Record only...1.50 - 3.00
    Picture sleeve only ....1.50 - 3.00
45, When I Think of You/Pretty Boy, A&M 2855, 1986
    Record only...1.50 - 3.00
    Picture sleeve only..1.50 - 3.00
LP, *Janet Jackson's Rhythm Nation 1814,* A&M SP-3920, 1989.........7.50 - 15.00

MVP:

12-inch single, State of the World, with 6 dance mixes plus the "State of the
    World Suite," A&M 75021 7523 1 [(2-record set), promo only,
    1991 ....20.00 - 40.00

LP, *Thriller*

    Epic QE 38112, 1982 ....4.00 - 8.00
    Epic 8E8 38867, 1983, picture disc in plastic cover ....10.00 - 20.00
    Epic HE 48112, 1982, "Half Speed Mastered" on cover.............20.00 - 40.00

45, Beat It/Get On the Floor, Epic 34-03759, 1983................................2.00 - 4.00

45, Ben/You Can Cry on My Shoulder, Motown 1207, 1972 ....2.50 - 5.00

45, Billie Jean/Can't Get Outta the Rain, Epic 34-03509, 1983 ....2.00 - 4.00

45, Black or White/(Instrumental), Epic 34-74100, 1991....................1.50 - 3.00

45, Don't Stop 'Til You Get Enough/I Can't Help It, Epic 9-50742,
    1979..2.00 - 4.00

45, Got to Be There/Maria (You Were the Only One), Motown 1191,
    1971..2.50 - 5.00

45, Remember the Time/Black or White (The Underground Club Mix),
    Epic 34-74200, 1992..1.50 - 3.00

45, Rock with You/Working Day and Night, Epic 9-50797, 1979..........2.00 - 4.00

45, Rockin' Robin/Love Is Here and Now You're Gone, Motown 1197,
    1972..2.50 - 5.00

45, Smooth Criminal/(Instrumental), Epic 34-08044, 1988
    Record only...1.50 - 3.00
    Picture sleeve only...1.50 - 3.00

LP, *Got to Be There*
    Motown M5-130V1, 1981, reissue..5.00 - 10.00
    Motown M 747, 1972, original..7.50 - 15.00

LP, *HIStory: Past, Present and Future — Book I* , Epic E3 59000
    (3-record set), 1995, box set with booklet ....10.00 - 20.00

LP, *Off the Wall*
    Epic FE 35745, 1979...4.00 - 8.00
    Epic HE 47545, 1982, "Half Speed Mastered" on cover.............20.00 - 40.00

MVP:

45, Someone in the Dark (same on both sides), MCA S45-1786, white label
    promotional copy only, 1982, record with picture sleeve ....50.00 - 100.00

LP, *100 Strings and Joni*

    MGM E-3755, mono, 1959, yellow label ....40.00 - 80.00

    MGM E-3755, mono, 1960, black label......................................20.00 - 40.00

    MGM SE-3755, stereo, 1959, yellow label ....60.00 - 120.00

    MGM SE-3755, stereo, 1960, black label ....25.00 - 50.00

45, Have You Heard/Wishing Ring, MGM K11390, 1953 ....10.00 - 20.00
45, How Important Can It Be?/This Is My Confession, MGM K11919, 1955
....10.00 - 20.00
45, There Goes My Heart/Funny
    MGM K12706, 1958 ....7.50 - 15.00
    MGM SK-12706, stereo, 1958...20.00 - 40.00
    MGM SK-12706, picture sleeve, 1958..25.00 - 50.00
45, Why Don't You Believe Me/Purple Shades, MGM K11333, 1952
....15.00 - 30.00
45, You Are My Love/I Lay Me Down to Sleep, MGM K12066, 1955
....10.00 - 20.00
LP, *Award Winning Album*
    MGM E-3346, mono, 1956, yellow label ....40.00 - 80.00
    MGM E-3346, mono, 1960, black label..20.00 - 40.00
LP, *Songs of Hank Williams*
    MGM E-3739, mono, 1959, yellow label ....40.00 - 80.00
    MGM E-3739, mono, 1960, black label..20.00 - 40.00
    MGM SE-3739, stereo, 1959, yellow label ....60.00 - 120.00
    MGM SE-3739, stereo, 1960, black label ....25.00 - 50.00
LP, *The Very Best of Joni James*
    MGM E-4151, mono, 1963...20.00 - 40.00
    MGM SE-4151, stereo, 1963..25.00 - 50.00

MVP:
45, Let There Be Love/My Baby Just Cares for Me, Sharp 46, 1952
....150.00 - 300.00

LP, *I Think We're Alone Now*

    Roulette R 25353, mono, 1967 ....15.00 - 30.00

    Roulette SR 25353, stereo, 1967, "footprints" cover ....12.50 - 25.00

    Roulette SR 25353, stereo, 1967, photo on cover ....7.50 - 15.00

45, Crimson and Clover/(I'm) Taken, Roulette 7028, 1968................7.50 - 15.00
45, Crimson and Clover/Some Kind of Love, Roulette 7028, 1968......5.00 - 10.00
45, Crystal Blue Persuasion/I'm Alive, Roulette 7050, 1969 ....5.00 - 10.00
45, Hanky Panky/Thunderbolt
   Red Fox 110, 1966, as "The Shondells," early reissue ....20.00 - 40.00
   Snap 102, 1966, as "The Shondells," with "Dist. by Red Fox Records,
   Pgh, Pa." on label, early reissue...15.00 - 30.00
   Roulette 4686, 1966, "hit" release...5.00 - 10.00
45, I Think We're Alone Now/Gone, Gone, Gone, Roulette 4720, 1967
   Record only...5.00 - 10.00
   Picture sleeve only...7.50 - 15.00
45, Mirage/Run, Run, Baby, Run, Roulette 4736, 1967
   Record only...4.00 - 8.00
   Picture sleeve only...7.50 - 15.00
45, Mony Mony/One Two Three and I Fell, Roulette 7008, 1968........5.00 - 10.00
45, Sweet Cherry Wine/Breakaway, Roulette 7039, 1969.....................4.00 - 8.00
LP, *The Best of Tommy James & The Shondells*,
   Roulette SR 42040, original version in a Unipak (gatefold must be opened
   to remove record)..10.00 - 20.00
   Roulette SR 42040, later versions have gatefold covers, but record is
   removed from outside ....7.50 - 15.00
LP, *Cellophane Symphony*, Roulette SR 42030, 1969 ....10.00 - 20.00
LP, *Crimson and Clover*, Roulette SR 42023, 1969..........................10.00 - 20.00

MVP:
45, Hanky Panky/Thunderbolt, Snap 102, 1963, as "The Shondells"; original
   issue, no mention of Red Fox Records on label (see above for other
   releases) ....40.00 - 80.00

LP, *Jan and Dean Take Linda Surfin'*
  Liberty LRP-3294, mono, 1963...25.00 - 50.00
  Liberty LST-7294, stereo, 1963...40.00 - 80.00

45, Baby Talk/Jeannette Get Your Hair Done, Dore 522, 1959 ....15.00 - 30.00

45, Batman/Bucket "T", Liberty 55860, 1966 ....12.50 - 25.00

45, Dead Man's Curve/The New Girl in School, Liberty 55672, 1964
    Record only..7.50 - 15.00
    Picture sleeve only..20.00 - 40.00

45, The Little Old Lady (From Pasadena)/My Mighty G.T.O., Liberty 55704, 1964
    Record only..7.50 - 15.00
    Picture sleeve only..20.00 - 40.00

45, Ride the Wild Surf/The Anaheim, Azusa and Cucamonga Sewing Circle, Book
    Review and Timing Association, Liberty 55724, 1964
    Record only..7.50 - 15.00
    Picture sleeve only ....20.00 - 40.00

45, Surf City/She's My Summer Girl, Liberty 55580, 1963
    Record only..7.50 - 15.00
    Picture sleeve only..20.00 - 40.00

LP, *Drag City*
    Liberty LRP-3339, mono, 1963..20.00 - 40.00
    Liberty LST-7339, stereo, 1963 ....25.00 - 50.00

LP, *Jan and Dean Meet Batman*
    Liberty LRP-3444, mono, 1966..25.00 - 50.00
    Liberty LST-7444, stereo, 1966 ....35.00 - 70.00

LP, *The Very Best of Jan and Dean* United Artists UA-LA443-E,
    1975..5.00 - 10.00

MVP:
LP, *Jan and Dean* , Dore LP-101, mono, 1960, original with blue label (add
    another 60.00-120.00 if bonus photo is included).................200.00 - 400.00

LP, *Crown of Creation*

    RCA Victor AYL1-3797, 1980, reissue ....4.00 - 8.00

    RCA Victor LSP-4058, 1968. black label, dog on top, original.....15.00 - 30.00

    RCA Victor LSP-4058, 1969, orange label.....................................6.00 - 12.00

    RCA Victor LSP-4058, 1975, tan label...5.00 - 10.00

45, Ballad of You & Me & Pooneil/Two Heads, RCA Victor 47-9297,
1967...5.00 - 10.00
45, Somebody to Love/She Has Funny Cars, RCA Victor 47-9140,
1967...7.50 - 15.00
45, Volunteers/We Can Be Together, RCA Victor 74-0245, 1969
Record only..3.00 - 6.00
Picture sleeve only..7.50 - 15.00
45, White Rabbit/Plastic Fantastic Lover, RCA Victor 47-9248, 1967...7.50 - 15.00

LP, *After Bathing at Baxter's*
RCA Victor LOP-1511, mono, 1967 ....25.00 - 50.00
RCA Victor LSO-1511, stereo, 1967, black label, dog on top.......10.00 - 20.00
RCA Victor LSO-1511, stereo, 1969, orange label.........................6.00 - 12.00
RCA Victor LSO-1511, stereo, 1975, tan label..............................5.00 - 10.00
RCA Victor AFL1-4545, 1981, reissue ....4.00 - 8.00
RCA Victor AYL1-4718, 1983, another reissue ....4.00 - 8.00

LP, *Surrealistic Pillow*
DCC Compact Classics LPZ-2033, stereo, 1997, 180-gram reissue.12.50 - 25.00
RCA Victor AYL1-3738, 1980, reissue ....4.00 - 8.00
RCA Victor LPM-3766, mono, 1967 ....30.00 - 60.00
RCA Victor LSP-3766, stereo, 1967, black label, dog on top ......15.00 - 30.00
RCA Victor LSP-3766, stereo, 1969, orange label ....6.00 - 12.00
RCA Victor LSP-3766, stereo, 1975, tan label ....5.00 - 10.00
Sundazed LP-5135, mono, 2002, 180-gram reissue ....7.50 – 15.00

MVP:
LP, *Jefferson Airplane Takes Off!*, (RCA Victor LSP-3584, stereo, 1966, with
"Runnin' 'Round This World" as the last song on side 1; count the number of
bands on Side 1 of the record, don't rely on the cover listing, as some jackets
list the title when it's not on the record (mono versions of this go for the
$2,250-$3,000 range; versions without this song are a lot less)
....3,500.00 – 5,000.00

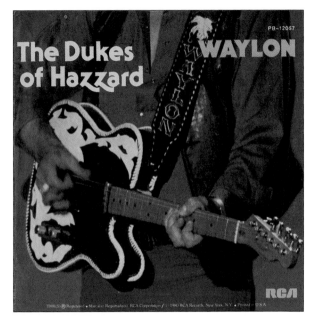

45, Theme from "The Dukes of Hazzard" (Good Ol' Boys)/It's Alright,
RCA PB-12067, 1980

Record only...2.00 - 4.00

Picture sleeve only..2.50 - 5.00

45, Amanda/Lonesome, On'ry and Mean, RCA PB-11596, 1979
    Record only..2.00 - 4.00
    Picture sleeve only ....2.50 - 5.00
45, Are You Sure Hank Done It This Way/Bob Wills Is Still the King, RCA
    Victor PB-10379, 1975..3.00 - 6.00
45, Don't You Think This Outlaw Bit's Done Got Out of Hand/Girl I Can Tell
    (You're Trying to Work It Out), RCA PB-11390, 1978.....................2.00 - 4.00
45, I've Always Been Crazy/I Never Said It Would Be Easy, RCA PB-11344,
    1978..2.00 - 4.00
45, Lucille (You Won't Do Your Daddy's Will)/Medley of Hits, RCA
    PB-13465, 1983..2.00 - 4.00
45, Luckenbach, Texas (Back to the Basics of Love)/Belle of the Ball, RCA
    PB-10924, 1977 ....2.50 - 5.00
45, Rose in Paradise/Crying Don't Even Come Close, MCA 53009,
    1987..1.50 - 3.00
45, This Time/Mona, RCA Victor APBO-0251, 1974............................3.00 - 6.00
45, The Wurlitzer Prize (I Don't Want to Get Over You)/Lookin' for a Feeling,
    RCA PB-11118, 1977..2.50 - 5.00
LP, *Greatest Hits*, RCA Victor AHL1-3378, 1979 ....5.00 - 10.00
LP, *Nashville Rebel*
    RCA Victor LPM-3736, mono, 1967...20.00 - 40.00
    RCA Victor LSP-3736, stereo, 1967..25.00 - 50.00
LP, *Ol' Waylon*
    RCA Victor AAL1-2317, 1980s, reissue ....4.00 - 8.00
    RCA Victor APL1-2317, 1977, original..5.00 - 10.00
    RCA Victor AYL1-5126, 1984, another reissue ....4.00 - 8.00

MVP:
LP, *Waylon Jennings at JD's*, Bat 1001, mono, 1964 (reissue on Sounds 1001
    worth 250.00-500.00)...350.00 - 700.00

LP, *Thick as a Brick*

    Chrysalis CHR 1003, 1973, green label, "3300 Warner Blvd."
address..6.00 - 12.00
    Chrysalis CHR 1003, 1977, blue label, New York address.............5.00 - 10.00
    Chrysalis FV 41003, 1983...4.00 - 8.00
    Mobile Fidelity 1-187, 1985, "Original Master Recording" at top of front
cover ....15.00 - 30.00
    Reprise MS 2072, 1972, original with intact "newspaper"............7.50 - 15.00

45, Living in the Past/Christmas Song, Chrysalis 2006, 1972 ....3.00 - 6.00
45, Living in the Past/Driving Song, Reprise 0845, 1969, white label
    promotional copy ....10.00 - 20.00
45, Bungle in the Jungle/Back Door Angels, Chrysalis 2101, 1974
    Record only..2.50 - 5.00
    Picture sleeve only ....5.00 - 10.00
LP, *Aqualung*
    Chrysalis CH4 1044, quadraphonic, 1974 ....20.00 - 40.00
    Chrysalis CHR 1044, 1973, green label, "3300 Warner Blvd."
    address..6.00 - 12.00
    Chrysalis CHR 1044, 1977, blue label, New York address ....5.00 - 10.00
    Chrysalis FV 41044, 1983..4.00 - 8.00
    Mobile Fidelity 1-061, 1980, "Original Master Recording" at top of front
    cover ....35.00 - 70.00
    Reprise MS 2035, 1971, original..7.50 - 15.00
LP, *M.U. — The Best of Jethro Tull*
    Chrysalis CHR 1078, 1975 , green label, "3300 Warner Blvd."
    address..6.00 - 12.00
    Chrysalis CHR 1078, 1977, blue label, New York address ....5.00 - 10.00
    Chrysalis FV 41078, 1983..4.00 - 8.00
LP, *A Passion Play*
    Chrysalis CHR 1040, 1973, green label, "3300 Warner Blvd."
    address..6.00 - 12.00
    Chrysalis CHR 1040, 1977, blue label, New York address ....5.00 - 10.00
    Chrysalis PV 41040, 1983..4.00 - 8.00

MVP:
LP, *Aqualung* , DCC Compact Classics LPZ 2033, 1997, reissue on 180-gram vinyl
    (see above for other variations) ....50.00 - 100.00

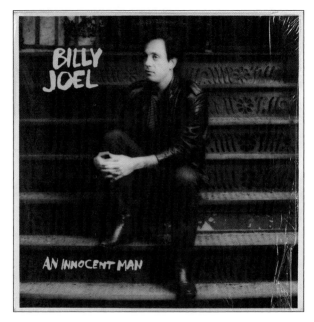

LP, *An Innocent Man*

    Columbia QC 38837, 1983 ....5.00 - 10.00

    Columbia HC 48837, 1983, "Half Speed Mastered" on front cover

    ....15.00 - 30.00

45, It's Still Rock and Roll to Me/Through the Long Night, Columbia 1-11276, 1980
   Record only..2.00 - 4.00
   Picture sleeve only ....3.00 - 6.00
45, Just the Way You Are/Get It Right the First Time, Columbia 3-10646, 1977..2.50 - 5.00
45, Only the Good Die Young/Get It Right the First Time, Columbia 3-10750, 1978 ....2.50 - 5.00
45, Piano Man/You're My Home, Columbia 4-45963, 1973 ....4.00 - 8.00
45, Tell Her About It/Easy Money, Columbia 38-04012, 1983
   Record only..1.50 - 3.00
   Picture sleeve only...2.00 - 4.00
45, We Didn't Start the Fire/House of Blue Light, Columbia 38-73021, 1989...1.50 - 3.00
LP, *52nd Street*
   Columbia FC 35609, 1978...5.00 - 10.00
   Columbia PC 35609, 1985, reissue..4.00 - 8.00
LP, *Glass Houses*
   Columbia FC 36384, 1980...5.00 - 10.00
   Columbia PC 36384, 1986, reissue..4.00 - 8.00
LP, *The Stranger*
   Columbia HC 34987, 1981, "Half Speed Mastered" on cover......15.00 - 30.00
   Columbia JC 34987, 1977, original ....5.00 - 10.00
   Columbia PC 34987, 1979, reissue with new prefix, bar code on back ....4.00 - 8.00
   Columbia HC 44987, 1982, "Half Speed Mastered" on cover, new number ....12.50 - 25.00

MVP:
LP, *Songs in the Attic*, Columbia HC 47461, 1982, must say "Half-Speed Mastered" on cover (regular version is common) ....35.00 - 70.00

LP, *Goodbye Yellow Brick Road*

    MCA 6894 (2-record set), 1980, reissue, blue labels with rainbow,
many copies in single sleeve rather than gatefold..........................5.00 - 10.00

    MCA 2-10003 (2-record set), 1973, original, black labels with
rainbow...7.50 - 15.00

    MCA 2-10003 (2-record set), 1977, tan labels..............................6.00 - 12.00

45, Crocodile Rock/Elderberry Wine
    MCA 40000, 1972, solid black label with white print, original ....3.00 - 6.00
    MCA 40000, 1973, black label with rainbow, silver print ....2.50 - 5.00
45, Daniel/Skyline Pigeon, MCA 40046, 1973, black label with
    rainbow...2.50 - 5.00
45, Empty Garden (Hey Hey Johnny)/Take Me Down to the Ocean, Geffen
    GFS 50049, 1982
    Record only...2.00 - 4.00
    Picture sleeve only ....2.50 - 5.00
45, I Guess That's Why They Call It the Blues/The Retreat, Geffen 7-29460, 1983
    Record only..1.50 - 3.00
    Picture sleeve only..1.50 - 3.00
45, Your Song/Take Me to the Pilot, Uni 55265, 1970.........................3.00 - 6.00
LP, *Madman Across the Water*
    DCC Compact Classics LPZ-2004, 1994, gold border on front cover,
    virgin vinyl edition ....60.00 - 120.00
    MCA 2016, 1973, second issue, with booklet...............................5.00 - 10.00
    MCA 3003, 1977, third edition ....4.00 - 8.00
    MCA 37200, 1982, fourth edition ....4.00 - 8.00
    Uni 93120, 1971, original, with booklet......................................7.50 - 15.00
LP, *Too Low for Zero* , Geffen GHS 4006, 1983 ....5.00 - 10.00

MVP:
45, Lady Samantha/All Across the Havens, DJM 70008, 1969, green label stock
    copy (white label promos are 50.00-100.00) ....150.00 - 300.00

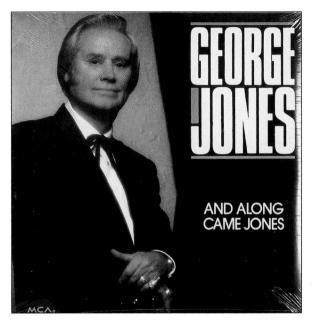

LP, *And Along Came Jones*, MCA 10398, 1991, vinyl issued only through the
Columbia House record club...10.00 - 20.00

45, A Good Year for the Roses/Let a Little Loving Come In, Musicor 1425,
1970..4.00 - 8.00

45, He Stopped Loving Her Today/A Hard Act to Follow, Epic 9-50867,
1980..3.00 - 6.00

45, I Always Get Lucky with You/I'd Rather Have What We Had, Epic
34-03883, 1983 ....1.50 - 3.00

45, She Thinks I Still Care/Sometimes You Just Can't Win, United Artists 424, 1962
Record only...5.00 - 10.00
Picture sleeve only...7.50 - 15.00

45, Tender Years/Battle of Love, Mercury 71804, 1961
Record only...6.00 - 12.00
Picture sleeve only...7.50 - 15.00

45, White Lightning/Long Time to Forget, Mercury 71406, 1959........7.50 - 15.00

45, Why Baby Why/Season of My Heart, Starday 202, 1955.............25.00 - 50.00

LP, *Anniversary — 10 Years of Hits*, Epic KE2 38323 (2-record set),
1982..6.00 - 12.00

LP, *George Jones' Greatest Hits*
Mercury MG-20621, mono, 1961...20.00 - 40.00
Mercury SR-60621, stereo, 1961...25.00 - 50.00

LP, *The Race Is On*
United Artists UAL-3422, mono, 1965, with cartoon on front .....10.00 - 20.00
United Artists UAL-3422, mono. 1965, with photo of George Jones on
front ....15.00 - 30.00
United Artists UAS-6422, stereo, 1965, with cartoon on front......12.50 - 25.00
United Artists UAS-6422, stereo, 1965, with photo of George Jones on
front ....20.00 - 40.00

MVP:
LP, *The Grand Ole Opry's New Star* , Starday SLP 101, mono, 1958
....600.00 – 1,200.00

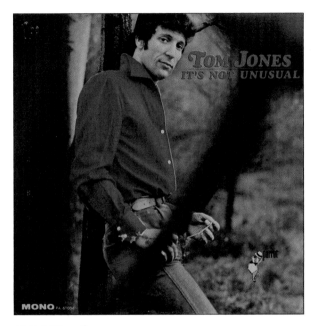

LP, *It's Not Unusual*
    Parrot PA 61004, mono, 1965...7.50 - 15.00
    Parrot PAS 71004, stereo, 1965 ....7.50 - 15.00

45, Delilah/Smile Away Your Blues, Parrot 40025, 1968 ....4.00 - 8.00
45, Green, Green Grass of Home/If I Had You, Parrot 40009, 1966.....4.00 - 8.00
45, It's Not Unusual/To Wait for Love (Is to Waste Your Life Away), Parrot
    9737, 1965..5.00 - 10.00
45, I'll Never Fall in Love Again/Once Upon a Time
    Parrot 40018, 1967, with four-plus-minute version of A-side ....6.00 - 12.00
    Parrot 40018, 1969, with 2:55 version of A-side ....4.00 - 8.00
45, Say You'll Stay Until Tomorrow/Lady Lay, Epic 8-50308, 1976........2.00 - 4.00
45, She's a Lady/My Way, Parrot 40058, 1971
    Record only..3.00 - 6.00
    Picture sleeve only...4.00 - 8.00
45, What's New Pussycat/Once Upon a Time, Parrot 9765, 1965
    Record only..5.00 - 10.00
    Picture sleeve only...7.50 - 15.00
LP, *A-Tom-Ic Jones*
    Parrot PA 61007, mono, 1966...7.50 - 15.00
    Parrot PAS 71007, stereo, 1966..7.50 - 15.00
LP, *She's a Lady*, Parrot PAS 71046, 1971 ....6.00 - 12.00
LP, *This Is Tom Jones*, Parrot PAS 71028, 1969 ....6.00 - 12.00
LP, *The Tom Jones Fever Zone*, Parrot PAS 71019, 1968...................6.00 - 12.00

MVP:
LP, *Special Tom Jones Interview,* Parrot XPAS-1, 1970, promo-only open-end
    interview with gatefold cover and script ....50.00 - 100.00

Kansas

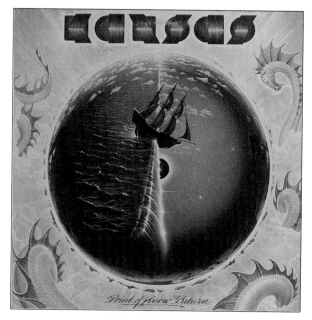

LP, *Point of Know Return*

    Kirshner JZ 34929, 1977, no bar code on cover ....5.00 - 10.00

    Kirshner JZ 34929, 1979, with bar code on cover..........................4.00 - 8.00

    Kirshner HZ 44929, 1982, "Half Speed Mastered" on cover ....20.00 - 40.00

45, All I Wanted/We're Not Alone Anymore, MCA 52958, 1986
    Record only..1.50 - 3.00
    Picture sleeve only..1.50 - 3.00
45, Carry On Wayward Son/Questions of My Childhood, Kirshner ZS8 4267,
    1976..2.50 - 5.00
45, Dust in the Wind/Paradox, Kirshner ZS8 4274, 1978.....................2.50 - 5.00
45, People of the South Wind/Stay Out of Trouble, Kirshner ZS8 4284,
    1979..2.00 - 4.00
45, Point of Know Return/Closet Chronicles, Kirshner ZS8 4273,
    1977..2.00 - 4.00
LP, *The Best of Kansas* CBS Associated QZ 39283, 1984....................4.00 - 8.00
LP, *Leftoverture*
    Kirshner JZ 34224, 1976, original, no bar code..........................5.00 - 10.00
    Kirshner PZ 34224, 1980s, reissue, bar code on back..................4.00 - 8.00
LP, *Masque*
    Kirshner PZ 33806, 1975, original, no bar code..........................6.00 - 12.00
    Kirshner PZ 33806, 1980s, reissue, bar code on back..................4.00 - 8.00
LP, *Power*, MCA 5838, 1986 ....4.00 - 8.00
LP, *Song for America*
    Kirshner PZ 33385, 1975, original, no bar code..........................6.00 - 12.00
    Kirshner PZ 33385, 1980s, reissue, bar code on back ....4.00 - 8.00

MVP:
LP, *Vinyl Confessions*, Kirshner HZ 48002, 1982, "Half-Speed Mastered" on
    cover (other versions are much less).......................................50.00 - 100.00

LP, *Wrap Around Joy*

    Ode PE 34953, 1977, reissue, no bar code .... 5.00 - 10.00

    Ode PE 34953, 1980s, reissue, with bar code .... 4.00 - 8.00

    Ode SP-77024, 1974, original .... 6.00 - 12.00

45, It Might As Well Rain Until September/Nobody's Perfect
   Companion 2000, 1962, original...150.00 - 300.00
   Dimension 2000, 1962, blue label ....6.00 - 12.00
   Dimension 2000, 1962, purple label ....7.50 - 15.00
45, It's Too Late/I Feel the Earth Move , Ode 66015, 1971
   Record only..2.00 - 4.00
   Picture sleeve only...2.50 - 5.00
45, One Fine Day, Capitol 4864, 1980
   Record only, with B-side "Rulers of This World"........................2.00 - 4.00
   Picture sleeve only, with B-side listed as "Recipients of History"   ...4.00 - 8.00
   Picture sleeve only, with no B-side listed ....2.00 - 4.00
45, So Far Away/Smackwater Jack , Ode 66019, 1971
   Record only..2.00 - 4.00
   Picture sleeve only...2.50 - 5.00
45, Sweet Seasons/Pocket Money, Ode 66022, 1971
   Record only..2.00 - 4.00
   Picture sleeve only...2.50 - 5.00
LP, *Fantasy*
   Ode PE 34962, 1977, reissue, no bar code................................5.00 - 10.00
   Ode PE 34962, 1980s, reissue, with bar code..............................4.00 - 8.00
   Ode SP-77018, 1973, original ....6.00 - 12.00
LP, *Tapestry*
   Ode FE 34946, 1979, reissue with new prefix and bar code.........5.00 - 10.00
   Ode PE 34946, 1977, reissue ....5.00 - 10.00
   Ode HE 44946, 1980, "Half Speed Mastered" on cover ....25.00 - 50.00
   Ode SP-77009, 1971, original ....6.00 - 12.00

MVP:
45, Oh, Neil/A Very Special Boy, Alpine 57, 1959 ....350.00 - 700.00

LP, *The Kingston Trio at Large*

Capitol ST 1199, stereo, 1959, black label with colorband, Capitol logo
at left ....20.00 - 40.00
Capitol T 1199, mono, 1959, black label with colorband, Capitol logo
and "Long Playing High-Fidelity" at left ....15.00 - 30.00
Capitol T 1199, mono, 1960, black label with colorband, Capitol logo
at left, white line replaces "Long Playing High-Fidelity" ....12.50 - 25.00
(Other label variations exist and sell for less.)

45, Greenback Dollar/New Frontier, Capitol 4898, 1963 ....5.00 - 10.00
45, M.T.A./All My Sorrows, Capitol F4221, 1959 ....10.00 - 20.00
45, Reverend Mr. Black/One More Round, Capitol 4951, 1963 ....5.00 - 10.00
45, The Tijuana Jail/Oh Cindy
    Capitol F4167, mono, 1959 ....10.00 - 20.00
    Capitol SF4167, stereo,1959 ....25.00 - 50.00
45, Tom Dooley/Ruby Red, Capitol F4049, 1958 ....12.50 - 25.00
45, A Worried Man/San Miguel, Capitol F4271, 1959 ....10.00 - 20.00
LP, *The Kingston Trio*
    Capitol DT 996 , "Duophonic" rechanneled stereo, 1960s............6.00 - 12.00
    Capitol T 996, mono, 1958, turquoise label ....25.00 - 50.00
    Capitol T 996, mono, 1958, black label with colorband, Capitol logo
    at left ....20.00 - 40.00
    Capitol T 996, mono, 1962, black label with colorband, Capitol logo
    at top ....10.00 - 20.00
LP, *Sold Out*
    Capitol ST 1352, stereo, 1960, black label with colorband, Capitol logo
    at left ....20.00 - 40.00
    Capitol ST 1352, stereo, 1962, black label with colorband, Capitol logo
    at top ....10.00 - 20.00
    Capitol T 1352, mono, 1960, black label with colorband, Capitol logo
    at left ....15.00 - 30.00
    Capitol T 1352, mono, 1962, black label with colorband, Capitol logo
    at top ....7.50 - 15.00

MVP:
LP, *Stereo Concert*, Capitol ST 1183, stereo, 1959, black label with colorband,
    Capitol logo at left (later editions are less) ....25.00 - 50.00

LP, *You Really Got Me*

    Reprise R-6143, mono, 1965 ....30.00 - 60.00

    Reprise RS-6143, stereo, 1965, pink, gold and green label.........40.00 - 80.00

    Reprise RS-6143, stereo, 1971, orange label with "r:" and steamboat

    at top...5.00 - 10.00

    Rhino R1 70315, 1988 ....6.00 - 12.00

45, All Day and All of the Night/I Gotta Move, Reprise 0334, 1964...10.00 - 20.00
45, Come Dancing/Noise
    Arista 1054, 1983, record only, original...2.00 - 4.00
    Arista 1054, 1983, picture sleeve only, original ....2.00 - 4.00
    Arista 9016, 1983, record only, early reissue ....1.50 - 3.00
    Arista 9016, 1983, picture sleeve only, early reissue ....1.50 - 3.00
45, Lola/Mindless Child of Motherhood, Reprise 0930, 1970.............5.00 - 10.00
45, Tired of Waiting for You/Come On Now, Reprise 0347, 1965 .....10.00 - 20.00
45, You Really Got Me/It's All Right, Reprise 0306, 1964
    Original, peach label ....12.50 - 25.00
    Second edition, orange and brown label ....7.50 - 15.00
LP, *Arthur (Or The Decline and Fall of the British Empire)*
    Reprise RS-6366, 1969 , two-tone orange label with "r: and "W7" logos
    with steamboat ....12.50 - 25.00
    Reprise RS-6366, 1971, orange label with "r:" and steamboat at top
    ....5.00 - 10.00
    Reprise SMAS-93034, 1970, Capitol Record Club edition............20.00 - 40.00
LP, *The Kinks Are the Village Green Preservation Society*
    Reprise RS-6327, 1969, two-tone orange label with "r: and "W7" logos
    with steamboat ....15.00 - 30.00
    Reprise RS-6327, 1971, orange label with "r:" and steamboat at
    top...5.00 - 10.00
LP, *Muswell Hillbillies*
    RCA Victor AYL1-4558, 1982, reissue ....4.00 - 8.00
    RCA Victor LSP-4644, 1971, original, orange label.....................15.00 - 30.00

MVP:
45, Long Tall Sally/I Took My Baby Home, Cameo 308, 1964 (stock copy;
    promos go for less, as does a reissue on Cameo 345) ....300.00 - 600.00

LP, *Rock and Roll Over*

    Casablanca NBLP 7037, 1976, tan label with desert scene, "Casablanca"
label; with sticker and Kiss Army paraphenalia order form ....10.00 - 20.00

    Casablanca NBLP 7037, 1977, tan label with desert scene, "Casablanca
Record and FilmWorks" label, with inserts....................................6.00 - 12.00

    Casablanca 824 150-1, 1984, reissue...4.00 - 8.00

45, Beth/Detroit Rock City
   Casablanca 863, 1976, with "Beth" listed as "Side A"; brown label with
   camel ....3.00 - 6.00
   Casablanca 863, 1977, with "Beth" listed as "Side A"; "Casablanca Record
   and FilmWorks" label...2.50 - 5.00
45, Detroit Rock City/Beth, Casablanca 863, 1976, with "Detroit Rock City"
   listed as "Side A" ....5.00 - 10.00
45, Forever/The Street Giveth and the Street Taketh Away, Mercury 876 716-7,
   1990..2.50 - 5.00
45, I Was Made for Lovin' You/Hard Times, Casablanca 983, 1979......2.50 - 5.00
45, Rock and Roll All Nite (Live)/Rock and Roll All Nite (Studio)
   Casablanca 850, 1975, blue label..5.00 - 10.00
   Casablanca 850, 1977, "Casablanca Record and FilmWorks"
   label ....6.00 - 12.00
LP, *Alive!* (2-record set)
   Casablanca NBLP 7020, 1975, dark blue labels; with booklet .....20.00 - 40.00
   Casablanca NBLP 7020, 1976, tan labels with desert scene, "Casablanca"
   label ....10.00 - 20.00
   Casablanca NBLP 7020, 1977, tan labels with desert scene, "Casablanca
   Record and FilmWorks" label ....7.50 - 15.00
   Casablanca 822 780-1, 1984, reissue..5.00 - 10.00
LP, *Lick It Up*, Mercury 814 297-1, 1983 ....6.00 - 12.00

MVP:
LP, *Alive II*, Casablanca NBLP 7076, (2-record set), 1977, with 8-page booklet,
   tattoo insert and "Combat Gear" order form; back cover lists three tracks —
   "Take Me," "Hooligan" and "Do You Love Me" — that were not included on
   the record; no records with these tracks were made; perhaps as few as 50
   copies of this cover were made (cover MUST list these tracks to be this
   valuable) ....200.00 - 400.00

LP, *If I Were Your Woman*, Soul SS 731, 1971 ....7.50 - 15.00

45, Best Thing That Ever Happened to Me/Once in a Lifetime, Buddah 403, 1974..2.50 - 5.00

45, Every Beat of My Heart/Room in Your Heart
Fury 1050, 1961, re-recordings of the same songs on Huntom and Vee Jay..12.50 - 25.00
Huntom 2510, 1961, original, as "The Pips"..........................250.00 - 500.00
Lost-Nite 382, 1970s, reissue of Fury versions.............................3.00 - 6.00
Vee Jay 386, 1961, reissue of Huntom single, by "Pips".............10.00 - 20.00
Vee Jay 386, 1961, by "Pips"; B-side called "Ain'tcha Got Some Room (In Your Heart for Me)"..10.00 - 20.00

45, Hero (The Wind Beneath My Wings)/Seconds, Columbia 38-04219, 1983...2.50 - 5.00

45, I Heard It Through the Grapevine/It's Time to Go Now, Soul 35039, 1967...5.00 - 10.00

45, If I Were Your Woman/The Tracks of My Tears, Soul 35078, 1970...3.50 - 7.00

45, Love Overboard/(Instrumental), MCA 53210, 1987
Record only..1.50 - 3.00
Picture sleeve only...1.50 - 3.00

45, Midnight Train to Georgia/(Instrumental), Buddah 383, 1973.......3.00 - 6.00

45, Midnight Train to Georgia/Window Raising Granny, Buddah 383, 1973
....2.50 - 5.00

45, Neither One of Us (Wants to Be the First to Say Goodbye)/Can't Give It Up No More, Soul 35098, 1972 ....3.00 - 6.00

LP, *Imagination*, Buddah BDS-5141, 1973 ....6.00 - 12.00

LP, *Neither One of Us*
Motown M5-193V1, 1981, reissue..6.00 - 12.00
Soul S 737L, 1973, original ....7.50 - 15.00

MVP:
LP, *Letter Full of Tears*, Fury 1003, mono, 1962 ....250.00 - 500.00

LP, *Emergency*, De-Lite 822 943-1, 1984...4.00 - 8.00

45, Celebration/Morning Star, De-Lite 807, 1980 ....2.00 - 4.00
45, Cherish/(Instrumental), De-Lite 880 869-7, 1985
    Record only..1.50 - 3.00
    Picture sleeve only ....2.00 - 4.00
45, Hollywood Swinging/Dujii, De-Lite 561, 1974 ....2.50 - 5.00
45, Jungle Boogie/North, East, South, West, De-Lite 559, 1973 ....2.50 - 5.00
45, Ladies Night/If You Feel Like Dancin', De-Lite 801, 1979 ....2.00 - 4.00
45, Open Sesame — Part 1/Open Sesame — Part 2, De-Lite 1586,
    1976..2.50 - 5.00
45, Too Hot/Tonight's the Night, De-Lite 802, 1979 ....2.00 - 4.00
LP, *As One*
    De-Lite 8505, 1982, original ....5.00 - 10.00
    De-Lite 822 535-1, 1984, reissue ....4.00 - 8.00
LP, *Celebrate!*
    De-Lite 9518, 1980, original ....5.00 - 10.00
    De-Lite 822 538-1, 1984, reissue ....4.00 - 8.00
LP, *Ladies Night*
    De-Lite 9513, 1979, original ....5.00 - 10.00
    De-Lite 822 537-1, 1984, reissue ....4.00 - 8.00
LP, *Wild and Peaceful* , De-Lite 2013, 1973.....................................5.00 - 10.00

MVP:
LP, *Kool and the Gang* , De-Lite 2003, 1969 ....12.50 - 25.00

LP, *Houses of the Holy*

    Atlantic SD 7255, 1973, "1841 Broadway" address on label.........6.00 - 12.00

    Atlantic SD 7255, 1974, "75 Rockefeller Plaza" address on label ...5.00 - 10.00

    Atlantic SD 7255, 2001, Classic Records reissue ....12.50 - 25.00

    Atlantic SD 19130, 1977, reissue..4.00 - 8.00

45, Black Dog/Misty Mountain Hop, Atlantic 2849, 1971 ....5.00 - 10.00
45, Immigrant Song/Hey, Hey, What Can I Do
    Atlantic 2777, 1970, first pressings with "Do What Thou Wilt Shalt Be the
    Whole of the Law" in trail-off ....12.50 - 25.00
    Atlantic 2777. 1971, second pressings without "Do What Thou Wilt Shalt
    Be the Whole of the Law" in trail-off ....7.50 - 15.00
    Atlantic 2777, 1977, third pressings with smaller, bolder type and
    Warner Communications logo in perimeter print ....2.50 - 5.00
45, Whole Lotta Love/Living Loving Maid (She's Just a Woman)
    Atlantic 2690, 1969, with A-side time of 3:12................................7.50 - 15.00
    Atlantic 2690, 1969, with A-side time of 5:33.............................10.00 - 20.00
LP, *Led Zeppelin (IV) (Runes)*
    Atlantic 7208, mono, white label, "Promotional DJ Copy Monaural Not for Sale"
    sticker on cover, 1971..150.00 - 300.00
    Atlantic SD 7208, stereo, 1971, white label, promotional copy .75.00 - 150.00
    Atlantic SD 7208, stereo, 1971, "1841 Broadway" address on
    label ....6.00 - 12.00
    Atlantic SD 7208, stereo, 1974, "75 Rockefeller Plaza" address on label
    ....5.00 - 10.00
    Atlantic SD 7208 , 2001, Classic Records reissue ....12.50 - 25.00
    Atlantic SD 19129, 1977, reissue...4.00 - 8.00
    Atlantic SMAS-94019, 1972, Capitol Record Club edition ....20.00 - 40.00
LP, *Led Zeppelin (Box Set)*, Atlantic 82144 (6-record set),
    1990..50.00 - 100.00

MVP:
LP, *Houses of the Holy*, Atlantic 7255, mono, white label, "Promotional DJ Copy
    Monaural Not for Sale" sticker on cover, 1973 (other versions go for much
    less; see previous page) ....500.00 – 1,000.00

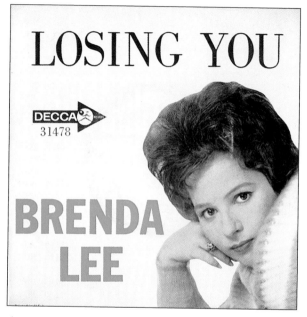

45, Losing You/He's So Heavenly, Decca 31478, 1963
  Record only..7.50 - 15.00
  Picture sleeve only ....12.50 - 25.00

45, Break It To Me Gently/So Deep, Decca 31348, 1962
Record only...7.50 - 15.00
Picture sleeve only..12.50 - 25.00
45, I Want to Be Wanted/Just a Little, Decca 31149, 1960
Record only...7.50 - 15.00
Picture sleeve only..20.00 - 40.00
45, I'm Sorry/That's All You Gotta Do, Decca 31093, 1960
Record only...10.00 - 20.00
Picture sleeve only..25.00 - 50.00
45, Rockin' Around the Christmas Tree/Papa Noel
Decca 9-30776, 1958, originals have black labels with star under
"Decca"..12.50 - 25.00
Decca 9-30776, 1960, second editions have black labels with
color bars..7.50 - 15.00
Decca 9-30776, 1960, picture sleeve only ....25.00 - 50.00
LP, *Brenda Lee*
Decca DL 4039, mono, 1960..12.50 - 25.00
Decca DL 74039, stereo, 1960 ....15.00 - 30.00
LP, *This Is...Brenda*
Decca DL 4082, mono, 1960..12.50 - 25.00
Decca DL 74082, stereo, 1960 ....15.00 - 30.00
LP, *The Versatile Brenda Lee*
Decca DL 4661, mono, 1965..10.00 - 20.00
Decca DL 74661, stereo, 1965 ....12.50 - 25.00

MVP:
45, Sweet Nothin's/Weep No More My Baby, Decca 9-30967, 1959, picture sleeve
only (record is 10.00 - 20.00) ....60.00 - 120.00

LP, *John Lennon Plastic Ono Band*

    Apple SW-3372, 1970 ....10.00 - 20.00
    Capitol SW-3372, 1978, purple label, large Capitol logo ....6.00 - 12.00
    Capitol SW-3372, 1982, black label, print in colorband ....10.00 - 20.00
    Capitol SW-3372, 1988, purple label, small Capitol logo ....15.00 - 30.00

45, Give Peace a Chance/Remember Love, Apple 1809, 1969, as
"Plastic Ono Band"

    Record only..2.50 - 5.00

    Picture sleeve only ....7.50 - 15.00

45, Imagine/It's So Hard, as "John Lennon Plastic Ono Band"

    Apple 1840, 1971, tan custom label ....4.00 - 8.00

    Apple 1840, 1975, green label with "All Rights Reserved" ....6.00 - 12.00

    Capitol 1840, 1978, purple late 1970s label.................3.00 - 6.00

    Capitol 1840, 1983, black colorband label ....3.00 - 6.00

    Capitol 1840, 1988, purple late-1980s label (wider) ....2.50 - 5.00

45, (Just Like) Starting Over/Kiss Kiss Kiss, Geffen GEF 49604, 1980,
B-side by Yoko Ono

    Record only..2.00 - 4.00

    Picture sleeve only ....2.00 - 4.00

LP, *Live Peace in Toronto 1969*, as "The Plastic Ono Band"

    Apple SW-3362, 1970, with calendar ....10.00 - 20.00

    Apple SW-3362, 1970, without calendar......................7.50 - 15.00

    Capitol ST-12239, 1982, reissue, purple Capitol label ....5.00 - 10.00

    Capitol ST-12239, 1983, black Capitol label ....25.00 - 50.00

LP, *Walls and Bridges*

    Apple SW-3416, 1974, with fold-open segmented front cover .....10.00 - 20.00

    Capitol SW-3416, 1978, purple label, large Capitol logo; standard front
cover ....7.50 - 15.00

    Capitol SW-3416, 1982, black label, print in colorband..............15.00 - 30.00

    Capitol SW-3416, 1989, purple label, small Capitol logo.............15.00 - 30.00

MVP:

LP, *Double Fantasy*, Nautilus NR-47, 1982, "Super Disc" on cover, with yellow
"sky" over John and Yoko's heads at top of cover and a red heart over John
and Yoko at the bottom; not to be confused with common versions of this
album 1982 ....1000.00 - 2000.00

LP, *The Lettermen In Concert*

    Capitol ST 1936, stereo, 1963 ....10.00 - 20.00

    Capitol T 1936. mono, 1963..7.50 - 15.00

45, Come Back Silly Girl/A Song for Young Love, Capitol 4699, 1962
Record only..6.00 - 12.00
Picture sleeve only ....10.00 - 20.00
45, Goin' Out of My Head-Can't Take My Eyes Off You/I Believe,
Capitol 2054, 1967...4.00 - 8.00
45, Theme from "A Summer Place"/Sealed with a Kiss, Capitol
5437, 1965...4.00 - 8.00
45, The Way You Look Tonight/That's My Desire, Capitol 4586, 1961
Record only..6.00 - 12.00
Picture sleeve only...10.00 - 20.00
45, When I Fall in Love/Smile, Capitol 4658, 1961
Record only..6.00 - 12.00
Picture sleeve only...10.00 - 20.00
LP, *The Best of the Lettermen*
Capitol ST 2554, stereo, 1966 ....7.50 - 15.00
Capitol T 2554, mono, 1966...6.00 - 12.00
Capitol SN-16071, 1980, reissue ....4.00 - 8.00
LP, *The Lettermen!!!... And "Live!"*
Capitol ST 2758, stereo, 1967 ....7.50 - 15.00
Capitol T 2758, mono, 1967...10.00 - 20.00
Capitol SM-11814, 1978, reissue.................................4.00 - 8.00
LP, *A Song for Young Love*
Capitol ST 1669, stereo, 1962 ....10.00 - 20.00
Capitol T 1669, mono, 1962...7.50 - 15.00

MVP:
LP, *A Time for Us*, Longines Symphonette 220 (5-record set), 1972
....15.00 - 30.00

LP, *Fore!,* Chrysalis OV 41534, 1986..4.00 - 8.00

45, Do You Believe in Love/Is It Me, Chrysalis 2589, 1981....................2.00 - 4.00
45, Heart and Soul/You Crack Me Up, Chrysalis VS4 42726, 1983
    Record only...1.50 - 3.00
    Picture sleeve only..1.50 - 3.00
45, The Heart of Rock and Roll/Workin' for a Livin' (Live), Chrysalis VS4 42782,
    1984
    Record only...1.50 - 3.00
    Picture sleeve only..1.50 - 3.00
45, I Want a New Drug/Finally Found a Home , Chrysalis VS4 42766, 1983
    Record only...1.50 - 3.00
    Picture sleeve only ....2.00 - 4.00
45, The Power of Love/Bad Is Bad, Chrysalis VS4 42876, 1985
    Record only, with title as "Power of Love".......................................2.50 - 5.00
    Record only, with title as "The Power of Love" ....1.50 - 3.00
    Picture sleeve only ....2.50 - 5.00
LP, *Huey Lewis and the News*
    Chrysalis CHR 1292, 1980..6.00 - 12.00
    Chrysalis FV 41292, 1983, reissue..4.00 - 8.00
    Chrysalis PV 41292, 1980s, later reissue ....3.00 - 6.00
LP, *Picture This*
    Chrysalis CHR 1340, 1982 ....5.00 - 10.00
    Chrysalis FV 41340, reissue, 1983...4.00 - 8.00

MVP:
LP, *Sports*, Mobile Fidelity 1-181, 1985, "Original Master Recording" at top of
    cover (other versions are less)..12.50 - 25.00

45, High School Confidential/Fools Like Me, Sun 296, 1958

    Record only..15.00 - 30.00

    Picture sleeve only..40.00 - 80.00

45, Breathless/Down the Line, Sun 288, 1958................................20.00 - 40.00

45, Chantilly Lace/Think About It Darlin, Mercury 73273, 1972 ....4.00 - 8.00

45, Great Balls of Fire/You Win Again, Sun 281, 1957
    Record only...20.00 - 40.00
    Picture sleeve only ....40.00 - 80.00

45, To Make Love Sweeter for You/Let's Talk About Us, Smash 2202, 1968
....5.00 - 10.00

45, What's Made Milwaukee Famous (Has Made a Loser Out of Me)/All the Good Is
Gone, Smash 2164, 1968 ....5.00 - 10.00

45, Whole Lot of Shakin' Going On/It'll Be Me, Sun 267, 1957 ....20.00 - 40.00

45, Would You Take Another Chance on Me/Me and Bobby McGee, Mercury
73248, 1971...4.00 - 8.00

LP, *The Best of Jerry Lee Lewis*, Smash SRS-67131, 1970 ....10.00 - 20.00

LP, *The Golden Hits of Jerry Lee Lewis*
    Smash MGS-27040, mono, 1964 ....12.50 - 25.00
    Smash SRS-67040, stereo, 1964, with original title ....15.00 - 30.00
    Smash SRS-67040, stereo, 1969, with new title *The Golden Rock Hits of Jerry Lee Lewis* ....7.50 - 15.00

LP, *Original Golden Hits — Volume 1*, Sun LP-102, 1969................7.50 - 15.00

LP, *Original Golden Hits — Volume 2*, Sun LP-103, 1969................7.50 - 15.00

LP, *Original Golden Hits — Volume 3*, Sun LP-128, 1972................7.50 - 15.00

MVP:
LP, *Jerry Lee's Greatest* , Sun SLP-1265, mono, 1961, white label promotional
    copy (regular yellow label stock copy is 125.00 - 250.00) .....400.00 - 800.00

LP, *The Specialty Sessions*, Specialty SP-8508 (5-record set), 1989
....20.00 - 40.00

45, Good Golly, Miss Molly/Hey-Hey-Hey-Hey!, Specialty 624, 1958
    Record only..15.00 - 30.00
    Picture sleeve only ....25.00 - 50.00
45, Great Gosh A-Mighty! (It's a Matter of Time)/The Ride, MCA 52780,
    1986, B-side by Charlie Midnight
    Record only..1.50 - 3.00
    Picture sleeve only..1.50 - 3.00
45, Jenny, Jenny/Miss Ann, Specialty 606, 1957
    Record only..20.00 - 40.00
    Picture sleeve only..30.00 - 60.00
45, Keep a Knockin'/Can't Believe You Wanna Leave, Specialty 611, 1957
    Record only..15.00 - 30.00
    Picture sleeve only..30.00 - 60.00
45, Long Tall Sally/Slippin' and Slidin' (Peepin' and Hidin'),
    Specialty 572, 1956 ....20.00 - 40.00
45, Rip It Up/Ready Teddy, Specialty 579, 1956..............................20.00 - 40.00
45, Tutti-Frutti/I'm Just a Lonely Guy, Specialty 561, 1955.................25.00 - 50.00
LP, *The Explosive Little Richard*
    Okeh OKM 12117, mono, 1967..12.50 - 25.00
    Okeh OKS 14117, stereo, 1967 ....10.00 - 20.00
LP, *Little Richard — His Biggest Hits*
    Specialty SP-2111, mono, 1963, thick vinyl ....25.00 - 50.00
    Specialty SP-2111, 1970s, reissue on thinner vinyl......................10.00 - 20.00

MVP:
45, Taxi Blues/Every Hour, RCA Victor 47-4392, 1951 ....450.00 - 900.00

LP, *Calendar Girl* , Liberty SL-9002, mono, 1956..........................50.00 - 100.00

45, Cry Me a River/S'Wonderful, Liberty 55006, 1955 .... 6.00 - 12.00
45, I'd Like You for Christmas/Saddle the Wind, Liberty 55108,
    1957 .... 6.00 - 12.00
LP, *The Best of Julie London*
    Liberty L-5501, mono, 1962 .... 15.00 - 30.00
    Liberty S-6601, stereo, 1962 .... 20.00 - 40.00
LP, *By Myself* , Columbia Record Club exclusive
    Liberty MCR-1 , mono, 1960s .... 12.50 - 25.00
    Liberty SCR-1, stereo, 1960s .... 15.00 - 30.00
LP, *Julie Is Her Name*
    Liberty LRP-3006, mono, 1956, green label .... 25.00 - 50.00
    Liberty LRP-3006, mono, 1960, black label, colorband and logo
        at left .... 10.00 - 20.00
    Liberty LST-7027, stereo, 1958, black label, silver print .... 20.00 - 40.00
    Liberty LST-7027, stereo, 1958, blue vinyl .... 50.00 - 100.00
    Liberty LST-7027, stereo, 1958, red vinyl .... 50.00 - 100.00
    Liberty LST-7027, stereo, 1960, black label, colorband and logo
        at left .... 12.50 - 25.00
LP, *Lonely Girl*
    Liberty LRP-3012, mono, 1956, green label .... 25.00 - 50.00
    Liberty LRP-3012, mono, 1960, black label, colorband and logo
        at left .... 10.00 - 20.00
    Liberty LST-7029, stereo, 1958, black label, silver print .... 20.00 - 40.00
    Liberty LST-7029, stereo, 1960, black label, colorband and logo
        at left .... 12.50 - 25.00

MVP:
LP, *Julie…At Home*, Liberty LST-7152, stereo, 1960, blue vinyl (regular black
    vinyl versions go for less) .... 50.00 - 100.00

LP, *Everything Playing*

    Kama Sutra KLP-8061, mono, 1968..15.00 - 30.00

    Kama Sutra KLPS-8061, stereo, 1968...10.00 - 20.00

45, Daydream/Night Owl Blues, Kama Sutra 208, 1966
  Record only, mostly red-orange label ....7.50 - 15.00
  Record only, mostly yellow label with "Kama Sutra" in red ....6.00 - 12.00
  Record only, mostly yellow label with "Kama Sutra" in black........5.00 - 10.00
  Picture sleeve only...7.50 - 15.00
45, Did You Ever Have to Make Up Your Mind/Didn't Want to Have to Do It,
  Kama Sutra 209, 1966
  Record only...5.00 - 10.00
  Picture sleeve only ....7.50 - 15.00
45, Do You Believe in Magic/On the Road Again
  Kama Sutra 201, 1965, mostly red-orange label...........................7.50 - 15.00
  Kama Sutra 201, 1966, mostly yellow label with "Kama Sutra"
  in red ....5.00 - 10.00
  Kama Sutra 201, 1966, mostly yellow label with "Kama Sutra"
  in black ....4.00 - 8.00
45, Summer in the City/Butchie's Tune, Kama Sutra 211, 1966
  Record only...5.00 - 10.00
  Picture sleeve only ....7.50 - 15.00
LP, *The Best of the Lovin' Spoonful* (add 5.00 –10.00 if all four bonus
  photos are with LP)
  Kama Sutra KLP-8056, mono, 1967..7.50 - 15.00
  Kama Sutra KLPS-8056, stereo, 1967 ....7.50 - 15.00

MVP:
EP, *The Lovin' Spoonful* (contents: It's Not Time Now/Nashville Cats//Henry
  Thomas/Darlin' Companion), Kama Sutra EK-1, 1967, promotional only item
  sent to country radio stations, picture sleeve and record together (record
  alone is 10.00 – 20.00) ....35.00 - 70.00

LP, *Loretta Lynn's Greatest Hits*

Decca DL 75000, 1968...12.50 - 25.00
Decca ST-91604, 1968, Capitol Record Club edition ....15.00 - 30.00
MCA 1, 1973, reissue, black label with rainbow..........................7.50 - 15.00
MCA 2341, 1978, reissue, tan label ....6.00 - 12.00
MCA 37235, 1980s, reissue, blue label with rainbow ....4.00 - 8.00

45, Coal Miner's Daughter/Man of the House, Decca 32749, 1970
    Record only..5.00 - 10.00
    Picture sleeve only..6.00 - 12.00
45, Don't Come Home a-Drinkin' (With Lovin' on Your Mind)/A Saint to a
    Sinner, Decca 32045, 1966 ....5.00 - 10.00
45, Fist City/Slowly Killing Me, Decca 32264, 1968 ....4.00 - 8.00
45, Here in Topeka/Kinfolks Holler, Decca 32900, 1971.................10.00 - 20.00
45, One's On the Way/Kinfolks Holler, Decca 32900, 1971, retitled version
    of "Here in Topeka" ....3.50 - 7.00
45, The Pill/Will You Be There, MCA 40358, 1975 ....2.50 - 5.00
45, Rated "X"/'Til the Pain Outwears the Shame, Decca 33039, 1972..3.50 - 7.00
45, Somebody Somewhere (Don't Know What He's Missin' Tonight)/Sundown
    Tavern, MCA 40607, 1976 ....2.50 - 5.00
LP, *Loretta Lynn's Greatest Hits Vol. II*
    MCA 420, 1974, original, black label with rainbow......................7.50 - 15.00
    MCA 2353, 1978, reissue, tan label...6.00 - 12.00
    MCA 37205, 1980s, reissue, blue label with rainbow....................4.00 - 8.00
LP, *You Ain't Woman Enough*
    Decca DL 4783, mono, 1966...12.50 - 25.00
    Decca DL 74783, stereo, 1966..15.00 - 30.00
    MCA 6, 1973, reissue ....7.50 - 15.00

MVP:
45, I'm a Honky Tonk Girl/Whispering Sea, Zero 107, 1960 ....250.00 - 500.00

LP, *Street Survivors*

    MCA 3029, 1977, originals with the band in flames on the front cover and a
smaller band photo on the back cover ....12.50 - 25.00
    MCA 3029, 1977, reissue after the band's plane crash; back cover photo
moved to the front, and the back cover has only the song titles ....5.00 - 10.00
    MCA 5223, 1980, reissue ....4.00 - 8.00
    MCA 37213, 1985, reissue ....4.00 - 8.00

45, Free Bird/Down South Jukin', MCA 40328, 1974, edited studio
version ....2.50 - 5.00
45, Free Bird/Searching, MCA 40665, 1976, edited live version ....2.50 - 5.00
45, Sweet Home Alabama/Take Your Time
   Sounds of the South 40258, 1974, yellow label ....4.00 - 8.00
   MCA 40258, 1974, black label with rainbow ....2.50 - 5.00
45, What's Your Name/I Know a Little, MCA 40819, 1977...................2.50 - 5.00
LP, *(pronounced leh-nerd skin-nerd)*
   Sounds of the South 363, 1973, original, yellow label ....10.00 - 20.00
   MCA 363, 1975, black label with rainbow ....6.00 - 12.00
   MCA 3019, 1976, reissue, black label with rainbow or tan label .....5.00 - 10.00
   MCA 5221, 1980, reissue, blue label with rainbow ....4.00 - 8.00
   MCA 37211, 1985, reissue ....4.00 - 8.00
LP, *Second Helping*
   Sounds of the South 413, 1974, original, yellow label ....10.00 - 20.00
   MCA 413, 1975, black label with rainbow ....6.00 - 12.00
   MCA 3020, 1976, reissue, black label with rainbow or tan label .....5.00 - 10.00
   MCA 5222, 1980, reissue, blue label with rainbow ....4.00 - 8.00
   MCA 37212, 1985, reissue ....4.00 - 8.00

MVP:
45, Need All My Friends/Michelle, Shade Tree 101, 1971, as "Lynard Skynard";
   approximately 300 copies pressed (not to be confused with the reissue on
   Atina, which goes for a lot less) ....750.00 – 1,500.00

45, Borderline/Think of Me, Sire 7-29354, 1984

Record only...2.00 - 4.00

Fold-open poster sleeve only..40.00 - 80.00

45, Crazy for You/No More Words, Geffen 7-29051, 1985, B-side by Berlin
    Record only..1.50 - 3.00
    Picture sleeve only...1.50 - 3.00
45, Like a Prayer/Act of Contrition, Sire 7-27539, 1989
    Record only..1.50 - 3.00
    Picture sleeve only...1.50 - 3.00
45, Like a Virgin/Stay, Sire 7-29210, 1984
    Record only..1.50 - 3.00
    Picture sleeve only...1.50 - 3.00
45, Material Girl/Pretender, Sire 7-29083, 1985
    Record only..1.50 - 3.00
    Picture sleeve only...1.50 - 3.00
45, Music/Cyberraga, Maverick 7-16826, 2000 ....2.00 - 4.00
45, Vogue (Single Version)/Vogue (Bette Davis Dub), Sire 7-19863,
    1990...1.50 - 3.00
LP, *The Immaculate Collection*, Sire 26440 (2-record set), 1990 ....7.50 - 15.00
LP, *Like a Prayer*, Sire 25844, 1989...5.00 - 10.00
LP, *Madonna*, Sire 23867, 1983
    With 4:48 version of "Burning Up"; this version has only been found
    on copies with a gold promotional stamp on the cover ....10.00 - 20.00
    With 3:49 version of "Burning Up," though some labels say "4:48";
    on the record, all the Side 1 tracks are roughly the same size ......5.00 - 10.00
LP, *True Blue*, Sire 25442, 1986, deduct 33% if poster is missing .....6.00 - 12.00

MVP:
12-inch single, Fever (12 mixes), Maverick PRO-A-6074 (2-record set), 1993,
    promotional only collection on red vinyl ....50.00 - 100.00

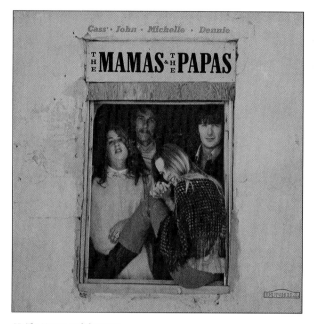

LP, *The Mamas and the Papas*

ABC Dunhill DS-50010, 1968, reissue with ABC logo next to "Dunhill"
on label ....6.00 - 12.00

Dunhill D-50010, mono, 1966 ....10.00 - 20.00

Dunhill DS-50010, stereo, 1966...12.50 - 25.00

Dunhill ST-90924, stereo, 1966, Capitol Record Club edition......20.00 - 40.00

Dunhill T-90924, mono, 1966, Capitol Record Club edition........15.00 - 30.00

45, California Dreamin'/Somebody Groovy, Dunhill 4020, 1966
    Record only...5.00 - 10.00
    Picture sleeve only ....150.00 - 300.00
45, Creeque Alley/Did You Ever Want to Cry, Dunhill 4083, 1967
    Record only...5.00 - 10.00
    Picture sleeve only ....20.00 - 40.00
45, Dedicated to the One I Love/Free Advice, Dunhill 4077, 1967 .....5.00 - 10.00
45, Monday, Monday/Got a Feeling, Dunhill 4026, 1966 ....5.00 - 10.00
45, Words of Love/Dancing in the Street, Dunhill 4057, 1966............5.00 - 10.00
LP, *If You Can Believe Your Eyes and Ears*
    ABC Dunhill DS-50006, 1968, reissue with "ABC" added to "Dunhill"
    logo on label ....6.00 - 12.00
    Dunhill D-50006, mono, 1966, with toilet completely visible in
    lower right..40.00 - 80.00
    Dunhill D-50006, mono, 1966, with scroll over toilet.................10.00 - 20.00
    Dunhill D-50006, mono, 1966, black cover with photo cropped to
    render toilet invisible...20.00 - 40.00
    Dunhill DS-50006, stereo, 1966, with toilet completely visible in
    lower right..50.00 - 100.00
    Dunhill DS-50006, stereo, 1966, with scroll over toilet..............12.50 - 25.00
    Dunhill DS-50006, stereo, 1966, black cover with photo cropped to
    render toilet invisible...25.00 - 50.00
    Dunhill ST-90797, stereo, 1966, Capitol Record Club edition......25.00 - 50.00
    Dunhill T-90797, mono, 1966, Capitol Record Club edition........25.00 - 50.00

MVP:
45, Monday, Monday/I Call Your Name, Dunhill 4026, 1966, picture sleeve only
    for unreleased single pairing (the records have "Got a Feeling" as the B-side,
    so most of the sleeves were destroyed before release) ....300.00 - 600.00

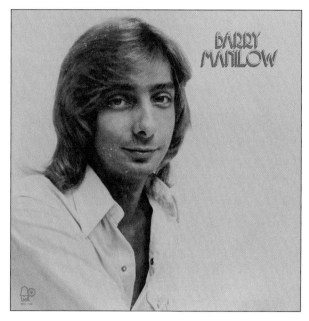

LP, *Barry Manilow*, Bell 1129, 1973, original issue without the
number "I"...12.50 - 25.00

45, Can't Smile Without You/Sunrise, Arista 0305, 1978.....................2.00 - 4.00
45, Copacabana (Short Version)/Copacabana (Long Version),
    Arista 0339, 1978...2.00 - 4.00
45, Could It Be Magic/I Am Your Child, Arista 0126, 1975...................2.00 - 4.00
45, I Write the Songs/A Nice Boy Like Me, Arista 0157, 1975...............2.00 - 4.00
45, It's a Miracle/One of These Days, Arista 0108, 1975 ....2.00 - 4.00
45, Looks Like We Made It/New York City Rhythm, Arista 0244,
    1977...2.00 - 4.00
45, Mandy/Something's Comin' Up, Bell 45,613, 1974.........................2.50 - 5.00
45, Read 'Em and Weep/One Voice, Arista 9101, 1983 ....— - 3.00
LP, *Barry Manilow II*
    Arista AB 4016, 1977, reissue of AL 4016 with new prefix ....4.00 - 8.00
    Arista AL 4016, 1975, reissue of Bell 1314 ....5.00 - 10.00
    Arista AQ 4016, 1975, quadraphonic ....7.50 - 15.00
    Arista AL5-8085, 1980s, reissue of 8370 ....3.00 - 6.00
    Arista AL8-8370, 1985, reissue of AB 4016 ....3.00 - 6.00
    Bell 1314, 1974, original ....7.50 - 15.00
LP, *Manilow Magic*, Arista NU 9740, 1982, manufactured by
    K-Tel...6.00 - 12.00

MVP:
LP, *Greatest Hits*, Arista A2L 8601 (2-record set), 1979, entire album on two
    picture discs; confusingly, this has the same catalog number as the regular
    black vinyl edition, which goes for much less ....20.00 - 40.00

LP, *Everybody Loves Somebody*

Reprise R-6130, mono, 1964 ....6.00 - 12.00

Reprise RS-6130, stereo, 1964 ....7.50 - 15.00

45, The Door Is Still Open to My Heart/Every Minute, Every Hour,
Reprise 0307, 1964...4.00 - 8.00
45, Everybody Loves Somebody/A Little Voice, Reprise 0281, 1964....5.00 - 10.00
45, Houston/Bumming Around, Reprise 0393, 1965...........................4.00 - 8.00
45, I Will/You're the Reason I'm in Love, Reprise 0415, 1965 ....4.00 - 8.00
45, Little Ole Wine Drinker, Me/I Can't Help Remembering You,
Reprise 0608, 1967..3.00 - 6.00
45, Memories Are Made of This/Change of Heart, Capitol F3295,
1955...6.00 - 12.00
45, Return to Me/Forgetting You, Capitol F3894, 1958.......................4.00 - 8.00
45, Standing on the Corner/Watching the World Go By, Capitol F3414,
1956...5.00 - 10.00
45, That's Amore/You're the Right One, Capitol F2589, 1953.............7.50 - 15.00
LP, *The Best of Dean Martin*
Capitol DT 2601, "Duophonic," 1966 ....6.00 - 12.00
Capitol SM-2601, 1970s, reissue with new prefix ....5.00 - 10.00
Capitol T 2601, mono, 1966..7.50 - 15.00
LP, *The Best of Dean Martin, Vol. 2*, Capitol SKAO-140, 1968 ....7.50 - 15.00
LP, *Dean Martin's Greatest Hits! Vol. 1*, Reprise RS-6301, 1968.......7.50 - 15.00
LP, *Dean Martin's Greatest Hits! Vol. 2*, Reprise RS-6320, 1968.......7.50 - 15.00

MVP:
LP, *Dean Martin Sings*, Capitol H 401, mono, 1953, 10-inch record
....50.00 - 100.00

LP, *Love Is Blue*

    Columbia CL 2837, mono, 1968...12.50 - 25.00
    Columbia CS 9637, stereo, 1968 ....7.50 - 15.00

45, A Certain Smile/Let It Rain, Columbia 4-41193, 1958
　　Record only...5.00 - 10.00
　　Picture sleeve only ....7.50 - 15.00
45, Chances Are/The Twelfth of Never, Columbia 4-40993, 1957
　　Record only...5.00 - 10.00
　　Picture sleeve only ....10.00 - 20.00
45, It's Not for Me to Say/Warm and Tender, Columbia 4-40851,
　　1957...6.00 - 12.00
45, Misty/The Story of Our Love, Columbia 4-41483, 1959
　　Record only...5.00 - 10.00
　　Picture sleeve only...7.50 - 15.00
45, Wonderful! Wonderful!/When Sunny Gets Blue, Columbia 4-40784,
　　1956...6.00 - 12.00
LP, *Johnny's Greatest Hits*
　　Columbia CL 1133, mono, 1958, red and black label with six "eye"
　　logos ....15.00 - 30.00
　　Columbia CL 1133, mono, 1962, red label with either "Guaranteed
　　High Fidelity" or "360 Sound Mono" ....7.50 - 15.00
　　Columbia CS 8634, rechanneled stereo, 1963, red "360 Sound Stereo"
　　label ....6.00 - 12.00
　　Columbia CS 8634, rechanneled stereo, 1970s, orange label ....4.00 - 8.00
　　LP, *Open Fire, Two Guitars*
　　Columbia CL 1270, mono, 1959, red and black label with six "eye"
　　logos ....15.00 - 30.00
　　Columbia CL 1270, mono, 1962, red label with either "Guaranteed
　　High Fidelity" or "360 Sound Mono" ....7.50 - 15.00
　　Columbia CS 8056, stereo, 1959, red and black label with six "eye"
　　logos ....20.00 - 40.00
　　Columbia CS 8056, stereo, 1962, red "360 Sound" label ....10.00 - 20.00

MVP:
LP, *Johnny Mathis*, Columbia CL 887, mono, 1957, red and black label with six
　　white "eye" logos ....25.00 - 50.00

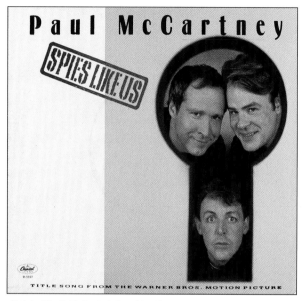

45, Spies Like Us/My Carnival, Capitol B-5537, 1985
Record only...1.50 - 3.00
Picture sleeve only ....3.00 - 6.00

45, Band on the Run/Nineteen Hundred and Eighty-Five, as "Paul McCartney
and Wings"
Apple 1873, 1974..4.00 - 8.00
Capitol 1873, 1976, black label...................................7.50 - 15.00
45, Goodnight Tonight/Daytime Nighttime Suffering, as "Wings," Columbia
3-10939, 1979 ....3.00 - 6.00
45, Live and Let Die/I Lie Around, as "Wings"
Apple 1863, 1973..4.00 - 8.00
Capitol 1863, 1976, black label...................................6.00 - 12.00
45, Maybe I'm Amazed/Soily, Capitol 4385, 1976, as "Wings"
Custom labels on both sides ....2.00 - 4.00
Black labels on both sides...10.00 - 20.00
45, My Love/The Mess, as "Paul McCartney and Wings"
Apple 1861, 1973, "Red Rose Speedway" label ....4.00 - 8.00
Capitol 1861, 1976, black label with "Capitol" at top.................10.00 - 20.00
LP, *Flaming Pie*, Capitol C1-56500, 1997...7.50 - 15.00
LP, *Wings at the Speed of Sound*, as "Wings"
Capitol SW-11525, 1976, custom "Speed of Sound" label............5.00 - 10.00
Columbia FC 37409, 1981, custom "Speed of Sound" label ....7.50 - 15.00
Columbia PC 37409, 1982, orange label ....7.50 - 15.00
LP, *Wings Over America*, as "Wings"
Capitol SWCO-11593 (3-record set), 1976, custom labels with
poster ....12.50 - 25.00
Columbia C3X 37990 (3-record set), 1982, custom labels, no
poster ....25.00 - 50.00

MVP:
LP, *Ram*, Apple MAS-3375, mono, 1971, by "Paul and Linda McCartney"; promotional copy, comes in a stereo cover, but the prefix on the record label *must*
be "MAS" and *not* "SMAS" to be the rare version; copies with "SMAS" on the
label are of minor value ....2,000.00 – 4,000.00

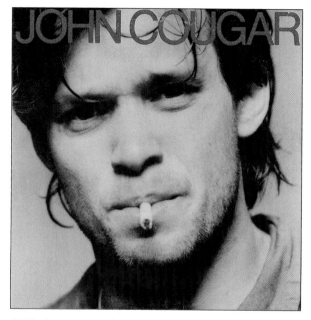

LP, *John Cougar*, Riva RVL 7401, 1979, as "John Cougar" ....5.00 - 10.00

45, Cherry Bomb/Shama Lama Ding Dong, Mercury 888 934-7, 1987, as
"John Cougar Mellencamp"
Record only..1.50 - 3.00
Picture sleeve only..1.50 - 3.00
45, Hurts So Good/Close Enough, Riva 209, 1982, as "John Cougar"
Record only..2.00 - 4.00
Picture sleeve only..5.00 - 10.00
45, Jack and Diane/Can You Take It, Riva 210, 1982, as "John Cougar".2.00 - 4.00
45, Pink Houses/Serious Business, Riva 215, 1983, as "John Cougar Mellencamp"
Record only..2.00 - 4.00
Picture sleeve only..3.00 - 6.00
45, Small Town/(Acoustic Version), Riva 884 202-7, 1985, as
"John Cougar Mellencamp"
Record only..1.50 - 3.00
Picture sleeve only..2.00 - 4.00
45, Wild Night/Brothers, Mercury 858 738-7, 1994, A-side with MeShell
NdegeOcello ....2.00 - 4.00
LP, *American Fool*, Riva RVL 7501, 1982, as "John Cougar"................4.00 - 8.00
LP, *John Mellencamp*, Columbia C 69602, 1998 ....7.50 - 15.00
LP, *The Lonesome Jubilee*, Mercury 832 465-1, 1987, as "John Cougar
Mellencamp" ....4.00 - 8.00
LP, *Scarecrow*, Riva 824 865-1, 1985, as "John Cougar Mellencamp"....4.00 - 8.00
LP, *Uh-Huh*, Riva RVL 7504, 1983, as "John Cougar Mellencamp".......4.00 - 8.00

MVP:
LP, *Chestnut Street Incident*, MCA 2225, 1977, as "Johnny Cougar"
....12.50 - 25.00

LP, *TV Sing Along with Mitch*
    Columbia CL 1628, mono, 1961, with lyric sheets.........................6.00 - 12.00
    Columbia CS 8428, stereo, 1961, with lyric sheets ....7.50 - 15.00

45, The Children's Marching Song/Carolina in the Morning, Columbia
4-41317, 1959
    Record only..4.00 - 8.00
    Picture sleeve only ....6.00 - 12.00
45, March from the River Kwai and Coloney Bogey/Hey Little Baby,
Columbia 4-41066, 1957..5.00 - 10.00
45, Theme Song from "Song for a Summer Night" (Vocal)/(Instrumental),
Columbia 4-40730, 1956..5.00 - 10.00
45, The Yellow Rose of Texas/Blackberry Winter, Columbia 4-40540,
1955...5.00 - 10.00
LP, *More Sing Along with Mitch*
    Columbia CL 1243, mono, 1958....................................7.50 - 15.00
    Columbia CS 8043, stereo, 1959 ....10.00 - 20.00
LP, *Sing Along with Mitch*
    Columbia CL 1160, mono, 1958, red and black label with 6 "eye"
    logos ....7.50 - 15.00
    Columbia CL 1160, mono, 1958, red label with "Guaranteed High Fidelity"
    or "360 Sound Mono"..5.00 - 10.00
    Columbia CS 8004, stereo, 1959, red and black label with 6 "eye"
    logos ....10.00 - 20.00
    Columbia CS 8004, stereo, 1963, red label with "360 Sound
    Stereo" ....6.00 - 12.00
    Columbia CS 8004, stereo, 1970, orange label................4.00 - 8.00
    Columbia PC 8004, stereo, 1980s, reissue with new prefix ....3.00 - 6.00
LP, *Your Request Sing Along with Mitch*
    Columbia CL 1671, mono, 1961.................................6.00 - 12.00
    Columbia CS 8471, stereo, 1961 ....7.50 - 15.00

MVP:
LP, *Mitch Miller with Horns and Chorus*, Columbia CL 6222, mono, early 1950s,
10-inch record ....15.00 - 30.00

LP, *Sailor*

    Capitol ST 2984, 1968, black label with colorband ....12.50 - 25.00

    Capitol ST 2984, 1970, lime green label.......................................7.50 - 15.00

    Capitol SN-16263, 1982, reissue ....4.00 - 8.00

45, Abracadabra, Capitol B-5126, 1982, picture sleeve only, no B-side
listed on sleeve..2.00 - 4.00

45, Abracadabra/Give It Up, Capitol B-5126, 1982, record only...........2.00 - 4.00

45, Abracadabra/Baby Wanna Dance, Capitol B-5126, 1982, record
only..1.50 - 3.00

45, The Joker/Something to Believe In, Capitol 3732, 1973 ....2.50 - 5.00

45, Living in the U.S.A./Quicksilver Girl, Capitol 2287, 1968..............6.00 - 12.00

45, Living in the U.S.A./Kow Kow Calqulator, Capitol 3884, 1974 ....2.50 - 5.00

45, Rockin' Me/Living in the U.S.A., Capitol 4323, 1976 ....2.50 - 5.00

45, Rock'n Me/Shu Ba Du Da Ma Ma Ma Ma Ma, Capitol 4323, 1976 ....2.00 - 4.00

LP, *Book of Dreams*
    Capitol SO-11630, 1977, regular issue ....5.00 - 10.00
    Capitol SEAX-11903, 1978. picture disc in die-cut sleeve..............7.50 - 15.00

LP, *Fly Like an Eagle*
    Capitol ST-11497, 1976, standard issue...5.00 - 10.00
    Capitol 21185, 1999, reissue on 180-gram vinyl ....10.00 - 20.00
    Mobile Fidelity 1-021, 1979, "Original Master Recording" on
    cover ....20.00 - 40.00

LP, *Greatest Hits 1974-1978*
    Capitol SOO-11872, 1978, standard issue ....5.00 - 10.00
    Capitol SOO-11872, 1978. blue vinyl, promotional issue only.....15.00 - 30.00
    DCC Compact Classics LPZ-2028, 1996, 180-gram virgin vinyl
    reissue...20.00 - 40.00

MVP:

LP, *Steve Miller/Quicksilver Messnger Service/The Band*, Capitol STCR-288
(3-record set), 1969, box set contaning the albums *Sailor, Quicksilver
Messenger Service* and *Music from Big Pink* ....20.00 - 40.00

LP, *Greatest Hits from the Beginning*

    Tamla T 254 (2-record set), mono, 1965 ....25.00 - 50.00

    Tamla TS 254 (2-record set), stereo, 1965 ....20.00 - 40.00

45, Do It Baby/I Wanna Be with You, Tamla 54248, 1974 ....2.50 - 5.00
45, Going to A-Go-Go/Choosey Beggar, Tamla 54127, 1965
    Record only ....7.50 - 15.00
    Picture sleeve only ....50.00 - 100.00
45, I Second That Emotion/You Must Be Love, Tamla 54159, 1967, as
    "Smokey Robinson and the Miracles" ....4.00 - 8.00
45, Love Machine (Part 1)/Love Machine (Part 2), Tamla 54262, 1975
    ....2.50 - 5.00
45, Mickey's Monkey/Whatever Makes You Happy, Tamla 54083, 1963
    ....10.00 - 20.00
45, Ooo Baby Baby/All That's Good, Tamla 54113, 1965 ....7.50 - 15.00
45, The Tears of a Clown/Promise Me, Tamla 54199, 1970, as
    "Smokey Robinson and the Miracles" ....3.00 - 6.00
45, The Tracks of My Tears/A Fork in the Road, Tamla 54118,
    1965 ....7.50 - 15.00
45, You've Really Got a Hold on Me/Happy Landing, Tamla 54073,
    1962 ....10.00 - 20.00
LP, *Away We a Go-Go*
    Motown M5-136V1, 1981, reissue ....4.00 - 8.00
    Tamla T 271, mono, 1966 ....12.50 - 25.00
    Tamla TS 271, stereo, 1966 ....15.00 - 30.00
LP, *Greatest Hits, Vol. 2,* as "Smokey Robinson and the Miracles"
    Motown M5-210V1, 1981, reissue ....4.00 - 8.00
    Tamla TS 280, 1968 ....12.50 - 25.00

MVP:
45, Bad Girl/I Love Your Baby, Motown G 1/G 2, also on Motown TLX-2207,
    1959, reissues on Chess are worth a lot less ....1,875.00 – 2,500.00

LP, *The Birds, the Bees & the Monkees*

    Colgems COM-109, mono, 1968..50.00 - 100.00

    Colgems COS-109, stereo, 1968..10.00 - 20.00

    Rhino RNLP-144, stereo, 1985 ....6.00 - 12.00

    Sundazed LP 5049, stereo, gold vinyl, 1996 ....5.00 - 10.00

45, Daydream Believer/Goin' Down, Colgems 66-1012, 1967

    Record only...7.50 - 15.00

    Picture sleeve only..15.00 - 30.00

45, Daydream Believer/Monkee's Theme, Arista 0201, 1976..............5.00 - 10.00

45, Daydream Believer/Randy Scouse Git, Arista 9532, 1986

    Record only...2.00 - 4.00

    Picture sleeve only..2.00 - 4.00

45, I'm a Believer/(I'm Not Your) Steppin' Stone, Colgems 66-1002, 1966

    Record only...7.50 - 15.00

    Picture sleeve only..15.00 - 30.00

45, Valleri/Tapioca Tundra, Colgems 66-1019, 1968.........................5.00 - 10.00

LP, *The Monkees*

    Arista AL-8524, 1988, reissue..6.00 - 12.00

    Colgems COM-101, mono, 1966, Side 1, Song 5 is "Papa Jean's

    Blues" ....12.50 - 25.00

    Colgems COM-101, mono, 1966, Side 1, Song 5 is "Papa Gene's

    Blues" (RE after number on upper right back cover) ....10.00 - 20.00

    Colgems COS-101, stereo, 1966, Side 1, Song 5 is "Papa Jean's

    Blues" ....12.50 - 25.00

    Colgems COS-101, stereo, 1966, Side 1, Song 5 is "Papa Gene's

    Blues" (RE after number on upper right back cover) ....10.00 - 20.00

    Rhino RNLP-70140, 1986, reissue..6.00 - 12.00

    Sundazed LP 5045, 1996, reissue on gold vinyl............................5.00 - 10.00

MVP:

45, A Little Bit Me, A Little Bit You/She Hangs Out, Colgems 66-1003, 1967, picture sleeve only, this record was never released, but the picture sleeve exists;
the photo was later used on the "Pleasant Valley Sunday" sleeve

    ....500.00 – 1,000.00

LP, *Every Good Boy Deserves Favour*

Mobile Fidelity 1-232, 1995, "Original Master Recording" on
cover ....12.50 - 25.00

Threshold THS 5, 1971, white label with purple logo;
gatefold cover..7.50 - 15.00

Threshold THS 5, mid 1970s, blue label, gatefold cover ....6.00 - 12.00

Threshold THS 5, late 1970s, blue label; no gatefold ....5.00 - 10.00

Threshold 820 160-1, 1985, reissue ....4.00 - 8.00

45, Gemini Dream/Painted Smile, Threshold 601, 1981......................2.00 - 4.00
45, Go Now!/Lose Your Money
    London 9726, 1965, white, purple and blue label......................10.00 - 20.00
    London 9726, 1965, blue swirl label, "London" in white............6.00 - 12.00
    London 9726, 1965, blue swirl label, "London" in black.............4.00 - 8.00
    London 9726, late 1970s, "sunrise" label ....3.00 - 6.00
45, I'm Just a Singer (In a Rock and Roll Band)/For My Lady, Threshold
    67012, 1973..2.50 - 5.00
45, Nights in White Satin/Cities
    Deram 85023, 1968, composer of "Nights in White Satin" listed as
    "Redwave"...5.00 - 10.00
    Deram 85023, early 1970s, composers of "Nights in White Satin"
    listed as "Redwave-Hayward" ....4.00 - 8.00
    Deram 85023, early 1970s, composer of "Nights in White Satin" listed as
    "Justin Hayward"..4.00 - 8.00
45, Tuesday Afternoon (Forever Afternoon)/Another Morning, Deram
    85028, 1968...4.00 - 8.00
45, Your Wildest Dreams/Talkin' Talkin', Polydor 883 906-7, 1986
    Record only...1.50 - 3.00
    Picture sleeve only..1.50 - 3.00
LP, *Seventh Sojourn*
    Mobile Fidelity 1-151, 1984, "Original Master Recording" on
    cover ....35.00 - 70.00
    Threshold THS 7, 1972, white label with purple logo, gatefold
    cover ....7.50 - 15.00
    Threshold THS 7, mid 1970s, blue label, gatefold cover ....6.00 - 12.00
    Threshold THS 7, late 1970s, blue label, no gatefold ....5.00 - 10.00
    Threshold 820 159-1, 1985, reissue ....4.00 - 8.00

MVP:

LP, *Days of Future Passed*, Deram DE 16012, mono, 1968, stereo copies on
    Deram DES 18102 go for a lot less ....125.00 - 250.00

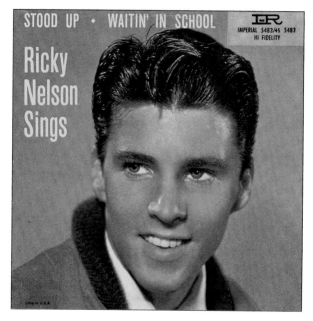

45, Stood Up/Waitin' in School, Imperial 5483, 1957
  Record only, black label..12.50 - 25.00
  Record only, red label ....20.00 - 40.00
  Picture sleeve only..35.00 - 70.00

45, Garden Party/So Long Mama, Decca 32980, 1972.........................5.00 - 10.00
45, It's Up to You/I Need You, Imperial 5901, 1962
    Record only...10.00 - 20.00
    Picture sleeve only..20.00 - 40.00
45, Lonesome Town/I Got a Feeling, Imperial 5545, 1958
    Record only, black vinyl ....15.00 - 30.00
    Record only, red vinyl..300.00 - 600.00
    Picture sleeve only..35.00 - 70.00
45, Poor Little Fool/Don't Leave Me This Way, Imperial 5528,
    1958..15.00 - 30.00
45, Travelin' Man/Hello Mary Lou, Imperial 5741, 1961
    Record only, black vinyl ....12.50 - 25.00
    Record only, red vinyl..400.00 - 800.00
    Picture sleeve only..35.00 - 70.00
LP, *Rick Nelson: 1957-1972*, Time-Life SRNR 31 (2-record set), 1989,
    part of "The Rock 'n' Roll Era" series, in box ....7.50 - 15.00
LP, *Ricky*
    Imperial LP 9048, mono, 1957, black label with stars ....50.00 - 100.00
    Imperial LP 9048, mono, 1964, black label with pink and white
    at left ....12.50 - 25.00
    Imperial LP 9048, mono, 1966, black label with green and white
    at left ....10.00 - 20.00
    Imperial LP 12392, rechanneled stereo, 1968 ....7.50 - 15.00
    United Artists LM-1004, 1980, reissue...5.00 - 10.00

MVP:
LP, *More Songs by Ricky*, Imperial LP 12059, stereo, 1960, blue vinyl, copies on
    black vinyl go for much less ....500.00 – 1,000.00

LP, *Always on My Mind*

Columbia FC 37951, 1982 ....5.00 - 10.00

Columbia PC 37951, 1984, reissue...4.00 - 8.00

Columbia HC 47951, 1982, "Half-Speed Mastered" on cover......25.00 - 50.00

45, Always on My Mind/The Party's Over, Columbia 18-02741,
1982 ....2.00 - 4.00
45, Angel Flying Too Close to the Ground/I Guess I've Come to Live Here
in Your Eyes, Columbia 11-11418, 1981 ....2.00 - 4.00
45, Blue Eyes Cryin' in the Rain/Bandera, Columbia 3-10176, 1975 ....2.50 - 5.00
45, City of New Orleans/Why Are You Pickin' On Me, Columbia 38-04568, 1984
Record only...1.50 - 3.00
Picture sleeve only..2.00 - 4.00
45, On the Road Again/Jumpin' Cotton-Eyed Joe, Columbia 11-11351, 1980,
B-side by Johnny Gimble...2.00 - 4.00
45, The Party's Over/Make Way for a Better Man, RCA Victor 47-9100,
1967..5.00 - 10.00
LP, ...And Then I Wrote
Liberty LRP-3239, mono, 1962...................................20.00 - 40.00
Liberty LST-7239, stereo, 1962 ....25.00 - 50.00
LP, Red Headed Stranger
Columbia PC 33482, 1975, no bar code........................7.50 - 15.00
Columbia PC 33482, 1979, with bar code ....4.00 - 8.00
LP, Shotgun Willie, Atlantic SD 7262, 1973....................10.00 - 20.00
LP, Stardust
Columbia JC 35305, 1978, no bar code ....5.00 - 10.00
Columbia JC 35305, 1979, with bar code........................4.00 - 8.00
Columbia JC 35305, 2000, "Manufactured and Distributed by Classic
Records" reissue ....12.50 - 25.00
Columbia HC 45305, 1981, "Half-Speed Mastered" on cover......35.00 - 70.00

MVP:
45, No Place for Me/The Lumberjack, Willie Nelson 628, 1957 ...150.00 - 300.00

LP, *Totally Hot*

    MCA 3067, 1978...5.00 - 10.00

    MCA 37123, 1981, reissue ....4.00 - 8.00

    Mobile Fidelity 1-040, 1980, "Original Master Recording" on cover

    ....15.00 - 20.00

45, Have You Never Been Mellow/Water Under the Bridge, MCA 40349,
1974...2.50 - 5.00
45, Hopelessly Devoted to You/Love Is a Many-Splendored Thing, RSO 903,
1978, B-side is instrumental...2.00 - 4.00
45, I Honestly Love You/Home Ain't Home Anymore, MCA 40280,
1974...2.50 - 5.00
45, If You Love Me (Let Me Know)/Brotherly Love, MCA 40209,
1974...2.50 - 5.00
45, Let Me Be There/Maybe Then I'll Think of You, MCA 40101,
1973...2.50 - 5.00
45, A Little More Love/Borrowed Time, MCA 40975, 1978
    Record only..2.00 - 4.00
    Picture sleeve only...2.50 - 5.00
45, Physical/The Promise (The Dolphin Song), MCA 51182, 1981
    Record only..1.50 - 3.00
    Picture sleeve only...2.00 - 4.00
45, Please Mr. Please/And In the Morning, MCA 40418, 1975
    Record only..2.50 - 5.00
    Picture sleeve only ....5.00 - 10.00
LP, *Have You Never Been Mellow*
    MCA 2133, 1975, original, black label with rainbow...................5.00 - 10.00
    MCA 3014, 1977, reissue, tan label ....4.00 - 8.00
LP, *Olivia Newton-John's Greatest Hits,* MCA 3028, 1977, originals have
tan label ....5.00 - 10.00
LP, *Physical*
    MCA 5229, 1981...4.00 - 8.00
    MCA 16011, 1982, "Audiophile" on cover ....12.50 - 25.00

MVP:
LP, *If Not for You*, Uni 73117, 1971 ....40.00 - 80.00

LP, *Nevermind*

    DGC 24425, 1991, all copies on black vinyl..............................10.00 - 20.00

    Mobile Fidelity 1-258, 1996, "Original Master Recording" on cover

    ....50.00 - 100.00

12-inch single, Smells Like Teen Spirit/Even In His Youth/Aneurysm, DGC
4344, 1991, promotional issue only, yellow vinyl ....10.00 - 20.00

45, Come As You Are/Drain You, DGC 19120, 1992 ....4.00 - 8.00

45, Sliver/Dive, Sub Pop 73, 1990
Blue vinyl...20.00 - 40.00
Clear pink/lavender vinyl ....25.00 - 50.00
Black vinyl, no California address on label...................................5.00 - 10.00
Later issues on pale yellow vinyl with California address on label ...3.50 - 7.00
Still later issues on black vinyl with California address on label ......1.50 - 3.00
Picture sleeve only, original fold-over, not seam sealed ....5.00 - 10.00
Picture sleeve only, later seam sealed ....1.50 - 3.00

45, Smells Like Teen Spirit/Even In His Youth, DGC 19050, 1991 ....4.00 - 8.00

LP, *From the Muddy Banks of the Wishkah*, DGC 25105
(2-record set), 1996 ....7.50 - 15.00

LP, *Incesticide*, DGC 24504, 1992, all copies on blue swirl vinyl .....15.00 - 30.00

LP, *In Utero*, DGC 24607, 1993, all copies on clear vinyl ....15.00 - 30.00

LP, *MTV Unplugged in New York*, DGC 24727, 1994, color of vinyl cannot
be determined without opening the shrink wrap
Black vinyl...10.00 - 20.00
White vinyl...10.00 - 20.00

MVP:
45, Love Buzz/Big Cheese, Sub Pop 23, 1988, hand-numbered edition of 1,000;
record and picture sleeve together ....500.00 – 1,000.00

LP, *Family Reunion*

    Philadelphia Int'l. PZ 33807, 1975, no bar code on back cover ...5.00 - 10.00

    Philadelphia Int'l. PZ 33807, 1980s, reissue with bar code.............4.00 - 8.00

    Philadelphia Int'l. PZQ 33807, 1975, quadraphonic ....7.50 - 15.00

45, Back Stabbers/Sunshine, Philadelphia Int'l. ZS7 3517, 1972..........2.50 - 5.00
45, For the Love of Money/People Keep Tellin' Me, Philadelphia Int'l.
  ZS7 3544, 1974...2.50 - 5.00
45, I Love Music (Part 1)/I Love Music (Part 2), Philadelphia Int'l.
  ZS8 3577, 1975...2.50 - 5.00
45, Lipstick Traces/Think It Over, Baby, Imperial 66102, 1965 ....5.00 - 10.00
45, Love Train/Who Am I, Philadelphia Int'l. ZS7 3524, 1973 ....2.50 - 5.00
45, Put Your Hands Together/You Got Your Hooks in Me, Philadelphia Int'l.
  ZS7 3535, 1973...2.50 - 5.00
45, Use Ta Be My Girl/This Time Baby, Philadelphia Int'l. ZS8 3642,
  1978..2.50 - 5.00
LP, *Back Stabbers*, Philadelphia Int'l. KZ 31712, 1972.....................6.00 - 12.00
LP, *The O'Jays in Philadelphia*
  Neptune 202, 1969..15.00 - 30.00
  Philadelphia Int'l. KZ 32120, 1973, reissue..................................6.00 - 12.00
LP, *Ship Ahoy*
  Philadelphia Int'l. KZ 32408, 1973, original.................................5.00 - 10.00
  Philadelphia Int'l. PZ 32408, 1980s, reissue ....4.00 - 8.00
  Philadelphia Int'l. PZQ 32408, 1974, quadraphonic ....7.50 - 15.00
LP, *So Full of Love*
  Philadelphia Int'l. JZ 35355, 1978...5.00 - 10.00
  Philadelphia Int'l. PZ 35355, 1980s, reissue ....4.00 - 8.00

MVP:
45, I'll Never Forget You/Pretty Words, Imperial 66162, 1966 ....40.00 - 80.00

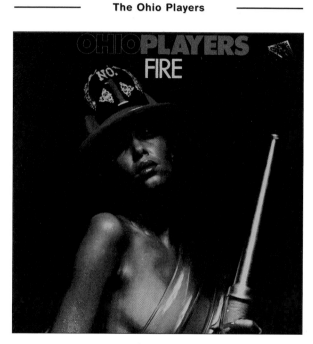

LP, *Fire*, Mercury SRM-1-1013, 1974 ....5.00 - 10.00

45, Fire/Together, Mercury 73643, 1974 .... 2.50 - 5.00
45, Funky Worm/Paint Me, Westbound 214, 1973 .... 3.00 - 6.00
45, Love Rollercoaster/It's All Over, Mercury 73734, 1975 .... 2.50 - 5.00
45, Skin Tight/Heaven Must Be Like This, Mercury 73609, 1974 .... 2.50 - 5.00
45, Sight for Sore Eyes/(Instrumental), Air City 402, 1984
    Record only .... 2.00 - 4.00
    Picture sleeve only .... 2.00 - 4.00
45, Who'd She Coo?/Bi-Centennial, Mercury 73814, 1976 .... 2.50 - 5.00
LP, *The Best of the Early Years*, Westbound 304, 1977 .... 7.50 - 15.00
LP, *Ecstasy*
    Westbound 222, 1976, reissue .... 6.00 - 12.00
    Westbound 2021, 1973, original .... 10.00 - 20.00
LP, *Honey*, Mercury SRM-1-1038, 1975 .... 5.00 - 10.00
LP, *Ohio Players Gold*
    Mercury SRM-1-1122, 1976, original .... 5.00 - 10.00
    Mercury 824 461-1, 1980s, reissue .... 4.00 - 8.00
LP, *Skin Tight*, Mercury SRM-1-705, 1974
    Red label .... 6.00 - 12.00
    Chicago skyline label .... 5.00 - 10.00

MVP:
LP, *Observations in Time*, Capitol ST-192, 1969 .... 25.00 - 50.00

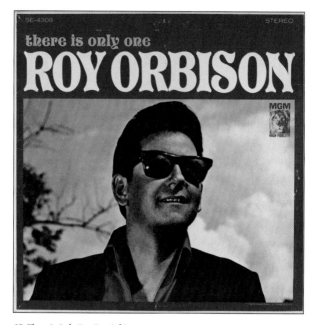

LP, *There Is Only One Roy Orbison*

    MGM E-4308, mono, 1965..12.50 - 25.00
    MGM SE-4308, stereo,1965...17.50 - 35.00
    MGM ST 90454, stereo, 1965, Capitol Record Club edition.........20.00 - 40.00
    MGM T 90454, mono, 1965, Capitol Record Club edition...........20.00 - 40.00

45, Crying/Candy Man
    Monument 447, 1961, record only...10.00 - 20.00
    Monument 447, 1961, picture sleeve only...................................20.00 - 40.00
    Monument 517, 1960s, reissue ....6.00 - 12.00
45, Dream Baby (How Long Must I Dream)/The Actress
    Monument 456, 1962, record only...10.00 - 20.00
    Monument 456, 1962, picture sleeve only...................................20.00 - 40.00
    Monument 519, 1960s, reissue ....6.00 - 12.00
45, Oh Pretty Woman/Yo Te Amo Maria, Monument 851, 1964, most copies
    have this A-side title..10.00 - 20.00
45, Pretty Woman/Yo Te Amo Maria, Monument 851, 1964, original copies
    have this A-side title..15.00 - 30.00
45, Running Scared/Love Hurts
    Monument 438, 1961, record only...10.00 - 20.00
    Monument 438, 1961, picture sleeve only...................................20.00 - 40.00
    Monument 514, 1960s, reissue ....6.00 - 12.00
LP, *Roy Orbison's Greatest Hits*
    Monument M-4009, mono, 1962, original ....25.00 - 50.00
    Monument MC-6619, stereo, 1977, reissue................................6.00 - 12.00
    Monument MLP-8000, mono, 1963, early reissue.....................15.00 - 30.00
    Monument SM-14009, stereo, 1962, original ....40.00 - 80.00
    Monument SLP-18000, stereo, 1963, early reissue....................20.00 - 40.00

MVP:
45, Ooby Dooby/Tryin' to Get to You, Je-Wel 101, 1956, by "The Teen Kings,"
    some copies have "Vocal: Roy Orbison" and others have "Vocal: Roy Oribson"
    on label at 3 o'clok; either one is equally rare ....2,750.00 – 4,000.00

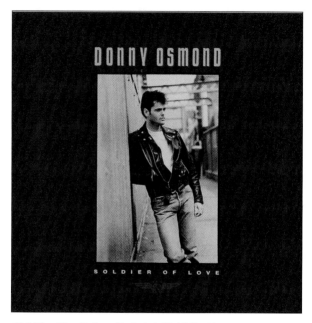

45, Soldier of Love/My Secret Touch, Capitol B-44369, 1989
  Record only...1.50 - 3.00
  Picture sleeve only..2.50 - 5.00

45, Go Away Little Girl/Time to Ride, MGM 14285, 1971......................3.00 - 6.00
45, Go Away Little Girl/The Wild Rover (Time to Ride), MGM 14285,
    1971, altered B-side title...2.50 - 5.00
45, Hey Girl/I Knew You When, MGM 14322, 1971.............................3.00 - 6.00
45, A Million to One/Young Love, MGM 14583, 1973...........................2.50 - 5.00
45, Puppy Love/Let My People Go, MGM 14367, 1972.........................3.00 - 6.00
45, Sweet and Innocent/Flirtin', MGM 14227, 1971
    Record only...3.00 - 6.00
    Picture sleeve only..4.00 - 8.00
45, The Twelfth of Never/Life Is Just What You Make It, MGM 14503, 1973
    Record only...2.50 - 5.00
    Picture sleeve only..4.00 - 8.00
LP, *Donny Osmond*, Capitol C1-92354, 1989....................................6.00 - 12.00
LP, *The Donny Osmond Album*, MGM SE-4782, 1971 ....6.00 - 12.00
LP, *My Best to You*, MGM SE-4872, 1972...5.00 - 10.00
LP, *Portrait of Donny*, MGM SE-4820, 1972.......................................5.00 - 10.00
LP, *To You with Love, Donny*, MGM SE-4797, 1971 ....5.00 - 10.00
LP, *Too Young*, MGM SE-4854, 1972..5.00 - 10.00

MVP:
LP, *Alone Together*, MGM SE-4886, 1973,with tear-off 10x10 photo intact, deduct
    60 percent if missing...12.50 - 25.00

LP, *Roll Out the Red Carpet for Buck Owens & The Buckaroos*

    Capitol ST 2443, stereo, 1966 ....12.50 - 25.00

    Capitol T 2443, mono, 1966..10.00 - 20.00

45, Act Naturally/Over and Over Again, Capitol 4937, 1963................7.50 - 15.00
45, I've Got a Tiger by the Tail/Cryin' Time, Capitol 5336, 1965
    Record only...5.00 - 10.00
    Picture sleeve only..7.50 - 15.00
45, Love's Gonna Live Here/Getting Used to Losing You, Capitol 5025,
    1963..6.00 - 12.00
45, Tall Dark Stranger/Sing That Kind of Song, Capitol 2570, 1969
    Record only...4.00 - 8.00
    Picture sleeve only..6.00 - 12.00
45, Waitin' in Your Welfare Line/In the Palm of Your Hand, Capitol
    5566, 1965...5.00 - 10.00
45, Your Tender Loving Care/What a Liar I Am, Capitol 5942, 1967
    Record only...4.00 - 8.00
    Picture sleeve only..6.00 - 12.00
LP, *The Best of Buck Owens*
    Capitol ST 2105, stereo, 1964 ....15.00 - 30.00
    Capitol T 2105, mono, 1964...12.50 - 25.00
LP, *The Best of Buck Owens, Vol. 2*, Capitol ST 2897, 1968 ....12.50 - 25.00
LP, *The Best of Buck Owens, Volume 3*, Capitol SKAO-145, 1969 ...10.00 - 20.00
LP, *The Best of Buck Owens, Vol. 4*, Capitol ST-830, 1971.................7.50 - 15.00
LP, *The Best of Buck Owens Volume 5*, Capitol ST-11273, 1973 ....7.50 - 15.00
LP, *The Best of Buck Owens, Volume 6*, Capitol ST-11471, 1976 ......7.50 - 15.00

MVP:
45, Hot Dog/Rhythm and Booze, Dixie 505, 1956, as "Corky Jones" (copies on
    Pep 107 are 125.00-250.00)..200.00 - 400.00

45, I Think I Love You/Somebody Wants to Love You, Bell 910, 1970

Record only...2.50 - 5.00

Picture sleeve only..3.00 - 6.00

45, Doesn't Somebody Want to Be Wanted/You Are Always on My Mind, Bell 963, 1971

    Record only..2.50 - 5.00

    Picture sleeve only..3.00 - 6.00

45, I Woke Up in Love This Morning/Twenty-Four Hours a Day, Bell 45, 130, 1971..2.50 - 5.00

45, I'll Meet You Halfway/Morning Rider on the Road, Bell 996, 1971..2.50 - 5.00

45, It's One of Those Nights (Yes Love)/One Night Stand, Bell 45,160, 1971..2.50 - 5.00

45, Lookin' for a Good Time/Money Money, Bell 45,414, 1973

    Record only (promo copies go for a lot less) ....20.00 - 40.00

    Picture sleeve only ....20.00 - 40.00

LP, *The Partridge Family Album*, Bell 6050, 1970

    With bonus photo ....15.00 - 30.00

    Without bonus photo ....10.00 - 20.00

LP, *The Partridge Family At Home with Their Greatest Hits*, Bell 1107, 1972..10.00 - 20.00

LP, *The Partridge Family Shopping Bag*, Bell 6072, 1972

    With shopping bag..15.00 - 30.00

    Without shopping bag...10.00 - 20.00

LP, *The Partridge Family Sound Magazine*, Bell 6064, 1971 ....10.00 - 20.00

LP, *The Partridge Family Up to Date*, Bell 6059, 1971

    With book cover ....15.00 - 30.00

    Without book cover..10.00 - 20.00

LP, *The World of the Partridge Family*, Bell 1319 (2-record set), 1974..20.00 - 40.00

MVP:

LP, *The Partridge Family Bulletin Board* , Bell 1137, 1973 ....25.00 - 50.00

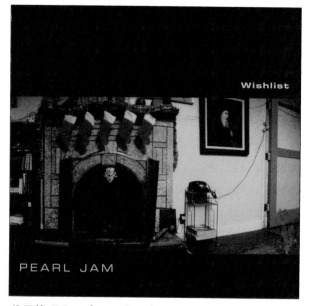

45, Wishlist//U/Brain of J, Epic 34-78896, 1998
   Record only..1.00 - 2.00
   Picture sleeve only..1.00 - 2.00

45, I Got ID/Long Road (*Merkinball* on sleeve), Epic 34-78199, 1995
   Record only...1.25 - 2.50
   Picture sleeve only, cardboard stock ....1.25 - 2.50
45, Jeremy/Alive
   Epic 34-74745, 1995, gray label with "Collectables" logo, reissue ....2.00 - 4.00
   Epic 34-74745, 1997, dark blue label, reissue................................1.50 - 3.00
   Epic Associated 35-74745, 1992, white label, original ....10.00 - 20.00
45, Not for You/Out of My Mind, Epic 34-77772, 1995
   Record only...1.50 - 3.00
   Picture sleeve only...1.50 - 3.00
45, Soldier of Love/Last Kiss, Epic ES7 41700,1998, "Ten Club" fan club single
   Record only.. 7.50 - 15.00
   Picture sleeve only...7.50 - 15.00
45, Spin the Black Circle/Tremor Christ, Epic 34-77771, 1994
   Record only...1.50 - 3.00
   Picture sleeve only...1.50 - 3.00
LP, *Binaural*, Epic E2 63365 (2-record set), 2000 ....6.00 - 12.00
LP, *Ten*, Epic Associated Z 47857, 1994, other formats were issued in
   1991...5.00 - 10.00
LP, *Vitalogy*, Epic E 66900, 1994 ....5.00 - 10.00
LP, *Vs.*, Epic E 53136, 1993..5.00 - 10.00
LP, *Yield*, Epic E 68164, 1998 ....6.00 - 12.00

MVP:
45, Let Me Sleep (Christmas Time)/Ramblings, Epic Associated ZS7 4354,1991,
   the first Pearl Jam "Ten Club" holiday fan club single and by far the rarest,
   small hole, plays at 33 1/3 rpm, record and picture sleeve together
   ....50.00 - 100.00

LP, *Peter, Paul and Mary*

    Warner Bros. W 1449, mono, 1962, gray label ....10.00 - 20.00

    Warner Bros. WS 1449, stereo, 1962, gold label.........................12.50 - 25.00

    Warner Bros. WS 1449, stereo, 1968, green label with "W7" box.6.00 - 12.00

    Warner Bros. WS 1449, stereo, 1970, any later label variation......5.00 - 10.00

45, Blowin' in the Wind/Flora, Warner Bros. 5368, 1963..................5.00 - 10.00

45, Don't Think Twice, It's All Right/Autumn to May, Warner Bros. 5385, 1963..5.00 - 10.00

45, I Dig Rock and Roll Music/The Great Mandella (The Wheel of Life), Warner Bros. 7067, 1967..5.00 - 10.00

45, If I Had a Hammer/Gone the Rainbow, Warner Bros. 5296, 1962..5.00 - 10.00

45, Leaving on a Jet Plane/The House Song, Warner Bros. 7340, 1969..5.00 - 10.00

45, Puff/Pretty Mary, Warner Bros. 5348, 1963, no subtitle on A-side..6.00 - 12.00

45, Puff (The Magic Dragon)/Pretty Mary, Warner Bros. 5348, 1963, with subtitle on A-side...5.00 - 10.00

LP, *Album 1700*

    Warner Bros. W 1700, mono, 1967...12.50 - 25.00

    Warner Bros. WS 1700, stereo, 1967, gold label........................12.50 - 25.00

    Warner Bros. WS 1700, stereo, 1968, green label with "W7" box...6.00 - 12.00

    Warner Bros. WS 1700, stereo, 1970, any later label variation......5.00 - 10.00

LP, *(Moving)*

    Warner Bros. W 1473, mono, 1963...10.00 - 20.00

    Warner Bros. WS 1473, stereo, 1963, gold label........................12.50 - 25.00

    Warner Bros. WS 1473, stereo, 1968, any later label variation.....5.00 - 10.00

LP, *Reunion*, Warner Bros. BSK 3231, 1978 ....5.00 - 10.00

MVP:

LP, *Peter, Paul and Mary In Concert*, Warner Bros. 2WS 1555 (2-record set), stereo, 1964, gold labels, mono copies and other label variations go for less
....15.00 - 30.00

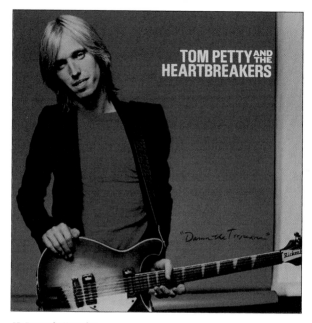

LP, *Damn the Torpedoes*
    Backstreet BSR-5105, 1979..5.00 - 10.00
    MCA 1486, 1987, reissue ....4.00 - 8.00

45, Breakdown/Fooled Again (I Can't Take It), Shelter 62008,
1977...3.00 - 6.00
45, Don't Come Around Here No More/Trailer, MCA 52496, 1985
    Record only, with 4:19 version of A-side ....2.00 - 4.00
    Record only, with 5-plus-minute version of A-side..........................2.00 - 4.00
    Picture sleeve only...2.00 - 4.00
45, Don't Do Me Like That/Casa Dega, Backstreet 41138, 1979
    Record only...2.00 - 4.00
    Picture sleeve only...2.50 - 5.00
45, Free Fallin'/Down the Line, MCA 53748, 1989 ....2.50 - 5.00
45, Refugee/It's Rainin' Again, Backstreet 41169, 1980
    Record only...2.00 - 4.00
    Picture sleeve only...2.50 - 5.00
45, You Don't Know How It Feels/Girl on LSD, Warner Bros. 7-18030,
1994...1.50 - 3.00
LP, *Full Moon Fever*, MCA 6253, 1989 ....5.00 - 10.00
LP, *Hard Promises*
    Backstreet BSR-5160, 1981...5.00 - 10.00
    MCA 37239, 1984, reissue ....4.00 - 8.00
LP, *Into the Great Wide Open*, MCA 10317, 1991............................7.50 - 15.00
LP, *The Last DJ*, Warner Bros. 47955, 2002 ....10.00 - 20.00

MVP:
LP, *Official Live 'Leg*, Shelter TP-12677, 1977, promotional only live album,
    includes letter to radio stations, counterfeits exist......................20.00 - 40.00

LP, *The Dark Side of the Moon*

Harvest SMAS-11163, 1973, with poster and two stickers, original
edition ....12.50 - 25.00
Mobile Fidelity 1-017, 1980, "Original Master Recording" on top of
cover ....25.00 - 50.00
Mobile Fidelity MFQR-017, 1982, "Ultra High Quality Recording"
in box..150.00 - 300.00
(Other versions exist and generally sell for less.)

45, Another Brick in the Wall (Part 2)/One of My Turns, Columbia 1-11187, 1980
    Record only, custom "wall" label ....2.50 - 5.00
    Record only, regular orange label ....2.00 - 4.00
    Picture sleeve only ....4.00 - 8.00
45, Money/Any Colour You Like, Harvest 3609, 1973.......................7.50 - 15.00
LP, *Animals*, Columbia JC 33474, 1977..5.00 - 10.00
LP, *Pulse*, EMI 32700 (4-record set), 1995, pressed in U.K. for U.S. release;
    box set with 12x12 hardback book; identical to British pressings except for
    American bar code (67065) on shrink wrap ....30.00 - 60.00
LP, *A Saucerful of Secrets*, Tower ST 5131, 1968
    Orange label...40.00 - 80.00
    Multi-colored striped label ....20.00 - 40.00
LP, *The Wall*
    Columbia PC2 36183 (2-record set), 1979.................................7.50 - 15.00
    Columbia HC2 46183 (2-record set), 1983, "Half-Speed Mastered"
    on cover ....125.00 - 250.00
LP, *Wish You Were Here*
    Columbia HC 33453, 1981, "Half-Speed Mastered" on cover......30.00 - 60.00
    Columbia PC 33453, 1975, with blue wraparound with title/artist sticker;
    most buyers threw this out upon opening the LP ....12.50 - 25.00
    Columbia PC 33453, 1975, no blue wraparound, no bar code......6.00 - 12.00
    Columbia PC 33453, 1980s, no blue wraparound, with bar code....4.00 - 8.00
    Columbia PCQ 33453, 1975, quadraphonic ....100.00 - 200.00
    Columbia HC 43453, 1982, "Half-Speed Mastered" on cover, later issue
    than HC 33453 ....20.00 - 40.00

MVP:
45, See Emily Play/Scarecrow, Tower 356, 1967, picture sleeve only, promotional
    issue with photo on sleeve; a different promotional picture sleeve with only
    text on it is 350.00-700.00; the record alone is 100.00-200.00 for stock
    copies, about half that for promos ....400.00 - 800.00

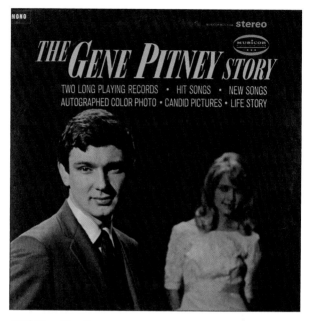

LP, *The Gene Pitney Story*

    Musicor M2-3148 (2-record set), mono, 1968, mono may be promotional
only, add 40% if bonus photo is included....................................20.00 - 40.00

    Musicor M2S-3148 (2-record set), stereo, 1968, add 40% if bonus photo
is included...12.50 - 25.00

45, I'm Gonna Be Strong/Aladdin's Lamp, Musicor 1045, 1964 ....10.00 - 20.00

45, I'm Gonna Be Strong/E Se Domani, Musicor 1045, 1964
    Record only...7.50 - 15.00
    Picture sleeve only...10.00 - 20.00

45, It Hurts to Be in Love/Hawaii, Musicor 1040, 1964
    Record only...7.50 - 15.00
    Picture sleeve only...10.00 - 20.00

45, (The Man Who Shot) Liberty Valance/Take It Like a Man, Musicor 1020,
    1962, brownish label...7.50 - 15.00

45, Only Love Can Break a Heart/If I Didn't Have a Dime, Musicor 1022, 1962,
    brownish label...7.50 - 15.00

45, Town Without Pity/Air Mail Special Delivery, Musicor 1009, 1961 ..7.50 - 15.00

45, Twenty-Four Hours from Tulsa/Lonely Night Dream, Musicor 1034, 1963
    Record only...7.50 - 15.00
    Picture sleeve only...10.00 - 20.00

LP, *Anthology (1961-1968)*, Rhino RNDA-1102 (2-record set), 1984
    ....6.00 - 12.00

LP, *Only Love Can Break a Heart*
    Musicor MM-2003, mono, 1962, brown label............................20.00 - 40.00
    Musicor MM-2003, mono, 1963, black label ....12.50 - 25.00
    Musicor MS-3003, stereo, 1962, brown label ....25.00 - 50.00
    Musicor MS-3003, stereo, 1963, black label ....15.00 - 30.00

MVP:
LP, *The Many Sides of Gene Pitney*, Musicor MM-2001, mono, 1962, brown
    label, black label versions go for half this amount ....25.00 - 50.00

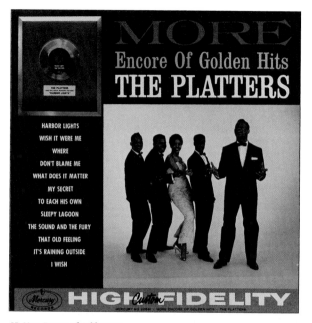

LP, *More Encore of Golden Hits*

    Mercury MG-20591, mono, 1960..12.50 - 25.00
    Mercury SR-60252, stereo, 1960..15.00 - 30.00
    Mercury 828 246-1, 1980s, reissue...4.00 - 8.00

45, The Great Pretender/I'm Just a Dancing Partner, Mercury 70753, 1955
 Maroon label ....20.00 - 40.00
 Black label ....10.00 - 20.00

45, My Prayer/Heaven on Earth, Mercury 70893, 1956
 Maroon label ....20.00 - 40.00
 Black label ....10.00 - 20.00

45, Only You (And You Alone)/Bark, Battle and Ball, Mercury 70633, 1955
 Pink label ....25.00 - 50.00
 Black label ....20.00 - 40.00

45, Smoke Gets In Your Eyes/No Matter What You Are
 Mercury 10001, stereo, 1959, blue label ....25.00 - 50.00
 Mercury 71383, 1958, black label ....12.50 - 25.00
 Mercury 71383, 1958, blue label ....15.00 - 30.00

45, With This Ring/If I Had a Love, Musicor 1229, 1967 ....5.00 - 10.00

45, (You've Got) The Magic Touch/Winner Take All, Mercury 70819, 1956
 Maroon label ....20.00 - 40.00
 Black label ....10.00 - 20.00

LP, *Encore of Golden Hits*
 Mercury MG-20472, mono, 1960 ....15.00 - 30.00
 Mercury SR-60243, stereo, 1960, black label, silver print, 12 songs on
 LP ....20.00 - 40.00
 Mercury SR-60243, stereo, 1965, red label, "MERCURY" in white across
 top, 12 songs on LP ....12.50 - 25.00
 Mercury SR-60243, stereo, 1975, Chicago skyline label, 10 songs
 on LP ....6.00 - 12.00
 Mercury 828 254-1, 1980s, reissue...4.00 - 8.00

MVP:
LP, *The Platters*, Federal 549, mono, 1957 ....800.00 – 1,600.00

LP, *The Pointer Sisters*, Blue Thumb BTS-48, 1973, grayish label......6.00 - 12.00

45, Fairytale/Love In Them Thar Hills
    ABC Blue Thumb 254, 1974, multicolor concentric circles label ....2.50 - 5.00
    Blue Thumb 254, 1974, grayish label, original.............................5.00 - 10.00
45, Fire/Love Is Like a Rolling Stone, Planet 45901, 1978
    Record only...2.00 - 4.00
    Picture sleeve only...3.00 - 6.00
45, He's So Shy/Movin' On, Planet 47916, 1980.................................2.00 - 4.00
45, Jump (For My Love)/Heart Beat, Planet YB-13780, 1984...............2.00 - 4.00
45, Slow Hand/Holdin' Out for Love, Planet 47929, 1981 ....2.00 - 4.00
45, Yes We Can Can/Jada, Blue Thumb 229, 1973...............................3.00 - 6.00
LP, *The Best of the Pointer Sisters*, ABC Blue Thumb BTSY-6026 (2-record set),
    1976...7.50 - 15.00
LP, *Break Out*
    Planet BXL1-4705, 1983, without "I'm So Excited" ....5.00 - 10.00
    Planet BEL1-4705A, 1984, with "I'm So Excited" plus a remix of "Jump
    (For My Love)" ....4.00 - 8.00
LP, *Energy*
    Planet P-1, 1978..5.00 - 10.00
    RCA Victor AYL1-5091, 1985, reissue ....4.00 - 8.00
LP, *Priority*
    Planet P-9003, 1979...5.00 - 10.00
    RCA Victor AYL1-5089, 1985, reissue ....4.00 - 8.00

MVP:
45, Destination No More Heartaches/Send Him Back, Atlantic 2893,
    1972...20.00 - 40.00

LP, *Synchronicity*, A&M SP-3735, 1983

    Black and white cover ....40.00 - 80.00

    Gold, silver and bronze color bands on cover ....20.00 - 40.00

    Blue, yellow and red color bands on cover; 93 versions of the cover exist,

    counting combinations of colors and the underlying photos ....5.00 - 10.00

45, De Do Do Do, De Da Da Da/Friends, A&M 2275, 1980
    Silver label with fading "A&M" logo ....2.00 - 4.00
    Yellowish custom label with blueish triangle ....1.50 - 3.00
    Red custom label with silver triangle..2.00 - 4.00
    Black title sleeve with large center hole..3.00 - 6.00
45, Every Breath You Take/Murder by Numbers, A&M 2542, 1983
    Record only..1.50 - 3.00
    Picture sleeve only...1.50 - 3.00
45, King of Pain/Someone to Talk To, A&M 2569, 1983
    Record only..1.50 - 3.00
    Picture sleeve only...1.50 - 3.00
45, Roxanne/Dead End Job, A&M 2096, 1978....................................3.00 - 6.00
45, Wrapped Around Your Finger/Tea in the Sahara (Live), A&M 2614, 1984
    Record only..1.50 - 3.00
    Picture sleeve only...1.50 - 3.00
LP, *Ghost in the Machine*
    A&M SP-3730, 1981, normal version ....5.00 - 10.00
    Nautilus NR-40, 1982, "Super Disc" on cover ....20.00 - 40.00
LP, *Zenyatta Mondatta*
    A&M SP-3720, 1980...5.00 - 10.00
    Nautilus NR-19, 1981, "Super Disc" on cover ....20.00 - 40.00

MVP:
LP, *Ghost in the Machine*, A&M SP-3730, 1981, promotional issue only,
    picture disc that actually lights up when placed on a turntable, thus is
    easily distinguishable from common copies ....500.00 – 1,000.00

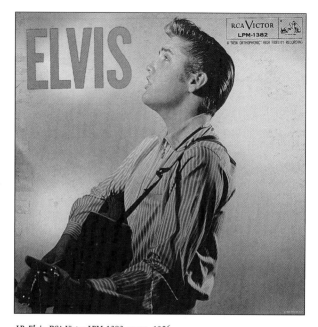

LP, *Elvis*, RCA Victor LPM-1382, mono, 1956

    Back cover has ads for other albums ....150.00 - 300.00

    Back cover has no ads for other albums; "Long Play" on label..150.00 - 300.00

    With tracks listed on labels as "Band 1" through "Band 6" ....200.00 - 400.00

    With alternate take of "Old Shep" on side 2, trail-off number on the

    "Old Shep" side ends in "15S," "17S" or "19S."....................400.00 - 800.00

(Other versions exist, but sell for less)

45, All Shook Up/That's When Your Heartaches Begin, RCA Victor 47-6870, 1957
    Record only..15.00 - 30.00
    Picture sleeve only ....45.00 - 90.00
45, Stuck on You/Fame and Fortune, RCA Victor 47-7740, 1960
    Record only..10.00 - 20.00
    Picture sleeve (die-cut) only ....30.00 - 60.00
45, Suspicious Minds/You'll Think of Me, RCA Victor 47-9764, 1969
    Record only..4.00 - 8.00
    Picture sleeve only ....10.00 - 20.00
45, Way Down/Pledging My Love, RCA PB-10998, 1977
    Record only..2.50 - 5.00
    Picture sleeve only ....5.00 - 10.00
LP, *A Legendary Performer, Volume 3*
    RCA Victor CPL1-3078, 1978, picture disc applied to blue vinyl LP; with booklet
    (deduct 40% if missing)..12.50 - 25.00
    RCA Victor CPL1-3082, 1978, black vinyl; with booklet (deduct 40% if missing)
    and die-cut hole in front cover ....12.50 - 25.00
    RCA Victor CPL1-3082, 1986, black vinyl; no die-cut hole in cover and no
    booklet..4.00 - 8.00
LP, *Moody Blue*
    RCA Victor AFL1-2428, 1977, blue vinyl ....5.00 - 10.00
    RCA Victor AFL1-2428, 1977, black vinyl...............................100.00 - 200.00
    RCA Victor AFL1-2428, 1977, any color except black or blue vinyl
    ....1,000.00 – 2,000.00
    RCA Victor AQL1-2428, 1979, reissue with new prefix ....12.50 - 25.00

MVP:
LP, *Elvis' Christmas Album*, RCA Victor LOC-1035, mono, 1957, unique red vinyl
    version, definitely not to be confused with a reissue on red vinyl from the
    Collectables label in 2002 ....11,250.00 – 15,000.00

LP, *1999*, Warner Bros. 23720 (2-record set), 1982.........................7.50 - 15.00

12-inch single, U Got the Look (Long Look 6:45) (Single Cut 3:58)/Housequake
(Album Cut 4:38) (7 Minutes MoQuake 7:15), Paisley Park 0-20727,
1987 ....7.50 - 15.00

45, I Wanna Be Your Lover/My Love Is Forever, Warner Bros. 49050,
1979 ....5.00 - 10.00

45, Little Red Corvette/All the Critics Love U in New York, Warner Bros. 7-29746,
1983 ....2.50 - 5.00

45, 1999/How Come U Don't Call Me Anymore?, Warner Bros. 7-29896, 1982
Record only..2.50 - 5.00
Picture sleeve only..5.00 - 10.00

45, When Doves Cry/17 Days, Warner Bros. 7-29286, 1984
Record only, black vinyl ....1.50 - 3.00
Record only, purple vinyl..10.00 - 20.00
Picture sleeve only ....1.50 - 3.00

LP, *Around the World in a Day*, Paisley Park 25286, 1985, with fold-over flap,
deduct at least 25% if missing ....5.00 - 10.00

LP, *For You*, Warner Bros. BSK 3150, 1978
"Burbank" palm trees label..10.00 - 20.00
White or tan label..6.00 - 12.00

LP, *Purple Rain*, Warner Bros. 25110, 1984
Black vinyl;, with poster ....5.00 - 10.00
Purple vinyl, with poster ....25.00 - 50.00

LP, *Sign "O" The Times*, Paisley Park 25577 (2-record set), 1987....7.50 - 15.00

MVP:

LP, *The Black Album*, Paisley Park 25677, 1987, withdrawn prior to release,
though a few copies escaped; only copies with this catalog number are worth
this much, copies on any label other than Paisley Park or Warner Bros. (1994
release) are counterfeits; this exists two ways, as a single record (1,000.00 –
2,000.00) and as two records that play at 45 rpm ....1,500.00 – 3,000.00

LP, *A Day at the Races*
  Elektra 6E-101, 1977, butterfly, red, or red/black labels...............5.00 - 10.00
  Mobile Fidelity 1-256, 1996, "Original Master Recording" on front
  cover ....25.00 - 50.00

45, Another One Bites the Dust/Don't Try Suicide, Elektra 47031,
1980..2.00 - 4.00
45, Bohemian Rhapsody/I'm in Love with My Car
Elektra 45297, 1975, butterfly label.................................4.00 - 8.00
Elektra 45297, 1976, red label...5.00 - 10.00
45, Crazy Little Thing Called Love/Spread Your Wings, Elektra 46579, 1979
....2.00 - 4.00
45, Killer Queen/Flick of the Wrist, Elektra 45226, 1975
Butterfly label...4.00 - 8.00
Caterpillar label..5.00 - 10.00
45, Radio Ga Ga/I Go Crazy, Capitol B-5317, 1984
Record only...2.00 - 4.00
Picture sleeve only...2.00 - 4.00
LP, *The Game*
Elektra 5E-513, 1980, with shiny silver cover................7.50 - 15.00
Elektra 5E-513, 1980, with dull gray cover ....5.00 - 10.00
Mobile Fidelity 1-211, 1995, "Original Master Recording" on front
cover ....15.00 - 30.00
LP, *News of the World*, Elektra 6E-112, 1977 ....5.00 - 10.00
LP, *A Night at the Opera*
DCC Compact Classics LPZ-2072, 2000, 180-gram virgin vinyl
reissue...12.50 - 25.00
Elektra 7E-1053, 1975, any label variation....................5.00 - 10.00
Mobile Fidelity 1-067, 1980, "Original Master Recording" on front
cover ....40.00 - 80.00

MVP:
LP, *News of the World* , Elektra 6E-112, 1977, promotional version only, white
label with oversized cover and enclosed press kit (see above for other ver-
sions) ....75.00 - 150.00

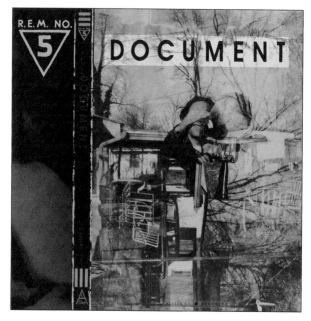

LP, *Document*

45, It's the End of the World As We Know It (And I Feel Fine)/Last Date ,
    I.R.S. 53220, 1987
        Record only..1.50 - 3.00
        Picture sleeve only ....1.50 - 3.00
45, Losing My Religion/Rotary Eleven, Warner Bros. 7-19392, 1991....1.50 - 3.00
45, The One I Love/Maps and Legends, I.R.S. 53171, 1987
        Record only..1.50 - 3.00
        Picture sleeve only ....1.50 - 3.00
45, So. Central Rain (I'm Sorry)/King of the Road, I.R.S. 9927, 1984
        Record only..3.00 - 6.00
        Picture sleeve only ....7.50 - 15.00
45, Stand/Memphis Train Blues, Warner Bros. 7-27688, 1988
        Record only..1.50 - 3.00
        Picture sleeve only ....1.50 - 3.00
LP, *Eponymous*, I.R.S. 6262. 1988..5.00 - 10.00
LP, *Fables of the Reconstruction*, I.R.S. 5592, 1985 ....6.00 - 12.00
LP, *Green*, Warner Bros. 25795, 1988..6.00 - 12.00
LP, *Lifes Rich Pageant*, I.R.S. 5783, 1986...6.00 - 12.00
LP, *Murmur*
        I.R.S. SP-70014, 1983, reissue ....6.00 - 12.00
        I.R.S. SP-70604, 1983, original ....7.50 - 15.00
        Mobile Fidelity 1-231, 1995, "Original Master Recording" on top of
        front cover..10.00 - 20.00

MVP:
45, Radio Free Europe/Sitting Still, Hib-Tone HT-0001, 1981, record and picture
    sleeve together, record has no address on label (versions with address on
    label go for about 12.50 - 25.00 less) ....75.00 - 150.00

LP, *Complete & Unbelievable…The Otis Redding Dictionary of Soul*

Volt 415, mono, 1966..20.00 - 40.00

Volt S-415, stereo, 1966 ....25.00 - 50.00

Sundazed LP-5063, 2001, reissue..6.00 – 12.00

45, I Can't Turn You Loose/Just One More Day, Volt 130, 1965 ....7.50 - 15.00

45, I've Been Loving You Too Long (To Stop Now)/I'm Depending on You,
    Volt 126, 1965...7.50 - 15.00

45, Respect/Ole Man Trouble, Volt 128, 1965 ....7.50 - 15.00

45, Satisfaction/Any Ole Way, Volt 132, 1966 ....7.50 - 15.00

45, (Sittin' On) The Dock of the Bay/Sweet Lorene
    Volt 157, 1968, black and red label , 1st press ....6.00 - 12.00
    Volt 157, 1968, multicolor (mostly brown) label, 2nd press ....5.00 - 10.00

LP, *History of Otis Redding*
    Volt 418, mono, 1967...20.00 - 40.00
    Volt S-418, stereo,1967 ....15.00 - 30.00
    Atco SD 33-261, 1968, reissue ....7.50 - 15.00

LP, *The Dock of the Bay*
    Volt S-419, 1968...15.00 - 30.00
    Atco SD 33-288, 1969, reissue ....7.50 - 15.00
    Sundazed LP-5172, 2003, reissue....................................6.00 – 12.00

MVP:

45, Shout Bamalama/Fat Girl, Orbit 135, 1961 (versions on Bethlehem,
    Confederate and King are much less) ....150.00 - 300.00

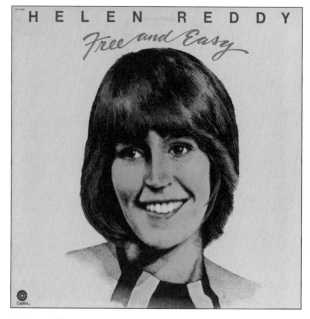

LP, *Free and Easy*

Capitol ST-11348, 1974, original, orange label..............................5.00 - 10.00

Capitol SN-16249, 1980s, reissue...4.00 - 8.00

45, Ain't No Way to Treat a Lady/Long Time Looking, Capitol 4128,
1975...2.00 - 4.00
45, Angie Baby/I Think I'll Write a Song, Capitol 3972, 1974...............2.00 - 4.00
45, Delta Dawn/If We Could Still Be Friends, Capitol 3645, 1973.........2.00 - 4.00
45, I Am Woman/More Than You Could Take, Capitol 3350, 1972
    Red and orange "target" label ....2.50 - 5.00
    Orange label, "Capitol" at bottom...2.00 - 4.00
45, I Don't Know How to Love Him/I Believe in Music, Capitol 3027,
1971...2.50 - 5.00
45, Leave Me Alone (Ruby Red Dress)/The Old Fashioned Way, Capitol
3768, 1973...2.00 - 4.00
45, You and Me Against the World/Love Song for Jeffrey, Capitol 3897,
1974...2.00 - 4.00
LP, *Helen Reddy's Greatest Hits*
    Capitol ST-11467, 1975 , orange label...5.00 - 10.00
    Capitol SW-11467, 1978, purple label...4.00 - 8.00
    Capitol SN-16333, 1984, reissue ....3.00 - 6.00
LP, *I Am Woman*
    Capitol ST-11068, 1972 ....5.00 - 10.00
    Capitol SN-16099, 1980, reissue ....4.00 - 8.00
LP, *Long Hard Climb*
    Capitol SMAS-11213, 1973 ....5.00 - 10.00
    Capitol SN-16101, 1980, reissue ....4.00 - 8.00

MVP:
45, One Way Ticket/Go, Fontana 1611, 1968.....................................7.50 - 15.00

LP, *Midnight Ride*

Columbia CL 2508, mono, 1966..12.50 - 25.00
Columbia CS 9308, stereo, 1966 ....15.00 - 30.00

45, Good Thing/Undecided Man, Columbia 4-43907, 1966
    Record only..5.00 - 10.00
    Picture sleeve only ....10.00 - 20.00
45, Him or Me — What's It Gonna Be?/Legend of Paul Revere, Columbia 4-44094, 1967
    Record only..5.00 - 10.00
    Picture sleeve only ....7.50 - 15.00
45, Hungry/There She Goes, Columbia 4-43678, 1966
    Record only..5.00 - 10.00
    Picture sleeve only..10.00 - 20.00
45, Indian Reservation (The Lament of the Cherokee Reservation Indian)/
    Terry's Tune, Columbia 4-45332, 1971, as "Raiders"
    Red label with black print ....4.00 - 8.00
    Orange label with "Columbia" background print ....3.00 - 6.00
45, Just Like Me/B.F.R.D.F. Blues, Columbia 4-43461, 1965..............5.00 - 10.00
45, Kicks/Shake It Up, Columbia 4-43556, 1966 ....5.00 - 10.00
LP, *Here They Come!*
    Columbia CL 2307, mono, 1965, "Guaranteed High Fidelity" on
    label ....15.00 - 30.00
    Columbia CL 2307, mono, 1965, "360 Sound Mono" on label....10.00 - 20.00
    Columbia CS 9107, stereo, 1965, "360 Sound Stereo" in black on
    label ....20.00 - 40.00
    Columbia CS 9107, stereo, 1965, "360 Sound Stereo" in white on
    label ....12.50 - 25.00
LP, *Just Like Us!*
    Columbia CL 2451, mono, 1966................................12.50 - 25.00
    Columbia CS 9251, stereo, 1966...............................15.00 - 30.00

MVP:
LP, *Paul Revere and the Raiders*, Sande S-1001, mono, 1963, original version
    with "Sande" and no mention of "Etiquette" in trail-off area (version with
    "Etiquette" in trail-off wax go for 12.50 – 25.00) ....600.00 – 1,200.00

45, (You're My) Soul and Inspiration/B Side Blues, Verve 10383, 1966
Record only..7.50 - 15.00
Picture sleeve only ....15.00 - 30.00

45, Ebb Tide/(I Love You) For Sentimental Reasons, Philles 130, 1965
  Record only..7.50 - 15.00
  Picture sleeve only ....15.00 - 30.00
45, Little Latin Lupe Lu/I'm So Lonely, Moonglow 215, 1963
  Black vinyl..10.00 - 20.00
  Red vinyl..25.00 - 50.00
45, Rock and Roll Heaven/I Just Wanna Be Me, Haven 7002, 1974 .....2.50 - 5.00
45, Unchained Melody/Hung on You
  Philles 129, 1965, with no producer credit on the "Unchained Melody" side
  ....15.00 - 30.00
  Philles 129, 1965, with "Producer: Phil Spector" on the "Unchained Melody"
  side ....7.50 - 15.00
  Verve 871 882-7, 1989, tan label reissue ....2.00 - 4.00
45, You've Lost That Lovin' Feelin'/There's a Woman, Philles 124, 1964
  ....7.50 - 15.00
LP, *Greatest Hits*
  Verve V-5020, mono, 1967 ....12.50 - 25.00
  Verve V6-5020, stereo, 1967 ....10.00 - 20.00
LP, *Some Blue-Eyed Soul*
  Moonglow MLP-1002, mono, 1964 ....20.00 - 40.00
  Moonglow MSP-1002, stereo, 1964................................30.00 - 60.00
LP, *You've Lost That Lovin' Feelin'*
  Philles PHLP-4007, mono, 1964......................................12.50 - 25.00
  Philles PHLPS-4007, stereo, 1964 ....20.00 - 40.00

MVP:
45 box set, *Celebrity Scene: The Righteous Brothers*, Verve CS-8-5, 1967, with
  box, yellow-label singles numbered 10520, 10521, 10522, 10523, and
  10524, jukebox title strips and short biography; price is for entire set
  ....30.00 - 60.00

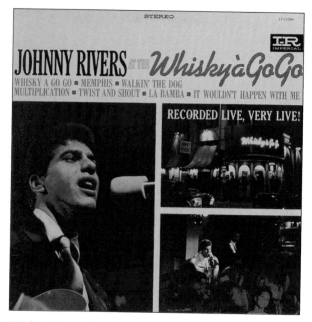

LP, *Johnny Rivers at the Whiskey A-Go-Go*
Imperial LP-9264, mono, 1964, black label with pink and white at left
....10.00 - 20.00
Imperial LP-12264, stereo, 1964, black label with pink and white at left
....12.50 - 25.00
(Copies with green and white at left of label go for less.)

45, Baby I Need Your Lovin'/Gettin' Ready for Tomorrow, Imperial 66227, 1967
    Record only...5.00 - 10.00
    Picture sleeve only..7.50 - 15.00
45, Memphis/It Wouldn't Happen with Me, Imperial 66032, 1964.....6.00 - 12.00
45, Rockin' Pneumonia-Boogie Woogie Flu/Come Home America, United Artists
    50960, 1972
    With long intro (about 35 seconds) ....3.00 - 6.00
    With short intro (about 20 seconds) ....3.00 - 6.00
45, Secret Agent Man/You Dig, Imperial 66159, 1966
    Record only...6.00 - 12.00
    Picture sleeve only..7.50 - 15.00
45, Summer Rain/Memory of the Coming Good, Imperial 66267,
    1967..5.00 - 10.00
45, Swayin' to the Music (Slow Dancin')/Outside Help, Big Tree 16094,
    1977..2.00 - 4.00
45, The Tracks of My Tears/Rewind Medley, Imperial 66244, 1967
    Record only...5.00 - 10.00
    Picture sleeve only..7.50 - 15.00
LP, *Johnny Rivers' Golden Hits*
    Imperial LP-9324, mono, 1966 ....7.50 - 15.00
    Imperial LP-12324, stereo, 1966...10.00 - 20.00
    Liberty LO-12324, 1980s, ...4.00 - 8.00
    Warner Bros. R133498, 1970s, "Burbank" palm trees label, RCA
    Music Service edition ....15.00 - 30.00
LP, *Realization*
    Imperial LP-9372, mono, 1968 ....20.00 - 40.00
    Imperial LP-12372, stereo, 1968...10.00 - 20.00

MVP:
45, Little Girl/Two by Two, Suede 1401, 1957, as "Johnny Ramistella"
    ....50.00 - 100.00

45, Ruby Ann/Won't You Forgive, Columbia 4-42614, 1962
    Record only..7.50 - 15.00
    Picture sleeve only ....12.50 - 25.00

45, Don't Worry/Like All the Other Times, Columbia 4-41922, 1961
    Record only...7.50 - 15.00
    Picture sleeve only..12.50 - 25.00
45, El Paso/Running Gun
    Columbia S7 30511, stereo, 1959, "Stereo Seven" (small hole, plays at
    33 1/3 rpm) ....15.00 - 30.00
    Columbia 4-41511, mono, standard issue ....10.00 - 20.00
    Columbia 4-41511, picture sleeve ....15.00 - 30.00
45, El Paso City/When I'm Gone, Columbia 3-10305, 1976 ....2.50 - 5.00
45, My Woman, My Woman, My Wife/Martha Ellen Jenkins, Columbia
    4-45091, 1970 ....2.50 - 5.00
45, Singing the Blues/I Can't Quit (I've Gone Too Far), Columbia 4-21508,
    1956...20.00 - 40.00
45, A White Sport Coat (And a Pink Carnation)/Grown Up Tears, Columbia
    4-40864, 1957
    Record only...12.50 - 25.00
    Picture sleeve only..20.00 - 40.00
LP, *Gunfighter Ballads and Trail Songs*
    Columbia CL 1349, mono, 1959, red and black label with six white "eye"
    logos ....15.00 - 30.00
    Columbia CL 1349, mono, 1963, red label with "Guaranteed High Fidelity"
    or "360 Sound Mono"..7.50 - 15.00
    Columbia CS 8158, stereo, 1959, red and black label with six white "eye"
    logos ....20.00 - 40.00
    Columbia CS 8158, stereo, 1963, red label with "360 Sound Stereo"
    ....10.00 - 20.00
    Columbia CS 8158, stereo, 1971, orange label............................5.00 - 10.00
    Columbia PC 8158, 1980s, reissue with new prefix ....4.00 - 8.00

MVP:
LP, Columbia CL 2601, *Rock 'N Roll 'N Robbins*, 1956, 10-inch LP
    ....500.00 - 1000.00

SECRETLY • MAKE ME A MIRACLE

R - 4070

ROULETTE
DYNAMIC HIGH FIDELITY

JIMMIE
RODGERS

45, Secretly/Make Me a Miracle, Roulette 4070, 1958
  Record only..10.00 - 20.00
  Picture sleeve only..20.00 - 40.00

45, Bimbombey/You Understand Me, Roulette 4116, 1958 ....7.50 - 15.00

45, Child of Clay/Turnaround, A&M 871, 1967 ....3.00 - 6.00

45, Honeycomb/Their Hearts Were Full of Spring, Roulette 4015, 1957,
   red label ....10.00 - 20.00

45, It's Over/Anita, You're Dreaming, Dot 16861, 1966 ....5.00 - 10.00

45, Kisses Sweeter Than Wine/Better Loved You'll Never Be, Roulette 4031,
   1957, red label ....10.00 - 20.00

45, Oh-Oh, I'm Falling in Love Again/The Long Hot Summer, Roulette 4045,
   1958,
   Red label ....10.00 - 20.00
   White label with colored spokes ....7.50 - 15.00

LP, *Child of Clay*
   A&M SP-130, mono, 1967 ....12.50 - 25.00
   A&M SP-4130, stereo, 1967 ....7.50 - 15.00

LP, *15 Million Sellers*
   Roulette R-25179, mono, 1962 ....12.50 - 25.00
   Roulette SR-25179, stereo, 1962, white label with colored spokes
   ....15.00 - 30.00
   Roulette SR-25179, stereo, 1960s, orange and yellow label ....10.00 - 20.00

LP, *Golden Hits/15 Hits of Jimmie Rodgers*
   Dot DLP-3815, mono, 1967 ....10.00 - 20.00
   Dot DLP-25815, stereo, 1967 ....7.50 - 15.00

LP, *Jimmie Rodgers*
   Roulette R-25020, mono, 1957, black label ....25.00 - 50.00
   Roulette R-25020, mono, 1959, white label with colored spokes
   ....12.50 - 25.00

MVP:
LP, *The Best of Jimmie Rodgers' Folk Tunes*, Roulette SR-25160, stereo, 1961,
   red vinyl (regular black vinyl goes for much less) ....125.00 - 250.00

IP, *The Gambler*

    Liberty LO-934, 1981, reissue ....4.00 - 8.00

    Liberty LN-10247, 1984, reissue..3.00 - 6.00

    Mobile Fidelity 1-044, 1981, "Original Master Recording" on front

    cover ....10.00 - 20.00

    United Artists UA-LA934-H, 1978..5.00 - 10.00

Kenny Rogers

45, Coward of the County/I Wanna Make You Smile, United Artists 1327,
1979...2.00 - 4.00
45, The Gambler/Momma's Waiting, United Artists XW1250, 1978.......2.00 - 4.00
45, Lady/Sweet Music Man, Liberty 1380, 1980
    Record only...2.00 - 4.00
    Picture sleeve only ....2.50 - 5.00
45, Love the World Away/Sayin' Goodbye-Requiem, United Artists 1359,
1980...2.00 - 4.00
45, Lucille/Till I Get It Right, United Artists XW929, 1976....................2.00 - 4.00
45, She Believes in Me/Morgana Jones, United Artists XW1273, 1979
    Record only...2.00 - 4.00
    Picture sleeve only ....2.50 - 5.00
45, You Decorated My Life/One Man's Woman, United Artists 1315, 1979
    Record only...2.00 - 4.00
    Picture sleeve only ....2.50 - 5.00
LP, *Kenny Rogers' Greatest Hits*
    Liberty LOO-1072, 1980 ....4.00 - 8.00
    Mobile Fidelity 1-049, 1981, "Original Master Recording" on front cover
    ....10.00 - 20.00
LP, *Ten Years of Gold*
    Liberty LO-835, 1981, reissue ....4.00 - 8.00
    Liberty LN-10254, 1984, reissue..3.00 - 6.00
    United Artists UA-LA835-H, 1978..5.00 - 10.00

MVP:
LP, *Eyes That See in the Dark*, RCA Victor AFL1-4697, 1983, picture disc on
    one side, regular RCA label on other, possibly an in-house demo at the
    RCA Indianapolis pressing plant, not to be confused with the common
    regular issues ....100.00 - 200.00

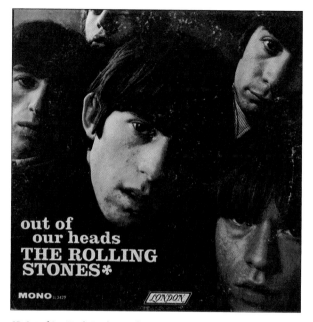

LP, *Out of Our Heads,* London LL 3429, mono

    1965, maroon label with "London/ffrr" in a box and "Made in England by the Decca Record Co. Ltd." at top edge ....100.00 - 200.00

    1965, maroon label with "London" unboxed at top of label........20.00 - 40.00

    1966, red or maroon label with "London" boxed at top ....12.50 - 25.00

12-inch single, Miss You/Far Away Eyes, Rolling Stones DK 4609, 1978
 With "Atlantic/Atco Disco" sleeve ....5.00 - 10.00
 With "The Rolling Stones Miss You" die-cut sleeve.......................6.00 - 12.00
45, (I Can't Get No) Satisfaction/The Under Assistant West Coast Promotion
 Man, London 9766
 1965, blue swirl label...10.00 - 20.00
 1965, picture sleeve only...200.00 - 500.00
 1970s, multicolor "sunrise" label ....4.00 - 8.00
 1980s, white label ....3.00 - 6.00
LP, *Their Satanic Majesties Request*
 London NP 2 , mono, 1967, maroon label ....125.00 - 250.00
 London NPS 2, stereo, 1967, blue label with 3-D cover..............20.00 - 40.00
 London NPS 2 , stereo, 1970s, without 3-D cover ....4.00 - 8.00
 London/Abkco 80021, stereo, 1986, "Digitally Remastered from Original
 Master Recording" on cover; red label...4.00 - 8.00
LP, *Sticky Fingers*
 Rolling Stones COC 39105, 1977, reissue with working zipper .....5.00 - 10.00
 Rolling Stones COC 39105, 1977, reissue with photo of zipper only
 ....4.00 - 8.00
 Rolling Stones FC 40488, 1986, reissue with photo of zipper only
 ....4.00 - 8.00
 Rolling Stones COC 59100, 1971, original with working zipper
 ....6.00 - 12.00
 Virgin 47863, 1999, reissue with 180-gram vinyl and working zipper
 ....12.50 - 25.00

MVP:
45, London 909, Street Fighting Man/No Expectations, 1968, picture sleeve only
 (record is 12.50-25.00) ....8,000.00 – 10,000.00

LP, *Living in the U.S.A.*

   Asylum 6E-155, 1978 ....5.00 - 10.00

   Asylum DP-401, 1978, picture disc ....9.00 - 18.00

45, Back in the U.S.A./White Rhythm and Blues, Asylum 45519, 1978
    Record only..2.00 - 4.00
    Picture sleeve only ....3.00 - 6.00
45, Blue Bayou/Old Paint, Asylum 45431, 1977 ....2.00 - 4.00
45, Heat Wave/Love Is a Rose, Asylum 45282, 1975...........................2.00 - 4.00
45, It's So Easy/Lo Siento Mi Vida, Asylum 45438, 1977....................2.00 - 4.00
45, Long Long Time/Nobody's, Capitol 2846, 1970...............................4.00 - 8.00
45, Ooh Baby Baby/Blowing Away, Asylum 45546, 1978......................2.00 - 4.00
45, That'll Be the Day/Try Me Again, Asylum 45340, 1976
    Clouds label...2.00 - 4.00
    All-blue label ....2.50 - 5.00
45, You're No Good/I Can't Help It (If I'm Still in Love with You), Capitol
    3990, 1974..2.00 - 4.00
LP, *Greatest Hits*
    Asylum 6E-106, 1977, reissue ....5.00 - 10.00
    Asylum 7E-1092, 1976, original ....6.00 - 12.00
LP, *Heart Like a Wheel*
    Capitol ST-11358, 1974, original ....6.00 - 12.00
    Capitol SW-11358, 1975, reissue ....5.00 - 10.00
LP, *Simple Dreams*
    Asylum 6E-104, 1977 ....5.00 - 10.00
    Nautilus NR-26, 1982, "Super Disc" on front cover ....25.00 - 50.00

MVP:
LP, *Greatest Hits*, DCC Compact Classics LPZ-2048, 1997, 180-gram virgin vinyl;
    other issues listed above...40.00 - 80.00

45, It's My Turn/Together, Motown 1496, 1980
   Record only...2.00 - 4.00
   Picture sleeve only ....6.00 - 12.00

45, Ain't No Mountain High Enough/Can't It Wait Until Tomorrow, Motown
    1169, 1970

    Record only...2.50 - 5.00

    Picture sleeve only ....6.00 - 12.00

45, I'm Coming Out/Give Up, Motown 1491, 1980 ....2.00 - 4.00

45, Last Time I Saw Him/Save the Children, Motown 1278, 1973.........2.50 - 5.00

45, Muscles/I Am Me, RCA PB-13348, 1982

    Record only...2.00 - 4.00

    Picture sleeve only..2.00 - 4.00

45, Theme from Mahogany (Do You Know Where You're Going To)/
    No One's Gonna Be a Fool Forever, Motown 1377, 1975

    Record only.. 2.50 - 5.00

    Picture sleeve only ....10.00 - 20.00

45, Touch Me in the Morning/I Won't Last a Day Without You, Motown
    1239, 1973...2.50 - 5.00

45, Upside Down/Friend to Friend, Motown 1494, 1980.....................2.00 - 4.00

LP, *All the Great Hits*, Motown M13-960C2 (2-record set), 1981 ......6.00 - 12.00

LP, *Diana*, Motown M8-936, 1980 ....5.00 - 10.00

LP, *Diana!*

    Motown M5-155V1, 1981, reissue...4.00 - 8.00

    Motown MS-719, 1971, original..7.50 - 15.00

LP, *Diana Ross*

    Motown M5-135V1, 1981, reissue...4.00 - 8.00

    Motown MS-711, 1970, original..7.50 - 15.00

MVP:

12-inch single, Love Hangover (7:49)/I Want You (Vocal 4:33) (Instrumental
    4:36), Motown PR-16, 1976, promotional only, "I Want You " is by Marvin
    Gaye, and that side has a Tamla label on it; a very early 12-inch single for
    Motown ....100.00 - 200.00

LP, *Santana*

    Columbia CS 9781, 1969, "360 Sound" on red label ....7.50 - 15.00

    Columbia CS 9781, 1970, orange label ....5.00 - 10.00

    Columbia PC 9781, 1980s, reissue with new prefix........................4.00 - 8.00

45, Evil Ways/Waiting, Columbia 4-45069, 1970 ....3.00 - 6.00
45, Black Magic Woman/Hope You're Feeling Better, Columbia 4-45270, 1970
    Record only...3.00 - 6.00
    Picture sleeve only...6.00 - 12.00
45, Hold On/Oxun, Columbia 38-03160, 1982......................................2.00 - 4.00
45, Hold On, B-side blank, Columbia CNR-03268, one-sided single,
    1982...3.00 - 6.00
45, Maria Maria (featuring The Product G&B)/Smooth (featuring Rob Thomas),
    Arista 13773, 2000...2.50 - 5.00
45, Oye Como Va/Samba Pa Ti, Columbia 4-45330, 1971
    Record only...2.50 - 5.00
    Picture sleeve only...4.00 - 8.00
LP, *Abraxas*
    Columbia CQ 30130, quadraphonic, 1972 ....10.00 - 20.00
    Columbia JC 30130, 1977, reissue...4.00 - 8.00
    Columbia KC 30130, 1970, original, with poster..........................7.50 - 15.00
    Columbia KC 30130, 1970s, with no poster..................................5.00 - 10.00
    Columbia PC 30130, 1985, reissue...4.00 - 8.00
LP, *Santana* (not the same album as CS 9761, this one is also known as *Santana III* or *The New Santana* Album)
    Columbia CQ 30595, quadraphonic, 1972 ....10.00 - 20.00
    Columbia KC 30595, 1971, original...6.00 - 12.00
    Columbia PC 30595, 1970s, reissue ....4.00 - 8.00

MVP:

LP, *Zebop!*, Columbia HC 47158, 1981, must have "Half-Speed Mastered: on
    cover (regular edition is common) ....20.00 - 40.00

EP, *Oh! Carol* (contents: Oh! Carol/Going Home to Mary Lou//The Girl for Me/I
Ain't Hurtin' No More), RCA Victor EPA-4353, 1959, record and cardboard
cover together ....60.00 - 120.00

45, Bad Blood/Your Favorite Entertainer, Rocket 40460, 1975 ....2.00 - 4.00
45, Breaking Up Is Hard to Do/As Long As I Live, RCA Victor 47-8046, 1962
    Record only..7.50 - 15.00
    Picture sleeve only ....12.50 - 25.00
45, Breaking Up Is Hard to Do/Nana's Song, Rocket 40500, 1975 ....2.00 - 4.00
45, Calendar Girl/The Same Old Fool, RCA Victor 47-7829, 1960
    Record only..7.50 - 15.00
    Picture sleeve only..12.50 - 25.00
45, Happy Birthday Sweet Sixteen/Don't Lead Me On, RCA Victor 47-7957,
    1961..7.50 - 15.00
45, Laughter in the Rain/Endlessly, Rocket 40313, 1974 ....2.00 - 4.00
45, Oh! Carol/One Way Ticket (To the Blues), RCA Victor 47-7595,
    1959..10.00 - 20.00
45, Stairway to Heaven/Forty Winks Away, RCA Victor 47-7709,
    1960..7.50 - 15.00
LP, *The Hungry Years*, Rocket PIG-2157, 1975 ....6.00 - 12.00
LP, *Neil Sedaka Sings His Greatest Hits*
    RCA Victor AFL1-0928, 1977, reissue with new prefix ....5.00 - 10.00
    RCA Victor APL1-0928, 1975, reissue..6.00 - 12.00
    RCA Victor LPM-2627, mono, 1962, black label, dog on top.......20.00 - 40.00
    RCA Victor LSP-2627, stereo, 1962, black label, dog on top, "Living Stereo"
    at bottom of label ....25.00 - 50.00
    RCA Victor LSP-2627, stereo, 1969, orange label ....10.00 - 20.00
    RCA Victor ANL1-3465, 1979, later reissue.....................................4.00 - 8.00

MVP:
45, Ring-a-Rockin'/Fly, Don't Fly on Me, Legion 133, 1958 (reissue on Guyden
    goes for less)..50.00 - 100.00

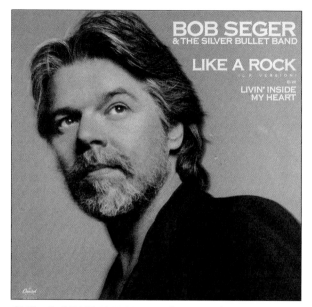

45, Like a Rock/Livin' Inside My Heart, Capitol B-5592, 1986
    Record only..1.50 - 3.00
    Picture sleeve only...1.50 - 3.00

45, Heavy Music/Heavy Music (Part 2), Cameo 494, 1967 ....10.00 - 20.00

45, Night Moves/Ship of Fools, Capitol 4369, 1976 ....2.00 - 4.00

45, Old Time Rock and Roll/Sunspot Baby, Capitol 4702, 1979
    Record only...2.00 - 4.00
    Picture sleeve only...3.00 - 6.00

45, Old Time Rock and Roll/Till It Shines, Capitol B-5276, 1983
    Record only...1.50 - 3.00
    Picture sleeve only...2.50 - 5.00

45, Ramblin' Gamblin' Man/Tales of Lucy Blue, Capitol 2297, 1968.....6.00 - 12.00

45, Shakedown/The Aftermath, MCA 53094, 1987
    Record only...1.50 - 3.00
    Picture sleeve, photo of Bob Seger on front ....2.00 - 4.00
    Picture sleeve, photo of Eddie Murphy on front ....7.50 - 15.00

45, Shame on the Moon/House Behind a House, Capitol B-5187, 1982
    Record only...1.50 - 3.00
    Picture sleeve only ....2.00 - 4.00

LP, *Beautiful Loser*
    Capitol ST-11378, 1975, orange label...5.00 - 10.00
    Capitol ST-11378, 1978, purple label ....4.00 - 8.00
    Capitol SN-16315, 1984, reissue ....4.00 - 8.00

LP, *Like a Rock*, Capitol PT-12398, 1986...5.00 - 10.00

LP, *Stranger in Town*, Capitol SW-11698, 1978 ....5.00 - 10.00

MVP:
LP, *Brand New Morning*, Capitol ST-731, 1971 ....50.00 - 100.00

LP, *The Shirelles' Greatest Hits*

    Scepter SPM-507, mono, 1962..20.00 - 40.00

    Scepter SPS-507, stereo, 1965..25.00 - 50.00

45, Baby It's You/Things I Want to Hear (Pretty Words), Scepter 1227,
1961..10.00 - 20.00
45, Dedicated to the One I Love/Look A Here Baby, Scepter 1203, 1958
    Red label..10.00 - 20.00
    White label...20.00 - 40.00
45, Foolish Little Girl/Not for All the Money in the World, Scepter 1248, 1963
    Record only..7.50 - 15.00
    Picture sleeve only..20.00 - 40.00
45, Mama Said/Blue Holiday, Scepter 1217, 1961 ....10.00 - 20.00
45, Soldier Boy/Love Is a Swingin' Thing, Scepter 1228, 1962 ....7.50 - 15.00
45, Tomorrow/Boys, Scepter 1211, 1960, later reissued as "Will You Love
Me Tomorrow"..20.00 - 40.00
45, Will You Love Me Tomorrow/Boys, Scepter 1211, 1960 ....15.00 - 30.00
LP, *Baby It's You*
    Scepter SPM-504, mono, 1962...............................50.00 - 100.00
    Scepter SPS-504, stereo, 1965................................50.00 - 100.00
LP, *The Shirelles' Greatest Hits, Volume 2*
    Scepter SPM-560, mono, 1967...............................10.00 - 20.00
    Scepter SPS-560, stereo, 1967................................12.50 - 25.00
LP, *The Very Best of the Shirelles*, United Artists UA-LA340-E,
1974..5.00 - 10.00

MVP:
45, I Met Him on a Sunday/I Want You to Be My Boyfriend, Tiara 6112, 1958,
versions on other labels go for a lot less ....400.00 - 800.00

LP, *Anticipation*, Elektra EKS-75016, 1971, butterfly label ....6.00 - 12.00

45, Coming Around Again/Itsy Bitsy Spider, Arista 9525, 1986
   Record only..1.50 - 3.00
   Picture sleeve only, with scenes from the movie *Heartburn* ....4.00 - 8.00
   Picture sleeve only, black and white photo of Carly Simon ....2.00 - 4.00
   Picture sleeve only, color photo of Carly Simon ....2.00 - 4.00
45, Haven't Got Time for the Pain/Mind on My Man, Elektra 45887,
   1974..2.50 - 5.00
45, That's the Way I've Always Heard It Should Be/Alone, Elektra 45724,
   1971..3.00 - 6.00
45, You Belong to Me/In a Small Moment, Elektra 45477, 1978
   Record only..2.00 - 4.00
   Picture sleeve only ....3.00 - 6.00
45, You're So Vain/His Friends Are More Than Fond of Robin, Elektra
   45824, 1972...3.00 - 6.00
LP, *The Best of Carly Simon*
   Elektra 7E-1048, 1975 ....5.00 - 10.00
   Elektra EQ-1048, quadraphonic, 1975 ....10.00 - 20.00
LP, *Hotcakes*
   Elektra 7E-1002, 1974 ....5.00 - 10.00
   Elektra EQ-1002, quadraphonic, 1974......................................10.00 - 20.00
LP, *Playing Possum*
   Elektra 7E-1033, 1975 ....5.00 - 10.00
   Elektra EQ-1033, quadraphonic,1975 ....10.00 - 20.00

MVP:
LP, *Boys in the Trees*, Direct Disk SD-16608, 1980, audiophile reissue, editions
   on Elektra go for a lot less ....25.00 - 50.00

LP, *Graceland*, Warner Bros. 25447, 1986...5.00 - 10.00

45, 50 Ways to Leave Your Lover/Some Folks Lives Roll Easy, Columbia
3-10270, 1975 ....2.50 - 5.00
45, Kodachrome/Tenderness, Columbia 4-45859, 1973
With no trademark disclaimer on label ....3.00 - 6.00
With sticker on label: "Kodachrome is a registered trademark for color
film." ....3.00 - 6.00
With printing on label: "Kodachrome is a registered trademark for color
film." ....2.50 - 5.00
45, Late in the Evening/How the Heart Approaches What It Yearns, Warner Bros.
49511, 1980
Record only...2.00 - 4.00
Picture sleeve only...2.50 - 5.00
45, Loves Me Like a Rock/Learn How to Fall, Columbia 4-45907,
1973..2.50 - 5.00
45, Mother and Child Reunion/Paranoia Blues, Columbia 4-45547, 1972
Orange label with "Columbia" repeated in background ....2.50 - 5.00
Gray label ....2.00 - 4.00
45, You Can Call Me Al/Gumboots, Warner Bros. 7-28667, 1986
Record only...1.50 - 3.00
Picture sleeve only ....1.50 - 3.00
LP, *Still Crazy After All These Years*
Columbia PC 33540, 1975, no bar code on back cover ....5.00 - 10.00
Columbia PC 33540, 1980, with bar code on back cover...............4.00 - 8.00
Columbia PCQ 33540, quadraphonic, 1975 ....10.00 - 20.00
Warner Bros. 25591, 1988, reissue..............................6.00 - 12.00

MVP:
45, I'm Lonely/I Wish I Weren't in Love, Canadian American 130, 1961, as
"Jerry Landis"; other singles under the name "Jerry Landis," though not
equally valuable, are quite hard to find and go in the 25.00 – 50.00 range
....50.00 - 100.00

LP, *Parsley, Sage, Rosemary and Thyme*

Columbia CL 2563, mono, 1966...10.00 - 20.00

Columbia CS 9363, stereo, 1966, "360 Sound Stereo" on red label

....7.50 - 15.00

Columbia CS 9363, stereo, 1970, orange label ....5.00 - 10.00

Columbia PC 9363, stereo, 1970s, reissue with new prefix ....4.00 - 8.00

45, Cecilia/The Only Living Boy in New York, Columbia 4-45133, 1970
Red label, "Columbia" in black at top ....3.00 - 6.00
Red label, continuous "Columbia Records" in white along outer
edge ....5.00 - 10.00
Picture sleeve only...4.00 - 8.00
45, Mrs. Robinson/Old Friends-Bookends, Columbia 4-44511, 1968
Label says "From the Motion Picture 'The Graduate'" ....5.00 - 10.00
Label says "From the Columbia Lp BOOKENDS," with no reference to
"The Graduate" ....4.00 - 8.00
45, The Sounds of Silence/We've Got a Groovey Thing Goin', Columbia
4-43396, 1965
With the "folk-rock" hit version of the A-side...............................5.00 - 10.00
With the original acoustic version of the A-side...........................25.00 - 50.00
LP, *Bridge Over Troubled Water*
CBS KCS 9914, 1970,"360 Sound Stereo" on label; pressed in U.S. for
export...7.50 - 15.00
Columbia JC 9914, 1970s, reissue with new prefix........................4.00 - 8.00
Columbia KCS 9914, 1970, "360 Sound Stereo" on red label, original
....6.00 - 12.00
Columbia KCS 9914, 1970, orange label ....5.00 - 10.00
Columbia KCS 9914, 2000, Classic Records reissue on audiophile
vinyl...12.50 - 25.00
Columbia PC 9914, 1980s, reissue with new prefix.......................4.00 - 8.00
Columbia CQ 30995, quadraphonic, 1971 ....12.50 - 25.00
Columbia PCQ 30995, quadraphonic, 1974, reissue with new prefix
....10.00 - 20.00
Mobile Fidelity 1-173, 1980s, audiophile reissue ....20.00 - 40.00

MVP:
LP, *Bookends*, Columbia KCL 2729, mono, 1968, red label with "Mono" at
bottom (all stereo versions on KCS 9729 are much less) ....50.00 - 100.00

LP, *Swing Easy/Songs for Young Lovers*, two albums originally released as 10-inch
records combined onto one 12-inch record

Capitol W 587, mono, 1955, gray label original ....20.00 - 40.00

Capitol W 587, mono, 1959, black label with colorband, large Capitol logo
at left (logo at top goes for less) ....12.50 - 25.00

45, High Hopes/All My Tomorrows, Capitol F4214, 1959
    Record only...7.50 - 15.00
    Picture sleeve only...100.00 - 200.00
45, Love and Marriage/The Impatient Years, Capitol F3260, 1955....10.00 - 20.00
45, My Way/Blue Lace, Reprise 0817, 1969 ....5.00 - 10.00
45, Strangers in the Night/Oh, You Crazy Moon, Reprise 0470, 1966....5.00 - 10.00
45, Theme from New York, New York/That's What God Looks Like to Me,
    Reprise 49233, 1980
    Record only...5.00 - 10.00
    Picture sleeve only..7.50 - 15.00
45, Young at Heart/Take a Chance , Capitol F2703, 1953 ....10.00 - 20.00
LP, *Frank Sinatra Sings for Only the Lonely*
    Capitol SW 1053, stereo, 1959, without "It's a Lonesome Old Town" and
    "Spring Is Here"...15.00 - 30.00
    Capitol SW 1053, stereo, 1960s, with "It's a Lonesome Old Town" and
    "Spring Is Here"...12.50 - 25.00
    Capitol W 1053, mono, 1958, gray label ....20.00 - 40.00
    Capitol W 1053, mono, 1959, black label with colorband, Capitol logo at left
    (Capitol logo at top is less) ....10.00 - 20.00
LP, *Moonlight Sinatra*
    Reprise F 1018, mono, 1966..7.50 - 15.00
    Reprise FS 1018, stereo, 1966...10.00 - 20.00
LP, *The Voice of Frank Sinatra*
    Columbia CL 6001, 10-inch LP, mono, 1949, original in pink paper cover
    with flap ....35.00 - 70.00
    Columbia CL 6001, 10-inch LP, mono, 1950, reissue in blue cardboard cover
    without flap ....30.00 - 60.00

MVP:
45, Reprise 20,157, California/America the Beautiful, 1963, promotoinal picture
    sleeve only (record, also promo only, goes for 125.00-250.00 by itself)
    ....375.00 - 750.00

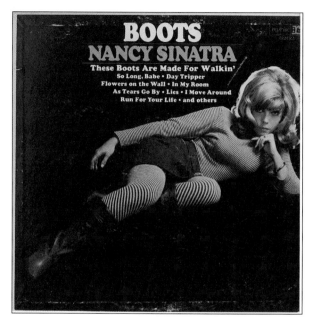

LP, *Boots*

Reprise R-6202, mono, 1966 .... 12.50 - 25.00

Reprise RS-6202, stereo, 1966 .... 15.00 - 30.00

Reprise ST-91341, stereo, 1967, Capitol Record Club edition ..... 20.00 - 40.00

45, How Does That Grab You, Darlin'?/The Last of the Secret Agents,
    Reprise 0461, 1966...5.00 - 10.00
45, Jackson/You Only Live Twice, Reprise 0595, 1967, A-side with Lee
    Hazlewood..5.00 - 10.00
45, Lightning's Girl/Until It's Time For You to Go, Reprise 0620, 1967
    Record only...5.00 - 10.00
    Picture sleeve only..10.00 - 20.00
45, Love Eyes/Coastin', Reprise 0559, 1967..5.00 - 10.00
45, Sugar Town/Summer Wine, Reprise 0527, 1966 ....6.00 - 12.00
45, These Boots Are Made for Walkin'/The City Never Sleeps at Night, Reprise
    0432, 1965..6.00 - 12.00
LP, *Boots: Nancy Sinatra's All-Time Hits (1966-1970)*, Rhino RNLP-70227,
    1987...5.00 - 10.00
LP, *How Does That Grab You?*
    Reprise R-6207, mono, 1966 ....10.00 - 20.00
    Reprise RS-6207, stereo, 1966 ....12.50 - 25.00
LP, *Nancy in London*
    Reprise R-6221, mono, 1966 ....10.00 - 20.00
    Reprise RS-6221, stereo, 1966 ....12.50 - 25.00
LP, *Sugar*
    Reprise R-6239, mono, 1967 ....12.50 - 25.00
    Reprise RS-6239, stereo, 1967 ....10.00 - 20.00
LP, *This Is Nancy Sinatra*, RCA Victor VPS-6078 (2-record set),
    1972...25.00 - 50.00

MVP:
45, Not Just Your Friend/Cuff Links and a Tie Clip, Reprise 20,017, 1961, picture
    sleeve only, record by itself is 10.00 – 20.00 ....30.00 - 60.00

LP, *Dance to the Music*

Epic LN 24371, mono, 1968...20.00 - 40.00
Epic BN 26371, stereo, 1968...7.50 - 15.00
Epic E 30334, 1971, reissue...6.00 - 12.00

45, Dance to the Music/Let Me Hear It from You, Epic 5-10256,
1967...5.00 - 10.00
45, Everyday People/Sing a Simple Song, Epic 5-10407, 1968
   Record only..5.00 - 10.00
   Picture sleeve only...6.00 - 12.00
45, Hot Fun in the Summertime/Fun, Epic 5-10497, 1969 ....5.00 - 10.00
45, If You Want Me to Stay/Babies Makin' Babies, Epic 5-11017,
1973...3.00 - 6.00
45, If You Want Me to Stay/Thankful N' Thoughtful, Epic 5-11017,
1973...3.00 - 6.00
45, Stand!/I Want to Take You Higher, Epic 5-10450, 1969
   Record only..5.00 - 10.00
   Picture sleeve only...6.00 - 12.00
45, Thank You Falettinme Be Mice Elf Agin/Everybody Is a Star, Epic
5-10555, 1969
   Record only..3.00 - 6.00
   Picture sleeve only...5.00 - 10.00
45, Family Affair/Luv N' Haight, Epic 5-10805 , 1971....................3.00 - 6.00
LP, *There's a Riot Goin' On*, Epic KE 30986, 1971
   Yellow label, gatefold cover, American flag cover ....6.00 - 12.00
   Non-gatefold, band photos on cover..4.00 - 8.00
LP, *A Whole New Thing*
   Epic LN 24324, mono, 1967...10.00 - 20.00
   Epic BN 26324, stereo, 1967...10.00 - 20.00
   Epic E 30335, 1971, reissue...6.00 - 12.00

MVP:
LP, *Sly and the Family Stone's Greatest Hits*, Epic EQ 30325, quadraphonic,
1971, has alternate mixes of "Hot Fun in the Summertime," "Thank You" and
"Everybody Is a Star," which are not rechanneled stereo as they are on KE or
PE 30325...50.00 - 100.00

LP, *Tunnel of Love*, Columbia OC 40999, 1987 ....5.00 - 10.00

45, Born to Run/Meeting Across the River, Columbia 3-10209, 1975
....10.00 - 20.00

45, Dancing in the Dark/Pink Cadillac

Columbia 38-04463, 1984, record only ....2.00 - 4.00

Columbia 38-04463, 1984, picture sleeve only ....2.50 - 5.00

Columbia 13-08408, 1988, gray label reissue ....1.50 - 3.00

45, My Hometown/Santa Claus Is Coming to Town

Columbia 38-05728, 1985, record only ....2.00 - 4.00

Columbia 38-05728, 1985, picture sleeve only ....2.00 - 4.00

Columbia 13-08414, 1988, gray label reissue ....1.50 - 3.00

LP, *Born to Run*

Columbia HC 33795, 1981, "Half Speed Mastered" on cover ......25.00 - 50.00

Columbia JC 33795, 1977, reissue ....4.00 - 8.00

Columbia PC 33795, 1975, promotional copy with white label
....50.00 - 100.00

Columbia PC 33795, 1975, original commercial edition, Jon Landau's name
is misspelled "John" on the back cover.......................................12.50 - 25.00

Columbia PC 33795, 1975, second commercial edition, with sticker with
the correct spelling of Jon Landau on back ....7.50 - 15.00

Columbia PC 33795, 1975, Jon Landau's name is correct on the back
cover ....5.00 - 10.00

Columbia PC 33795, 1999, Classic Records reissue, identified as such on
back cover; no gatefold ....20.00 - 40.00

Columbia PC 33795, 1999, Classic Records reissue, identified as such on
back cover; with gatefold..12.50 - 25.00

Columbia HC 43795, 1982, "Half Speed Mastered" on cover, reissue with new
number ....20.00 - 40.00

MVP:

LP, *Born to Run*, Columbia PC 33795, 1975, promo-only test pressing package
with "Bruce Springsteen — Born to Run" in script print on cover rather than
the normal light block print; also includes mailing envelope, letter from CBS
and orange patch ....800.00 – 1,200.00

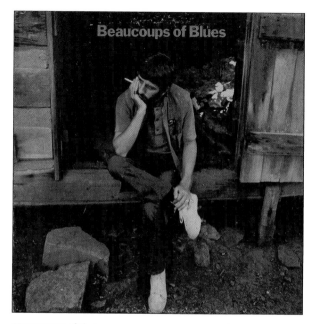

LP, *Beaucoups of Blues*
> Apple SMAS-3368, 1970 ....10.00 - 20.00
> Capitol SN-16235, 1980s, reissue ....10.00 - 20.00

45, It Don't Come Easy/Early 1970
    Apple 1831, 1971, no star on A-side label ....4.00 - 8.00
    Apple 1831, 1971, with star on A-side label ....6.00 - 12.00
    Apple 1831, 1971, picture sleeve only ....15.00 - 30.00
    Apple 1831, 1975, with "All rights reserved" on label..............15.00 - 30.00
    Capitol 1831, 1976, orange label ....12.50 - 25.00
    Capitol 1831, 1978, purple late-1970s label ....3.00 - 6.00
    Capitol 1831, 1983, black colorband label ....3.00 - 6.00
    Capitol 1831, 1988, purple late-1980s label (wider) ....2.50 - 5.00
45, Photograph/Down and Out
    Apple 1865, 1973, custom star label...3.00 - 6.00
    Apple 1865, 1973, picture sleeve only ....10.00 - 20.00
    Capitol 1865, 1978, purple late-1970s label ....4.00 - 8.00
    Capitol 1865, 1983, black colorband label ....4.00 - 8.00
    Capitol 1865, 1988, purple late-1980s label (wider) ....3.00 - 6.00
LP, *Goodnight Vienna*
    Apple SW-3417, 1974..6.00 - 12.00
    Capitol SN-16219, 1980s, reissue...12.50 - 25.00

MVP:
LP, *Ringo* , Apple SWAL-3413, 1973, with "Six O'Clock" listed AND playing 5:26;
   the tricky part is that later labels still say "5:26" but the disc only plays for
   4:05; all known copies with the long version have a promo punch hole in the
   top corner of the jacket; also, upon visual examination of Side 2, "Six
   O'Clock" will be obviously wider than any other track because it is the longest
   song on the side; regular versions go for a lot less than this ...200.00 - 400.00

LP, *Can't Buy a Thrill*

    ABC ABCX-758, 1972, black label..6.00 - 12.00

    ABC ABCX-758, 1974, multicolor concentric circles label............5.00 - 10.00

    ABC Dunhill SMAS-94976, 1973, Capitol Record Club edition pressed on the

    wrong label ....12.50 - 25.00

    Command QD-40009, quadraphonic, 1974................................10.00 - 20.00

    MCA 1591, 1987, reissue ....3.00 - 6.00

    MCA 37040, 1980, reissue, blue label with rainbow ....4.00 - 8.00

45, Deacon Blues/Home at Last, ABC 12355, 1978 ....2.00 - 4.00
45, Do It Again/Fire in the Hole, ABC 11338, 1972 ....2.00 - 4.00
45, Hey Nineteen/Bodhisattva, MCA 51036, 1980 ....2.00 - 4.00
45, Peg/I Got the News, ABC 12320, 1977.....................................2.00 - 4.00
45, Reeling In the Years/Only a Fool Would Say That, ABC 11352, 1973
   First edition, with "abc" children's blocks in a white triangle on
   label ....2.50 - 5.00
   Second edition, with "abc" in a rainbow box ....2.00 - 4.00
45, Rikki Don't Lose That Number/Any Major Dude Will Tell You
   ABC 11439, 1974 ....2.00 - 4.00
   ABC 12014, 1974, early reissue...3.00 - 6.00
LP, *Aja*
   ABC AA-1006, 1977, original..6.00 - 12.00
   MCA AA-1006, 1980, early reissue...5.00 - 10.00
   MCA 1688, 1987, later reissue ....3.00 - 6.00
   Mobile Fidelity 1-033, 1980, "Original Master Recording" at top of
   cover ....25.00 - 50.00
LP, *Countdown to Ecstasy*
   ABC ABCX-779, 1973, black label..6.00 - 12.00
   ABC ABCX-779, 1974, multicolor concentric circles label............5.00 - 10.00
   Command QD-40010, quadraphonic,1974...................................10.00 - 20.00
   MCA 1592, 1987, reissue ....3.00 - 6.00
   MCA 37041, 1980, reissue, blue label with rainbow ....4.00 - 8.00

MVP:
LP, *Katy Lied* ,Mobile Fidelity 1-007, 1979, "Original Master Recording" at top of
   cover (other editions go for less)..40.00 - 80.00

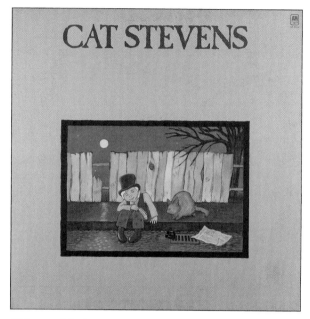

LP, *Teaser and the Firecat*
   A&M SP-4313, 1971, brown label ....6.00 - 12.00
   A&M SP-4313, 1974, mostly silver label with gradually fading
   "A&M"...5.00 - 10.00
   Mobile Fidelity 1-244, 1996, "Original Master Recording" at top of
   cover ....20.00 - 40.00

45, Another Saturday Night/Home in the Sky, A&M 1602, 1974
  Record only..2.00 - 4.00
  Picture sleeve only...3.00 - 6.00
45, Moon Shadow/I Think I See the Light, A&M 1265, 1971 ....2.00 - 4.00
45, Morning Has Broken/I Want to Live in a Wigwam, A&M 1335, 1972
  Record only..2.00 - 4.00
  Picture sleeve only ....3.00 - 6.00
45, Peace Train/Where Do the Children Play, A&M 1291, 1971
  Record only..2.00 - 4.00
  Picture sleeve only...3.00 - 6.00
45, Wild World/Miles from Nowhere, A&M 1231, 1970 ....2.50 - 5.00
LP, *Buddha and the Chocolate Box*
  A&M SP-3623, stereo, 1974 ....6.00 - 12.00
  A&M QU-53623, quadraphonic, 1974 ....10.00 - 20.00
LP, *Catch Bull at Four*, A&M SP-4365, 1972.....................6.00 - 12.00
LP, *Greatest Hits*
  A&M SP-4519, stereo, 1975 ....6.00 - 12.00
  A&M SP-54519, quadraphonic, 1975 ....10.00 - 20.00
LP, *Izitso*
  A&M SP-4702, 1977 ....6.00 - 12.00
  Mobile Fidelity 1-254, 1996, "Original Master Recording" at top of
  cover ....12.50 - 25.00

MVP:
LP, *Tea for the Tillerman*, Mobile Fidelity MFQR-035, 1984, "Ultra High Quality
  Recording" in custom box, other versions go for much less
  ....60.00 - 120.00

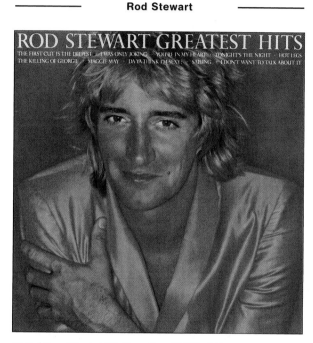

LP, *Rod Stewart Greatest Hits*, Warner Bros. HS 3373, 1979 ....5.00 - 10.00

45, Da Ya Think I'm Sexy?/Scarred and Scared, Warner Bros. 8724, 1978
 Record only, "Burbank" palm trees label ....4.00 - 8.00
 Record only, whtitsh label ....2.00 - 4.00
 Picture sleeve only ....2.50 - 5.00
45, Maggie May/Reason to Believe, Mercury 73224, 1971 ....3.00 - 6.00
45, Tonight's the Night (Gonna Be Alright)/Fool for You, Warner Bros.
 8262, 1976...2.00 - 4.00
45, You Wear It Well/True Blue, Mercury 73330, 1972
 Record only..2.50 - 5.00
 Picture sleeve only ....7.50 - 15.00
45, You're In My Heart (The Final Acclaim)/You Got a Nerve, Warner Bros.
 8475, 1977...2.00 - 4.00
LP, *Camouflage*, Warner Bros. 25095, 1984, issued with 16 different back
 covers, all of equal value, that, when assembled, form a giant poster 4.00 - 8.00
LP, *Every Picture Tells a Story*
 Mercury SRM-1-609, 1971, red label, with attached perforated
 poster ....7.50 - 15.00
 Mercury SRM-1-609, 1971, red label, with poster detached ....5.00 - 10.00
 Mercury SRM-1-609, 1974, Chicago skyline label ....5.00 - 10.00
 Mercury 822 385-1, 1984, reissue..4.00 - 8.00
LP, *A Night on the Town*
 Warner Bros. BS 2938, 1976, original...5.00 - 10.00
 Warner Bros. BSK 3116, 1977, reissue..4.00 - 8.00
LP, *Tonight I'm Yours*, Warner Bros. BSK 3602, 1981 ....5.00 - 10.00

MVP:
12-inch single, The Killing of Georgie (6:31) (same on both sides), Warner Bros.
 PRO 680, 1977, promotional issue only on red vinyl, other colors of vinyl go
 for less ....50.00 - 100.00

LP, *People*

    Columbia CL 2215, mono, 1964, "Guaranteed High Fidelity" on
    label ....10.00 - 20.00
    Columbia CS 9015, stereo, 1964, "360 Sound Stereo" in black on
    label ....12.50 - 25.00
    (Other label variations exist and sell for less.)

45, Love Theme from "A Star Is Born" (Evergreen)/I Believe in Love, Columbia
3-10450, 1976
    Record only...2.50 - 5.00
    Picture sleeve only...3.00 - 6.00
45, People/I Am Woman, Columbia 4-42965, 1964 ....5.00 - 10.00
45, Stoney End/I'll Be Home, Columbia 4-45236, 1970 ....2.50 - 5.00
45, The Way We Were/What Are You Doing the Rest of Your Life, Columbia
4-45944, 1973 ....2.50 - 5.00
45, Woman in Love/Run Wild, Columbia 1-11364, 1980.....................2.00 - 4.00
LP, *The Barbra Streisand Album*
    Columbia CL 2007, mono. 1963, "Guaranteed High Fidelity" on
    label ....10.00 - 20.00
    Columbia CL 2007, mono, 1966, "360 Sound Mono" on label......6.00 - 12.00
    Columbia CS 8807, stereo, 1963, "360 Sound Stereo" in black on
    label ....12.50 - 25.00
    Columbia CS 8807, stereo, 1966, "360 Sound Stereo" in white on
    label ....7.50 - 15.00
    Columbia CS 8807, stereo, 1970, orange label ....5.00 - 10.00
    Columbia PC 8807, stereo, 1970s, reissue with new prefix ....4.00 - 8.00
LP, *Barbra Streisand Featuring The Way We Were and All In Love Is Fair*,
    Columbia PC 32801, 1974, no title on front cover and this title on both
    the spine and the record label ....10.00 - 20.00
LP, *The Way We Were*
    Columbia JC 32801, 1970s, reissue with new prefix.......................4.00 - 8.00
    Columbia PC 32801, 1974, with this title on spine, label and front
    cover ....6.00 - 12.00
    Columbia PCQ 32801, quadraphonic, 1974 ....12.50 - 25.00

MVP:
LP, *The Second Barbra Streisand Album*, Columbia CL 2054, mono, 1963, white
    label, blue vinyl (editions with red labels and black vinyl are less)
    ....100.00 - 200.00

LP, *The Grand Illusion*

   A&M SP-3223, 1984, reissue...4.00 - 8.00

   A&M SP-4637, 1977, original, add 1.00-2.00 if poster is enclosed

   ....5.00 - 10.00

   Mobile Fidelity 1-026, 1979, "Original Master Recording" at top of cover

   ....15.00 - 30.00

45 Babe/I'm O.K., A&M 2188, 1979 ....2.00 - 4.00
45, Come Sail Away/Put Me On, A&M 1977, 1977
    Record only...2.00 - 4.00
    Picture sleeve only...3.00 - 6.00
45, Lady/Children of the Land
    Wooden Nickel WB-10102, 1974 ....2.50 - 5.00
    Wooden Nickel GB-10492, 1975, Gold Standard Series reissue .....2.00 - 4.00
45, Lady/You Better Ask, Wooden Nickel 65-0116, 1973...................5.00 - 10.00
45, Mr. Roboto/Snowblind, A&M 2525, 1983
    Record only...1.50 - 3.00
    Picture sleeve only...1.50 - 3.00
LP, *Cornerstone*
    A&M SP-3239, 1984, reissue...4.00 - 8.00
    A&M SP-3711, 1979, black vinyl ....5.00 - 10.00
    A&M SP-3711, 1979, silver vinyl..15.00 - 30.00
    Nautilus NR-27, 1982, "Super Disc" edition ....10.00 - 20.00
LP, *Man of Miracles*, Wooden Nickel BWL1-0638, 1974
    Original version, with "Lies"...15.00 - 30.00
    Second version, with "Best Thing"..10.00 - 20.00
LP, *Miracles*, RCA Victor AFL1-3596, 1979, retitled version of *Man of Miracles*
    ....5.00 - 10.00

MVP:
LP, *Styx Radio Special* , A&M SP-17053 (3-record set), 1978, promotional only
....20.00 - 40.00

LP, *Bad Girls*

    Casablanca NBLP 7150 (2-record set), 1979 ....6.00 - 12.00
    Casablanca 822 557-1 (2-record set), 1984, reissue ....5.00 - 10.00

45, Bad Girls/On My Honor, Casablanca 988, 1979..............................2.00 - 4.00

45, Can't We Just Sit Down (And Talk It Over)/I Feel Love, Casablanca 884, 1977, original copies have "Can't We Just Sit Down" labeled as "Side A" ....3.00 - 6.00

45, Hot Stuff/Journey to the Center of Your Heart, Casablanca 978, 1979..2.00 - 4.00

45, I Feel Love/Can't We Just Sit Down (And Talk It Over), Casablanca 884, 1977, second pressings have "I Feel Love" listed as "Side A"..........2.50 - 5.00

45, Love to Love You Baby/Need-A-Man Blues, Oasis 401 A /B, 1975, "Love to Love You Baby" has a radically different mix on this first pressing 6.00 - 12.00

45, Love to Love You Baby (4:55)/Love to Love You Baby (3:24), Oasis 401 AA/BB, 1975, both sides are remixed compared to the original 45 mix......3.00 - 6.00

45, Mac Arthur Park/Once Upon a Time, Casablanca 939, 1978..........2.00 - 4.00

45, She Works Hard for the Money/I Do Believe (I'll Fall in Love), Mercury 812 370-7, 1983
Record only..2.00 - 4.00
Picture sleeve only..2.50 - 5.00

LP, *The Best of Live and More*, Casablanca NBPIX 7119, 1979, picture disc ....10.00 - 20.00

LP, *Live and More*
Casablanca NBLP 7119 (2-record set), 1978 ....6.00 - 12.00
Casablanca 811 123-1 (2-record set), 1985, reissue ....5.00 - 10.00

LP, *Love to Love You Baby*, Oasis OCLP 5003, 1975, add 50% if poster is included ....6.00 - 12.00

LP, *Once Upon a Time...*, Casablanca NBLP 7078 [2-record set], 1977 ....6.00 - 12.00

LP, *The Wanderer*, Geffen GHS 2000, 1980 ....5.00 - 10.00

MVP:
12-inch single, The Power of One (8 versions), Atlantic DMD 2574 (2-record set), promotional only, 2000 ....15.00 - 30.00

LP, *Crime of the Century*

A&M SP-3647, 1974 ....6.00 - 12.00

Mobile Fidelity 1-005, 1979, "Original Master Recording" at top of cover
....20.00 - 40.00

Mobile Fidelity MFQR-005, 1983, "Ultra High Quality Recording" in box
....60.00 - 120.00

45, Bloody Well Right/Dreamer, A&M 1660, 1975.................................2.50 - 5.00
45, Give a Little Bit/Downstream, A&M 1938, 1977
    Record only...2.00 - 4.00
    Picture sleeve only ....3.00 - 6.00
45, Goodbye Stranger/Even in the Quietest Moments, A&M 2162, 1979
    Record only...2.00 - 4.00
    Picture sleeve only ....2.50 - 5.00
45, It's Raining Again/Bonnie, A&M 2502, 1982
    Record only...2.00 - 4.00
    Picture sleeve only...2.00 - 4.00
45, The Logical Song/Just Another Nervous Wreck, A&M 2128, 1979
    Record only...2.00 - 4.00
    Picture sleeve only ....2.50 - 5.00
LP, *Even in the Quietest Moments...*
    A&M SP-3215, 1982, reissue ....4.00 - 8.00
    A&M SP-4634, 1977, original..6.00 - 12.00
    Sweet Thunder 5, 1980s, audiophile edition ....20.00 - 40.00
LP, *Indelibly Stamped*
    A&M SP-3129, 1980s, reissue ....4.00 - 8.00
    A&M SP-4311, 1971, brown label ....10.00 - 20.00
    A&M SP-4311, 1974, silverish label with fading "A&M" logo ....5.00 - 10.00

MVP:

LP, *Breakfast in America*, A&M SP-3708, 1979, special custom-made picture
    discs, made in-house at A&M, featuring staff members posing with the cover
    model, regular copies go for 5.00 – 10.00 ....250.00 - 500.00

LP, *Where Did Our Love Go*

Motown M 621, mono, 1964...15.00 - 30.00

Motown MS 621, stereo, 1964...20.00 - 40.00

Motown 5270 ML, stereo, 1982, reissue ....4.00 - 8.00

45, Baby Love/Ask Any Girl, Motown 1066, 1964
    Record only..10.00 - 20.00
    Picture sleeve only..15.00 - 30.00
45, Back in My Arms Again/Whisper You Love Me Boy, Motown 1075, 1965
    Record only..7.50 - 15.00
    Picture sleeve only ....15.00 - 30.00
45, Come See About Me/Always in My Heart, Motown 1068, 1964...10.00 - 20.00
45, Love Child/Will This Be the Day, Motown 1135, 1968, as "Diana Ross and
    the Supremes"..4.00 - 8.00
45, Someday We'll Be Together/He's My Sunny Boy, Motown 1156, 1969, as
    "Diana Ross and the Supremes"......................................4.00 - 8.00
45, Stoned Love/Shine on Me, Motown 1172, 1970............................3.00 - 6.00
45, Stop! In the Name of Love/I'm in Love Again, Motown 1074, 1965
    Record only..7.50 - 15.00
    Picture sleeve only..15.00 - 30.00
45, Where Did Our Love Go/He Means the World to Me, Motown 1060, 1964
    Record only..10.00 - 20.00
    Picture sleeve only..15.00 - 30.00
LP, *The Supremes A' Go-Go*
    Motown M5-138V1, 1981, reissue....................................6.00 - 12.00
    Motown M 649, mono, 1966..12.50 - 25.00
    Motown MS 649, stereo, 1966..15.00 - 30.00

MVP:
LP, *Meet the Supremes*, Motown M 606, mono, 1963, with group sitting on
    stools; later album cover, with soft-focus close-up of the group's faces, goes
    for much less..450.00 - 900.00

45, Take Me to the River/Thank You for Sending Me an Angel (Version),
  Sire 1032, 1978
    Record only..2.00 - 4.00
    Picture sleeve only ....2.00 - 4.00

45, And She Was/And She Was (Dub), Sire 7-28917, 1985
  Record only..1.00 - 2.00
  Picture sleeve only ....1.00 - 2.00
45, Burning Down the House/I Get Wild-Wild Gravity, Sire 7-29565, 1983
  Record only..1.50 - 3.00
  Picture sleeve only..1.50 - 3.00
45, Psycho Killer/Psycho Killer (Acoustic), Sire 1013, 1978
  Record only..4.00 - 8.00
  Picture sleeve only ....4.00 - 8.00
LP, *Fear of Music*, Sire SRK 6076, 1979 ....5.00 - 10.00
LP, *More Songs About Buildings and Food*
  Sire SR 6058, 1978 ....6.00 - 12.00
  Sire SRK 6058, 1979, reissue with new prefix ....4.00 - 8.00
LP, *The Name of This Band Is Talking Heads*, Sire 2SR 3590 (2-record set),
  1982..10.00 - 20.00
LP, *Remain in Light* , Sire SRK 6095, 1981.....................................5.00 - 10.00
LP, *Speaking in Tongues*
  Sire 23771, 1983, clear vinyl in oversize plastic container with
  Robert Rauschenberg artwork...10.00 - 20.00
  Sire 23883, 1983, standard issue ....5.00 - 10.00
LP, *Stop Making Sense (Soundtrack)*
  Sire 25121, 1984, first issue with booklet and black & white cover
  ....7.50 - 15.00
  Sire 25186, 1984, second issue with no booklet and color cover
  ....5.00 - 10.00

MVP:
LP, *Talking Heads Live on Tour*, Warner Bros. WBMS-104, 1979, promotional
  only, part of "The Warner Bros. Radio Show" series ....12.50 - 25.00

LP, *James Taylor*

    Apple SKAO 3352, 1969, with title in black print..........................12.50 - 25.00

    Apple SKAO 3352, 1970, with title in orange print ....10.00 - 20.00

45, Fire and Rain/Anywhere Like Heaven, Warner Bros. 7423, 1970 ...4.00 - 8.00

45, Handy Man/Bartender's Blues, Columbia 3-10557, 1977 ....2.00 - 4.00

45, How Sweet It Is (To Be Loved By You)/Sarah Maria, Warner Bros. 8109, 1975..2.50 - 5.00

45, You've Got a Friend/You Can Close Your Eyes, Warner Bros. 7498, 1971..3.00 - 6.00

45, Your Smiling Face/If I Keep My Heart Out of Sight, Columbia 3-10602, 1977..2.00 - 4.00

LP, *Greatest Hits*

    Warner Bros. BS 2979, 1976, original..6.00 - 12.00

    Warner Bros. BSK 3113, 1977, new number, "Burbank" palm trees label ....5.00 - 10.00

    Warner Bros. BSK 3113, 1979, tan or white label ....4.00 - 8.00

LP, *JT*

    Columbia JC 34811, 1977 ....5.00 - 10.00

    Columbia PC 34811, 1980s, reissue ....4.00 - 8.00

LP, *Sweet Baby James*

    Warner Bros. WS 1843, 1970, green label with "W7" logo ....12.50 - 25.00

    Warner Bros. WS 1843, 1970, green "WB" label with no reference to other songs on front cover ....7.50 - 15.00

    Warner Bros. WS 1843, 1970, green "WB" label with "Contains Fire and Rain and Country Road" added to front cover ....5.00 - 10.00

    Warner Bros. WS 1843, 1973, "Burbank" palm trees label or tan/white label ....4.00 - 8.00

    Warner Bros. ST-93138, 1970, Capitol Record Club edition ....10.00 - 20.00

MVP:

45, Carolina in My Mind/Taking It In, Apple 1805, 1969, must have this B-side for this price range (versions with "Something's Wrong" on the sliced apple side are worth much less) ....150.00 - 300.00

LP, *Gettin' Ready*

    Gordy G 918, mono, 1966...12.50 - 25.00

    Gordy GS 918, stereo, 1966, script "Gordy" at top of label ....15.00 - 30.00

    Gordy GS 918, stereo, 1967, block "GORDY" inside "G" on left of label

    ....10.00 - 20.00

45, Ain't Too Proud to Beg/You'll Lose a Precious Love, Gordy 7054,
1966..7.50 - 15.00
45, Ball of Confusion (That's What the World Is Today)/It's Summer, Gordy
7099, 1970
Record only..3.00 - 6.00
Picture sleeve only...10.00 - 20.00
45, Beauty Is Only Skin Deep/You're Not an Ordinary Girl, Gordy 7055, 1966
Record only...7.50 - 15.00
Picture sleeve only...20.00 - 40.00
45, Cloud Nine/Why Did She Have to Leave Me, Gordy 7081, 1968......4.00 - 8.00
45, I Can't Get Next to You/Running Away (Ain't Gonna Help You, Gordy
7093, 1969..4.00 - 8.00
45, I Wish It Would Rain/I Truly, Truly Believe, Gordy 7068, 1967.....5.00 - 10.00
45, Just My Imagination (Running Away with Me)/You Make Your Own Heaven
and Hell Right Here on Earth, Gordy 7105, 1971............................3.00 - 6.00
45, Papa Was a Rollin' Stone/(Instrumental), Gordy 7121, 1972.........3.00 - 6.00
45, The Way You Do the Things You Do/Just Let Me Know, Gordy 7028,
1964..7.50 - 15.00
LP, *All Directions*, Gordy G 962L, 1972..10.00 - 20.00
LP, *The Temptations' Greatest Hits*
Gordy G 919, mono, 1966...12.50 - 25.00
Gordy GS 919, stereo, 1966, script "Gordy" at top of label.........15.00 - 30.00
Gordy GS 919, stereo, 1967, block "GORDY" inside "G" on left of label
....10.00 - 20.00

MVP:
45, My Girl/Nobody But My Baby, Gordy 7038, 1965, picture sleeve only (record
is 7.50-15.00) ....60.00 - 120.00

LP, *Three Dog Night*
   ABC Dunhill DS-50048, 1968, without the word "One" on the front cover
   ....7.50 - 15.00
   ABC Dunhill DS-50048, 1969, with the word "One" on the front cover
   ....6.00 - 12.00

45, Black and White/Freedom for the Stallion, ABC Dunhill 4317, 1972..2.50 - 5.00

45, Easy to Be Hard/Dreaming Isn't Good for You, ABC Dunhill 4203, 1969..4.00 - 8.00

45, Joy to the World/I Can Hear You Calling, ABC Dunhill 4272, 1971..2.50 - 5.00

45, Mama Told Me (Not to Come)/Rock and Roll Widow, ABC Dunhill 4239, 1970

    Record only..3.00 - 6.00

    Picture sleeve only ....6.00 - 12.00

45, An Old Fashioned Love Song/Jam, ABC Dunhill 4294, 1971 ....2.50 - 5.00

45, One/Chest Fever, ABC Dunhill 4191, 1969..........................4.00 - 8.00

45, Shambala/Our "B" Side, ABC Dunhill 4352, 1973

    First pressings have "Dunhill" spelled out in children's blocks on label ....2.50 - 5.00

    Transitional pressings have "Dunhill" in children's blocks on one label and "Dunhill" in a box on the other label...............................2.50 - 5.00

    Later pressings have "Dunhill" in a box on both labels (1968-72 style) ....2.00 - 4.00

45, The Show Must Go On/On the Way Back Home, ABC Dunhill 4382, 1974..2.00 - 4.00

LP, *Joy to the World: Their Greatest Hits*

    ABC Dunhill DSD-50178, 1974, with gatefold cover ....6.00 - 12.00

    ABC Dunhill DSD-50178, 1975, with standard cover....................5.00 - 10.00

    MCA 37120, 1980, reissue ....4.00 - 8.00

LP, *Suitable for Framing* , ABC Dunhill DS-50058, 1969..................6.00 - 12.00

MVP:

LP, *It Ain't Easy*, ABC Dunhill DS-50078, 1970, original cover with band members in the nude (other version goes for much less) ....50.00 - 100.00

45, Happy Together/Like the Seasons, White Whale 244, 1967
  Record only..4.00 - 8.00
  Picture sleeve only..20.00 - 40.00

45, Elenore/Surfer Dan, White Whale 276, 1968
   Record only...4.00 - 8.00
   Picture sleeve only...6.00 - 12.00
45, Guide for the Married Man/Think I'll Run Away, White Whale 251, 1967,
   withdrawn shortly after release...20.00 - 40.00
45, It Ain't Me, Babe/Almost There, White Whale 222, 1965 ....6.00 - 12.00
45, She'd Rather Be with Me/The Walking Song, White Whale 249, 1967
   Record only...4.00 - 8.00
   Picture sleeve only...12.50 - 25.00
45, She's My Girl/Chicken Little Was Right, White Whale 260, 1967
   All-blue label...5.00 - 10.00
   White concentric circles on mostly blue label 4.00 - 8.00
   Picture sleeve only ....10.00 - 20.00
45, You Know What I Mean/Rugs of Woods and Flowers, White Whale 254, 1967
   Record only...4.00 - 8.00
   Picture sleeve only...7.50 - 15.00
45, You Showed Me/Buzz Saw, White Whale 292, 1969
   Record only...4.00 - 8.00
   Picture sleeve only...6.00 - 12.00
LP, *The Turtles! Golden Hits*
   White Whale WW 115, mono, 1967 ....12.50 - 25.00
   White Whale WWS 7115, stereo,1967..10.00 - 20.00
LP, *The Turtles Present the Battle of the Bands*
   Rhino RNLP 70156, 1986, reissue...5.00 - 10.00
   White Whale WWS 7118, 1968 ....12.50 - 25.00

MVP:
45, The Story of Rock and Roll/Can't You Hear the Cows, White Whale 273, 1968.
   picture sleeve only (reoord is 4.00-8.00) ....25.00 - 50.00

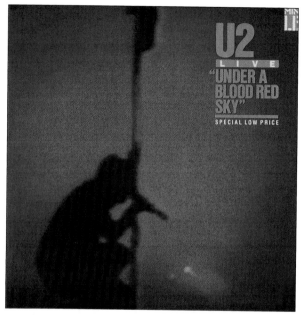

LP, *Under a Blood Red Sky*
  Island 90127-1-B, 1983, white labels with "Mini LP" logo; with version of "The Electric Co." in which Bono sings snippets of "A-Me-Ri-Ca" from *West Side Story* and "Send In The Clowns" during the instrumental break ...7.50 - 15.00
  Island 90127-1-B, 1983, white labels with "Mini LP" logo; with edited version of "The Electric Co." ....5.00 - 10.00

45, Desire/Hallelujah Here She Comes, Island 7-99250, 1988
Record only..1.50 - 3.00
Picture sleeve only, gatefold cardboard ....3.00 - 6.00
Picture sleeve only, standard paper ....1.50 - 3.00
45, I Still Haven't Found What I'm Looking For//Spanish Eyes/Deep in the
Heart, Island 7-99430, 1987
Record only, A-side plays at 45 rpm, B-side at 33 1/3 rpm ....1.50 - 3.00
Picture sleeve only, slick paper version ....1.50 - 3.00
Picture sleeve only, cardboard version ....2.00 - 4.00
45, I Still Haven't Found What I'm Looking For/Spanish Eyes, Island 7-99431,
1987, black label, both sides play at 45 rpm..................................6.00 - 12.00
45, With or Without You/Walk on the Water, Island 7-99453, 1987, white label,
both sides play at 45 rpm...10.00 - 20.00
45, With or Without You/Luminous Times (Hold On to Love)/Walk on the
Water, Island 7-99469, 1987
Record only, A-side plays at 45 rpm, B-side at 33 1/3 rpm ....1.50 - 3.00
Picture sleeve only, slick paper version ....1.50 - 3.00
Picture sleeve only, cardboard version ....2.00 - 4.00
LP, *Boy*
Island ILPS 9646, 1980, original ....7.50 - 15.00
Island 90040, 1983, reissue, dark purple label.............................6.00 - 12.00
Island 90040, 1984, reissue, light blue label................................5.00 - 10.00
Island 90040, 1985, reissue, black label..4.00 - 8.00
LP, *The Unforgettable Fire*
Island 90231, 1984 ....5.00 - 10.00
Mobile Fidelity 1-207, 1994, "Original Master Recording" at top of
cover ....12.50 - 25.00

MVP:
LP, *Two Sides Live* , Warner Bros. WBMS-117, 1981, promo only, part of
"The Warner Bros. Music Show" series; legitimate copies are on black
vinyl (colored vinyl versions are counterfeits).........................60.00 - 120.00

45, Jump/House of Pain, Warner Bros. 7-29384, 1984
Record only..1.50 - 3.00
Picture sleeve only ....1.50 - 3.00

45, Dance the Night Away/Outta Love Again, Warner Bros. 8823, 1979
  Record only...2.00 - 4.00
  Picture sleeve only ....6.00 - 12.00
45, (Oh) Pretty Woman/Happy Trails, Warner Bros. 50003, 1982, reissue
  with subtitle
  Record only...2.00 - 4.00
  Picture sleeve only ....2.00 - 4.00
45, Pretty Woman/Happy Trails, Warner Bros. 50003, 1982, original with
  no subtitle
  Record only...2.50 - 5.00
  Picture sleeve only...2.50 - 5.00
45, Why Can't This Be Love/Get Up, Warner Bros. 7-28740, 1986
  Record only...1.50 - 3.00
  Picture sleeve only...1.50 - 3.00
45, You Really Got Me/Atomic Punk, Warner Bros. 8515, 1978 ....2.50 - 5.00
LP, *5150*, Warner Bros. 25394, 1986 ....5.00 - 10.00
LP, *OU812*, Warner Bros. 25732, 1988...5.00 - 10.00
LP, *Van Halen*
  DCC Compact Classics LPZ-2066, 1998, 180-gram virgin vinyl
  reissue...20.00 - 40.00
  Warner Bros. BSK 3075, 1978, "Burbank" palm trees label ....6.00 - 12.00
  Warner Bros. BSK 3075, 1979, white or tan label ....5.00 - 10.00
LP, *Van Halen II*, Warner Bros. HS 3312, 1979 ....5.00 - 10.00
LP, *Women and Children First*, Warner Bros. HS 3415, 1980 ....5.00 - 10.00

MVP:
LP, *Looney Tunes*, Warner Bros. PRO 705, 1978, promotional item only,
  sampler on red vinyl ....30.00 - 60.00

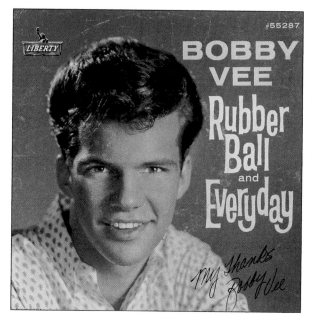

45, Rubber Ball/Everyday, Liberty 55287, 1960
   Record only...10.00 - 20.00
   Picture sleeve only ....15.00 - 30.00

Bobby Vee

45, Come Back When You Grow Up/Swahili Serenade, Liberty 55964,
1967 ....4.00 - 8.00
45, Come Back When You Grow Up/That's All There Is to That, Liberty
55964, 1967 ....4.00 - 8.00
45, Devil or Angel/Since I Met You Baby, Liberty 55270, 1960
   Record only ....10.00 - 20.00
   Picture sleeve only ....15.00 - 30.00
45, The Night Has a Thousand Eyes/Anonymous Phone Call, Liberty 55521,
1962 ....6.00 - 12.00
45, Please Don't Ask About Barbara/I Can't Say Goodbye, Liberty 55419,
1962
   Record only ....7.50 - 15.00
   Picture sleeve only ....12.50 - 25.00
45, Run to Him/Walkin' with My Angel, Liberty 55388, 1961 ....10.00 - 20.00
45, Take Good Care of My Baby/Bashful Bob, Liberty 55354, 1961....7.50 - 15.00
LP, *Bobby Vee*
   Liberty LRP-3181, mono, 1961...20.00 - 40.00
   Liberty LST-7181, stereo, 1961...25.00 - 50.00
LP, *Bobby Vee's Golden Greats*
   Liberty LRP-3245, mono, 1962...15.00 - 30.00
   Liberty LST-7245, stereo, 1962...20.00 - 40.00
   Liberty LM-51008, 1980s, reissue ....4.00 - 8.00
   United Artists LT-1008, 1980, reissue ....5.00 - 10.00

MVP:
LP, *Legendary Masters Series*, United Artists UA-LA025-G2 (2-record set),
1973, withdrawn before or shortly after release....................150.00 - 300.00

LP, *Walk Don't Run*

Dolton BLP 2003, mono, 1960, pale blue label with dolphins on
top..25.00 - 50.00
Dolton BLP 2003, mono, 1963, dark label, logo on left.............10.00 - 20.00
Dolton BST 8003, stereo, 1960, pale blue label with dolphins on
top..30.00 - 60.00
Dolton BST 8003, stereo, 1963, dark label, logo on left.............12.50 - 25.00
(Other versions exist and sell for less.)

45, Hawaii Five-O/Soul Breeze , Liberty 56068, 1968..........................4.00 - 8.00
45, Perfidia/No Trespassing, Dolton 28, 1960
    Record only..10.00 - 20.00
    Picture sleeve only..25.00 - 50.00
45, Walk — Don't Run/Home, Dolton 25, 1960 ....12.50 - 25.00
45, Walk — Don't Run/The McCoy, Dolton 25X, 1960....................10.00 - 20.00
45, Walk... Don't Run '64/The Cruel Sea, Dolton 96, 1964
    Record only..7.50 - 15.00
    Picture sleeve only ....15.00 - 30.00
LP, *Golden Greats by the Ventures*
    Liberty LRP-2053, mono, 1967..10.00 - 20.00
    Liberty LST-8053, stereo, 1967..10.00 - 20.00
    Liberty LTAO-8053, stereo, 1981, reissue, new prefix, gray label.....4.00 - 8.00
LP, *Play Guitar with the Ventures*
    Dolton BLP 16501, mono, 1965.......................................12.50 - 25.00
    Dolton BST 17501, stereo, 1965 ....15.00 - 30.00
LP, *The Ventures Play Telstar, The Lonely Bull*
    Dolton BLP 2019, mono, 1962...15.00 - 30.00
    Dolton BST 8019, stereo, 1962 ....20.00 - 40.00
    Liberty LN-10155, 1981, reissue.......................................4.00 - 8.00
LP, *The Ventures' Christmas Album*
    Dolton BLP-2038, mono, 1965...15.00 - 30.00
    Dolton BST-8038, stereo, 1965 ....10.00 - 20.00

MVP:
45, Walk-Don't Run/Home, Blue Horizon 101, 1960 (versions on other labels
    are much less) ....1,250.00 – 2,500.00

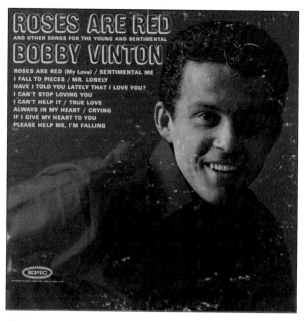

LP, *Roses Are Red*

    Epic LN 24020, mono, 1962..7.50 - 15.00

    Epic BN 26020, stereo, 1962...10.00 - 20.00

    Columbia Limited Edition LE 10139, 1970s, reissue ....5.00 - 10.00

45, Blue Velvet/Is There a Place (Where I Can Go), Epic 5-9614, 1963
Record only..6.00 - 12.00
Picture sleeve only..7.50 - 15.00
45, I Love How You Love Me/Little Barefoot Boy, Epic 5-10397, 1968
Record only..3.00 - 6.00
Picture sleeve only..5.00 - 10.00
45, Mr. Lonely/It's Better to Have Loved, Epic 5-9730, 1964
Record only..5.00 - 10.00
Picture sleeve only..6.00 - 12.00
45, My Melody of Love/I'll Be Loving You, ABC 12022, 1974
Black label..2.50 - 5.00
Multi-colored label..2.00 - 4.00
45, There! I've Said It Again/The Girl with the Bow in Her Hair, Epic 5-9638, 1963
Record only..6.00 - 12.00
Picture sleeve only ....7.50 - 15.00
LP, *Bobby Vinton's Greatest Hits*
Epic LN 24098, mono, 1964..6.00 - 12.00
Epic BN 26098, stereo, 1964...7.50 - 15.00
Epic PE 26098, stereo, dark blue label, reissue with new prefix .....4.00 - 8.00
LP, *There! I've Said It Again*
Epic LN 24081, mono, 1964..7.50 - 15.00
Epic BN 26081, stereo, 1964...10.00 - 20.00

MVP:
LP, *Blue On Blue*, Epic LN 24068, mono, 1963, white label promotional copy,
    blue vinyl (yellow label black vinyl copies are a lot less) ....75.00 - 150.00

LP, *Promises, Promises*, Scepter SPS-571, 1968 ....7.50 - 15.00

45, Anyone Who Had a Heart/The Love of a Boy, Scepter 1262,
    1963..6.00 - 12.00
45, Do You Know the Way to San Jose?/Let Me Be Lonely, Scepter 12216,
    1968..4.00 - 8.00
45, Don't Make Me Over/I Smiled Yesterday, Scepter 1239, 1962 ......6.00 - 12.00
45, Heartbreaker/I Can't See Anything But You, Arista 1015, 1982.......2.00 - 4.00
45, I Say a Little Prayer/(Theme from) Valley of the Dolls, Scepter 12203,
    1967..4.00 - 8.00
45, I'll Never Fall in Love Again/What the World Needs Now Is Love, Scepter
    12273, 1970...3.50 - 7.00
45, I'll Never Love This Way Again/In Your Eyes, Arista 0419, 1979 .....2.00 - 4.00
45, Message to Michael/Here Where There Is Love, Scepter 12133,
    1966..4.00 - 8.00
45, Walk On By/Any Old Time of Day, Scepter 1274, 1964 ....6.00 - 12.00
LP, *Dionne*
    Arista AB 4230, 1979, original ....5.00 - 10.00
    Arista AL 8295, 1985, reissue ....4.00 - 8.00
LP, *Dionne Warwick's Golden Hits, Part One*
    Scepter SPS-565, stereo, 1967..7.50 - 15.00
    Scepter SRM-565, mono, 1967...10.00 - 20.00
LP, *Dionne Warwick's Golden Hits, Part 2*, Scepter SPS-577,
    1969..7.50 - 15.00
LP, *Here Where There Is Love*
    Scepter SPS-555, stereo, 1966..7.50 - 15.00
    Scepter SRM-555, mono, 1966..6.00 - 12.00

MVP:
LP, *Valley of the Dolls*, Scepter SRM-568, mono, 1968. may only exist as a white
    label promotional copy (stereo version is much less) ....25.00 - 50.00

LP, *Who's Next*

    Decca DL 79182, 1971, original..12.50 - 25.00

    MCA 2023, 1973, reissue, black label with rainbow....................6.00 - 12.00

    MCA 3024, 1977, reissue, tan label..5.00 - 10.00

    MCA 5220, 1979, reissue, blue label with rainbow ....4.00 - 8.00

    MCA 11164, 1995, reissue, "Heavy Vinyl" logo, gatefold cover ...12.50 - 25.00

45, Behind Blue Eyes/My Wife, Decca 32888, 1971 ....5.00 - 10.00

45, I Can See for Miles/Mary-Anne with the Shaky Hands, Decca 32206, 1967..10.00 - 20.00

45, My Generation/Out in the Street (You're Going to Know Me), Decca 31877, 1965..15.00 - 30.00

45, Pinball Wizard/Dogs Part Two, Decca 32465, 1969

    Record only...5.00 - 10.00

    Picture sleeve only ....10.00 - 20.00

45, Squeeze Box/Success Story, MCA 40475, 1975

    Record only...2.50 - 5.00

    Picture sleeve only (promotional only) ....15.00 - 30.00

LP, *Live at Leeds*

    Decca DL 79175, 1970, original, in folder-style gatefold with poster and many inserts that appear to be authentic documents, such as contracts, song lyrics, etc., but all are reproductions ....20.00 - 40.00

    MCA 1577, 1988, late reissue...4.00 - 8.00

    MCA 2022, 1973, first reissue, in regular cover ....6.00 - 12.00

    MCA 3023, 1977, tan label ....5.00 - 10.00

    MCA 37000, 1979, blue label with rainbow..................................4.00 - 8.00

LP, *Tommy*

    Decca DXSW 7205 (2-record set), 1969, with booklet ....20.00 - 40.00

    MCA 2-10005 (2-record set), 1973, reissue, black labels with rainbow..7.50 - 15.00

    MCA 2-10005 (2-record set), 1978, reissue, tan labels ....6.00 - 12.00

    MCA 2-10005 (2-record set), 1980, reissue, blue labels with rainbow..5.00 - 10.00

MVP:

45, Young Man (Blues)/Substitute, Decca 32737, 1970, picture sleeve only (stock copy record goes for 125.00 - 250.00; promotional copy record goes for 75.00 – 150.00) ....250.00 - 500.00

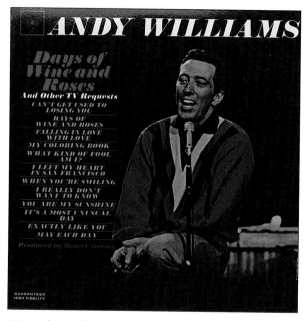

LP, *Days of Wine and Roses*

 Columbia CL 2015, mono, 1963, "Guaranteed High Fidelity" on
label ....6.00 - 12.00

 Columbia CS 8815, stereo, 1963, "360 Sound Stereo" in black on
label ....7.50 - 15.00

45, Battle Hymn of the Republic/Ave Maria, Columbia 4-44650, 1968
    Record only...2.50 - 5.00
    Picture sleeve only ....3.00 - 6.00
45, Butterfly/It Doesn't Take Very Long, Cadence 1308, 1957 ....6.00 - 12.00
45, Can't Get Used to Losing You/Days of Wine and Roses, Columbia 4-42674, 1963
    Record only...4.00 - 8.00
    Picture sleeve only...5.00 - 10.00
45, Canadian Sunset/High Upon a Mountain, Cadence 1297, 1956 ....6.00 - 12.00
45, I Like Your Kind of Love/Stop Teasin' Me, Cadence 1323, 1957 ...6.00 - 12.00
45, Lonely Street/Summer Love, Cadence 1370, 1959 ....5.00 - 10.00
45, (Where Do I Begin) Love Story/Something, Columbia 4-45317, 1971
    ....2.00 - 4.00
LP, *The Andy Williams Christmas Album*
    Columbia CL 2087, mono, 1963, red label with "Guaranteed High Fidelity"
    at bottom (other label versions are less) ....6.00 - 12.00
    Columbia CS 8887, stereo, 1963, red label with "360 Sound Stereo" in black at
    bottom (other label versions are less) ....6.00 - 12.00
LP, *Dear Heart*
    Columbia CL 2338, mono, 1965................................6.00 - 12.00
    Columbia CS 9138, stereo, 1965, red label with "360 Sound Stereo"
    at bottom (orange label is less) ....7.50 - 15.00
LP, *Moon River and Other Great Movie Themes*
    Columbia CL 1809, mono, 1962, black and red label with six white "eye"
    logos (other label versions are less).........................6.00 - 12.00
    Columbia CS 8609, stereo, 1962, black and red label with six white "eye"
    logos (other label versions are less) ....7.50 - 15.00

MVP:
LP, *Two Time Winners,* Cadence CLP 25026, stereo, 1959, red vinyl record
    (black vinyl is 15.00-30.00) ....40.00 - 80.00

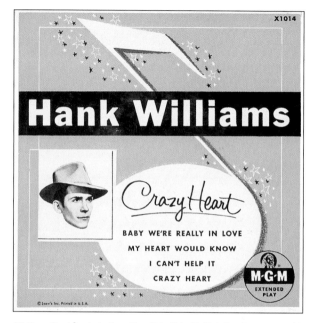

EP, *Crazy Heart* [contents: Crazy Heart/Baby We're Really in Love//My Heart Would
Know/I Can't Help It (If I'm Still in Love with You)]

MGM X-1014, 1953, record only, yellow label.............................40.00 - 80.00

MGM X-1014, 1960, record only, black label ....10.00 - 20.00

MGM X-1014, 1953, cardboard picture cover only ....10.00 - 20.00

45, Cold, Cold Heart/Dear John, MGM K10904, 1951 (78 rpms go for less)
....15.00 - 30.00

45, Hey, Good Lookin'/My Heart Would Know, MGM K11000, 1951
(78 rpms go for less) ....15.00 - 30.00

45, I Can't Help It (If I'm Still in Love with You)/Howlin' at the Moon,
MGM K10961, 1951 (78 rpms go for less)........................15.00 - 30.00

45, I'll Never Get Out of This World Alive/I Could Never Be Ashamed,
MGM K11366, 1952 (78 rpms go for less) ....15.00 - 30.00

45, Jambalaya (On the Bayou)/Window Shopping, MGM K11283, 1952 (78 rpms
go for less) ....15.00 - 30.00

45, Kaw-Liga/Your Cheatin' Heart, MGM K11416, 1953 (78 rpms go for
less) ....15.00 - 30.00

45, Lovesick Blues/Never Again (Will I Knock on Your Door)
MGM 8010, 1949, original 45 rpm issue.............................35.00 - 70.00
MGM K10352, 1950, reissue has original 45 rpm number in parentheses
under this number (78 rpms go for less) ....25.00 - 50.00

LP, *Memorial Album*
MGM E-202, mono, 1953, 10-inch LP...................................200.00 - 400.00
MGM E-3272, mono, 1955, yellow label ....50.00 - 100.00
MGM E-3272, mono, 1960, black label......................................20.00 - 40.00
MGM E-3272, mono, 1968, blue and gold label........................10.00 - 20.00

LP, *The Very Best of Hank Williams*
MGM E-4168 , mono, 1963..15.00 - 30.00
MGM SE-4168, rechanneled stereo, 1963, black label ....7.50 - 15.00
MGM SE-4168, rechanneled stereo, 1968, blue and gold label .....6.00 - 12.00

MVP:
LP, *Hank Williams Sings*, MGM E-107, mono, 1952, 10-inch LP (other Hank
Williams 10-inch LPs with an "E" prefix and a three-digit number are in the
same range) ....200.00 - 400.00

LP, *Body and Soul*

Brunswick BL 54105, mono, 1962, all-black label......................25.00 - 50.00

Brunswick BL 54105, mono, 1964, black label with color

bars..10.00 - 20.00

Brunswick BL 754105, stereo, 1962, all-black label ....40.00 - 80.00

Brunswick BL 754105, stereo, 1964, black label with color

bars..12.50 - 25.00

45, Baby Workout/I'm Going Crazy, Brunswick 55239, 1963, orange
label ....10.00 - 20.00
45, Lonely Teardrops/In the Blue of Evening, Brunswick 9-55105, 1958,
maroon label ....15.00 - 30.00
45, Night/Doggin' Around
Brunswick 55166, 1960, maroon label ....20.00 - 40.00
Brunswick 55166, 1960, orange label..7.50 - 15.00
Brunswick 55166, 1960, picture sleeve only................................25.00 - 50.00
Brunswick 55166, late 1960s, black label, color-bar arrow ....5.00 - 10.00
45, Reet Petite (The Finest Girl You Ever Want to Meet)/By the Light of the
Silvery Moon, Brunswick 9-55024, 1957, maroon label..............15.00 - 30.00
45, (Your Love Keeps Lifting Me) Higher and Higher/I'm the One to Do It,
Brunswick 55336, 1967 ....5.00 - 10.00
LP, *Baby Workout*
Brunswick BL 54110, mono, 1963, all-black label....................25.00 - 50.00
Brunswick BL 54110, mono, 1963, black label with color
bars ....10.00 - 20.00
Brunswick BL 754110, stereo, 1963, all-black label ....40.00 - 80.00
Brunswick BL 754110, stereo, 1963, black label with color
bars ....12.50 - 25.00
LP, *Higher and Higher*
Brunswick BL 54130, mono, 1967..12.50 - 25.00
Brunswick BL 754130 , stereo, 1967 ....15.00 - 30.00
LP, *The Jackie Wilson Story* Epic EG 38623 (2-record set), 1983 ...10.00 - 20.00

MVP:
LP, *Jackie Sings the Blues*, Brunswick BL 754055, stereo, 1960, all-black label
(other versions are less) ....100.00 - 200.00

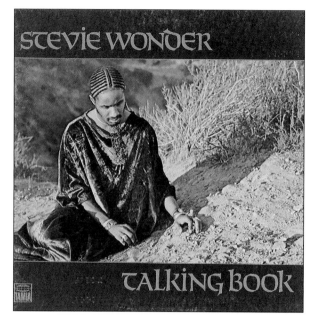

LP, *Talking Book*
    Tamla T 319L, 1972, original with note in braille on cover...........7.50 - 15.00
    Tamla T 319L, 1973, no braille note on cover...............................5.00 - 10.00

45, Boogie On Reggae Woman/Seems So Long, Tamla 54254, 1974
    With incorrect spelling of A-side ("Raggae") ....3.00 - 6.00
    With correct spelling of A-side..2.50 - 5.00
45, Fingertips — Pt. 2/Fingertips — Pt. 1, Tamla 54080, 1963
    Record only..10.00 - 20.00
    Picture sleeve only..25.00 - 50.00
45, I Wish/You and I, Tamla 54274, 1976..2.50 - 5.00
45, My Cherie Amour/ I Don't Know Why, Tamla 54180, 1969, original
    edition ....5.00 - 10.00
45, My Cherie Amour/Don't Know Why I Love You, Tamla 54180, 1969,
    second edition ....4.00 - 8.00
45, Superstition/You've Got It Bad Girl, Tamla 54226, 1972................2.50 - 5.00
45, You Are the Sunshine of My Life/Tuesday Heartbreak, Tamla 54232,
    1973..2.50 - 5.00
45, Yester-Me, Yester-You, Yesterday/I'd Be a Fool Right Now, Tamla 54188,
    1969..4.00 - 8.00
LP, *Fulfillingness' First Finale*, Tamla T6-332S1, 1974....................7.50 - 15.00
LP, *Innervisions*, Tamla T 326L, 1973...7.50 - 15.00
LP, *Signed Sealed and Delivered*
    Motown M5-176V1, 1981, reissue..6.00 - 12.00
    Tamla TS 304, 1970, original ....10.00 - 20.00
LP, *Songs in the Key of Life*, Tamla T13-340C2 (2-record set),1976, with
    booklet and bonus 7-inch EP ....10.00 - 20.00

MVP:
LP, *Tribute to Uncle Ray*, Tamla T 232, mono only, 1962, twin "globes" label
    (other versions are less) ....75.00 - 150.00

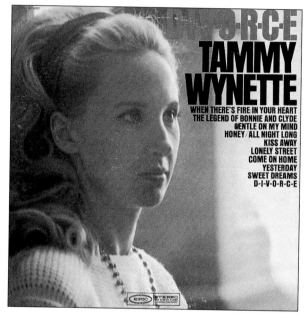

LP, *D-I-V-O-R-C-E*

    Epic LN 24392, mono, 1968, yellow label stock copy ....25.00 - 50.00

    Epic BN 26392, stereo, 1968, yellow label ....10.00 - 20.00

Tammy Wynette

45, Apartment No. 9/I'm Not Mine to Give, Epic 5-10095, 1966 ....5.00 - 10.00
45, Bedtime Story/Reach Out Your Hand, Epic 5-10818, 1971.............3.00 - 6.00
45, D-I-V-O-R-C-E/Don't Make It Now, Epic 5-10315, 1968 ....4.00 - 8.00
45, He Loves Me All the Way/One Last Night Together, Epic 5-10612,
    1970..3.00 - 6.00
45, Stand By Your Man/I Stayed Long Enough, Epic 5-10398, 1968...5.00 - 10.00
45, 'Til I Can Make It on My Own/Love Is Something Good for Everybody,
    Epic 8-50196, 1976..2.50 - 5.00
45, Your Good Girl's Gonna Go Bad/Send Me No Roses, Epic 5-10134,
    1967..4.00 - 8.00
LP, *Anniversary: 20 Years of Hits*, Epic EG 40625 (2-record set),
    1987..7.50 - 15.00
LP, *Christmas with Tammy*, Epic E 30343, 1970, yellow label........10.00 - 20.00
LP, *Tammy's Greatest Hits*
    Epic BN 26486, 1969, yellow label..10.00 - 20.00
    Epic BN 26486, 1970s, orange label ....6.00 - 12.00
    Epic PE 26486, 1980s, dark blue label ....4.00 - 8.00
LP, *Tammy's Greatest Hits, Volume II*
    Epic E 30733, 1971, yellow label ....10.00 - 20.00
    Epic E 30733, 1970s, orange label ....6.00 - 12.00
    Epic PE 30733, 198?, dark blue label...4.00 - 8.00

MVP:
LP, *D-I-V-O-R-C-E* , Epic LN 24392, mono, 1968, yellow label stock copy (stereo
    is less) ....25.00 - 50.00

———————   ———————

LP, *Fragile*

    Atlantic SD 7211, 1972...6.00 - 12.00

    Atlantic SD 19132, 1977, reissue...4.00 - 8.00

45, America/Total Mass Retain, Atlantic 2899, 1972..........................2.50 - 5.00
45, Owner of a Lonely Heart/Our Song, Atco 7-99817, 1983
    Record only..1.50 - 3.00
    Picture sleeve only...1.50 - 3.00
45, Roundabout/Long Distance Runaround, Atlantic 2854, 1972 ....2.50 - 5.00
45, Your Move/Clap, Atlantic 2819, 1971 ....2.50 - 5.00
LP, Close to the Edge
    Atlantic 7244, mono, 1972, "DJ Copy Monaural" sticker on cover, white
    label, banded for airplay ....25.00 - 50.00
    Atlantic SD 7244, 1972..6.00 - 12.00
    Atlantic SD 19133,1977, reissue......................................4.00 - 8.00
    Mobile Fidelity 1-077, 1982, "Original Master Recording" at top of
    cover ....30.00 - 60.00
LP, *90125*, Atco 90125, 1984 ....4.00 - 8.00
LP, *The Yes Album*
    Atlantic 8283, mono, 1971, "DJ Copy Monaural" sticker on cover, white
    label ....20.00 - 40.00
    Atlantic SD 8283, 1971..6.00 - 12.00
    Atlantic SD 19131, 1977, reissue......................................4.00 - 8.00
    Rhino R1 73788, 2003, new vinyl issue..........................7.50 - 15.00
LP, *Yessongs*, Atlantic SD 3-100 (3-record set), 1973 ....9.00 - 18.00

MVP:
45, Roundabout (mono/stereo), Atlantic 2854, 1972, promotional only, yellow
    vinyl (black vinyl versions are much less) ....50.00 - 100.00

LP, *Time Fades Away*

    Reprise M 2151, mono, 1973, special mono pressing for radio stations
only ....50.00 - 100.00
Reprise MS 2151, stereo, 1973, with cardboard inner sleeve, withdrawn after
the earliest pressing ....100.00 - 200.00
Reprise MS 2151, stereo, 1973, with paper insert........................5.00 - 10.00

45, Cinnamon Girl/Sugar Mountain, Reprise 0911, 1970 .... 2.50 - 5.00
45, Comes a Time/Motorcycle Mama, Reprise 1395, 1978
    Record only .... 2.00 - 4.00
    Picture sleeve only .... 2.00 - 4.00
45, Heart of Gold/Sugar Mountain, Reprise 1065, 1971
    Without reference to "Harvest" LP on label .... 2.00 - 4.00
    With reference to "Harvest" LP on label .... 2.50 - 5.00
45, Only Love Can Break Your Heart/Birds, Reprise 0958, 1970 .... 2.50 - 5.00
LP, *Everybody Knows This Is Nowhere*
    Reprise MSK 2282, 1978, reissue with new number, orange
    label .... 4.00 - 8.00
    Reprise RS 6349, 1969, original, two-tone orange label with "r:"
    and "W7" logos .... 15.00 - 30.00
    Reprise RS 6349, 1970, one-color orange label with only "r:" ...... 7.50 - 15.00
LP, *Harvest*
    Nautilus NR-44, 1982, "Super Disc" on cover .... 75.00 - 150.00
    Reprise MS 2032, 1972, first pressings have textured cover and lyric
    insert .... 7.50 - 15.00
    Reprise MS 2032, 1972, with smooth cover and no insert .... 5.00 - 10.00
    Reprise MSK 2277, 1978, reissue with new number, orange
    label .... 4.00 - 8.00
LP, *Rust Never Sleeps*, Reprise HS 2295, 1979 .... 5.00 - 10.00
LP, *Sleeps with Angels*, Reprise 45749 (2-record set), 1994 .... 7.50 - 15.00

MVP:
LP, *Give to the Wind* , Reprise MSK 2266, 1978, test pressing with plain white
    jacket with inserts and *stock copy label* (not a white label); when this album
    was issued for real, it was called *Comes a Time* .... 500.00 – 1,000.00

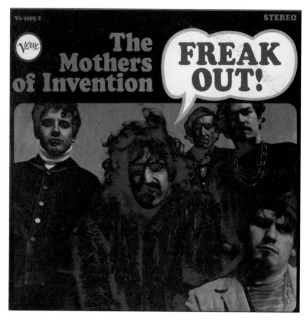

LP, *Freak Out!* (by The Mothers of Invention)

Verve V-5005-2 (2-record set), mono, 1966, with blurb on inside gatefold on how to get a map of "freak-out hot spots" in L.A....................100.00 - 200.00

Verve V6-5005-2 (2-record set), stereo, 1966, with blurb on inside gatefold on how to get a map of "freak-out hot spots" in L.A........................40.00 - 80.00

(Versions without the "freak-out hot spots" blurb get about 75 percent of the above prices.)

45, Dancin' Fool/Baby Snakes, Zappa Z-10, 1979 ....5.00 - 10.00
45, Don't Eat the Yellow Snow/Cosmic Debris, DiscReet 1312,
    1974..7.50 - 15.00
45, Valley Girl/You Are What You Is, Barking Pumpkin WS9-02972, 1982,
    with Moon Zappa
    Record only..1.50 - 3.00
    Picture sleeve only..3.50 - 7.00
LP, *Absolutely Free*
    Verve V-5013, mono, 1967 ....60.00 - 120.00
    Verve V6-5013, stereo, 1967 ....30.00 - 60.00
LP, *Apostrophe (')*
    DiscReet DS 2175, 1974, original..7.50 - 15.00
    DiscReet DS4 2175, 1974, quadraphonic....................................17.50 - 35.00
    DiscReet DSK 2289, 1977, reissue..6.00 - 12.00
LP, *Frank Zappa Meets the Mothers of Prevention*, Barking Pumpkin
    ST-74203, 1985...5.00 - 10.00
LP, *Sheik Yerbouti*, Zappa SRZ-2-1501 (2-record set), 1979...........10.00 - 20.00
LP, *Ship Arriving Too Late to Save a Drowning Witch*, Barking Pumpkin
    FW 38066, 1982..6.00 - 12.00
LP, *Weasels Ripped My Flesh*
    Bizarre MS-2028, 1970, blue label original................................12.50 - 25.00
    Bizarre MS-2028, 1973, reissue with brown Reprise label............7.50 - 15.00
LP, *Zoot Allures*, Warner Bros. BS 2970, 1976 ....7.50 - 15.00

MVP:
LP, *Lather*, Columbia (no #) (4-record set), 1977, test pressing only (not to be
    confused with the later Japanese edition or many bootlegs)....375.00 - 750.00

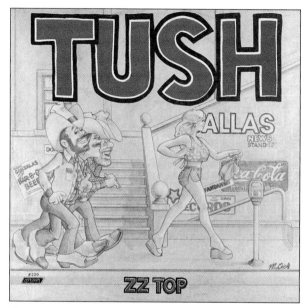

45, Tush/Blue Jean Blues, London 5N-220, 1975
  Record only...4.00 - 8.00
  Picture sleeve only..6.00 - 12.00

45, *Gimme All Your Lovin/If I Could Only Flag Her Down*, Warner Bros.
7-29693, 1983
Record only...2.00 - 4.00
Picture sleeve only ....2.50 - 5.00
45, *La Grange/Just Got Paid*, London 45-203, 1973................................4.00 - 8.00
45, *Legs/Bad Girl*, Warner Bros. 7-29272, 1984
Record only...2.00 - 4.00
Picture sleeve only...2.00 - 4.00
45, *Sharp Dressed Man/I Got the Six*, Warner Bros. 7-29576, 1983.....2.00 - 4.00
LP, *Afterburner*, Warner Bros. 25342, 1985...4.00 - 8.00
LP, *Eliminator*, Warner Bros. 23774, 1983...4.00 - 8.00
LP, *Fandango!*
London PS 656, 1975, original..6.00 - 12.00
Warner Bros. BSK 3271, 1979, reissue..4.00 - 8.00
LP, *Recycler*, Warner Bros. 26265, 1990...7.50 - 15.00
LP, *Rio Grande Mud*
London PS 612, 1972, original..6.00 - 12.00
Warner Bros. BSK 3269, 1979, reissue..4.00 - 8.00
LP, *Tres Hombres*
London XPS 631, 1973, original ....6.00 - 12.00
Warner Bros. BSK 3270, 1979, reissue..4.00 - 8.00

MVP:
45, *Salt Lick/Miller's Farm*, Scat 500, 1969 (reissue on London goes for a lot
less) ....100.00 - 200.00

Badfinger

LP, *Ass,* Apple SW-3411, 1973..10.00 – 20.00

LP, *Different Light*
    Columbia BFC 40039, 1986, original with short bar code ....6.00 – 12.00
    Columbia FC 40039, 1986, reissue with longer bar code ....4.00 – 8.00

LP, *Songs, Pictures and Stories of the Fabulous Beatles*
  Vee Jay LP 1092, mono, labels say "Introducing the Beatles,"
  1964..250.00 - 500.00
  Vee Jay VJS 1092, stereo, labels say "Introducing the Beatles,"
  1964...1,600.00–2,400.00
NOTE: Any non-gatefold copy or any copy called "Songs and Pictures of the
  Fabulous Beatles" is a counterfeit.

LP, *Let It Be*
  Apple AR-34001, 1970, red Apple label; originals have "Bell Sound" stamped
  in trail-off area, counterfeits do not..12.50 - 25.00
  Capitol SW-11922, 1979, purple label, large Capitol logo; with poster and
  custom innersleeve...7.50 - 15.00

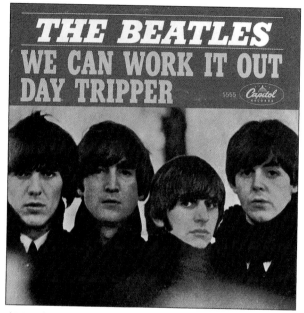

45, Capitol 5555, We Can Work It Out/Day Tripper
  Record only, 1965, original, orange and yellow swirl label without "A
  Subsidiary of Capitol Industries" in perimeter label print ....15.00 - 30.00
  Picture sleeve only ....30.00 - 60.00

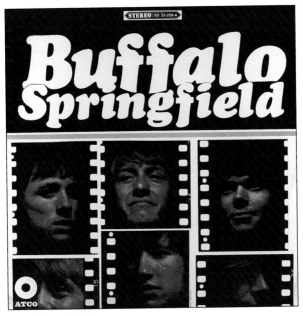

LP, *Buffalo Springfield*

    Atco 33-200 A, mono, 1967, revised, with "For What It's
Worth"..12.50 – 25.00

    Atco SD 33-200 A, stereo, 1967, revised, with "For What It's Worth,"
purple and brown label...12.50 – 25.00

    (Other label versions of SD 33-200A go for less.)

LP, *Johnny Burnette*
  Liberty LRP-3183, mono, 1961...20.00 - 40.00
  Liberty LST-7183, stereo, 1961...30.00 - 60.00

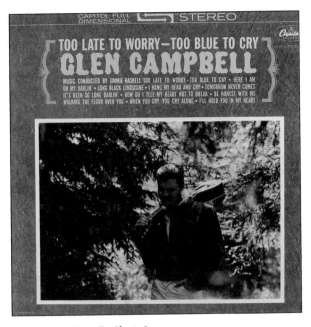

LP, *Too Late to Worry – Too Blue to Cry*
    Capitol ST 1881, stereo, 1963 ....12.50 – 25.00
    Capitol T 1881, mono, 1963...10.00 – 20.00

LP, *Boogie with Canned Heat*

    Liberty LRP-3541, mono, 1968, stock copy in stereo cover with "Audition
Mono LP Not for Sale" sticker ....20.00 – 40.00
    Liberty LST-7541, stereo, 1968 ....10.00 – 20.00
    Liberty LN-10105, 1981, reissue ....4.00 – 8.00
    United Artists LM-1015, 1980, reissue ....6.00 – 12.00

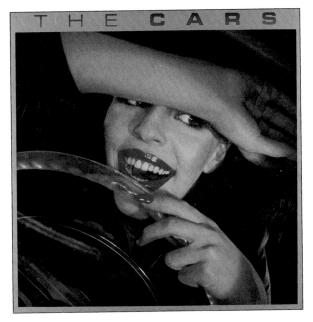

LP, *The Cars*
Elektra 6E-135, 1978, red label .... 5.00 – 10.00
Nautilus NR-14, 1981, "Super Disc" on cover .... 15.00 – 30.00

45, Should I Stay or Should I Go/Cool Confusion, Epic 34-03547, 1983, reissue
   Record only..2.00 – 4.00
   Picture sleeve only..2.00 – 4.00

LP, *The Best of the Cowsills*, MGM SE-4597, 1968............................7.50 – 15.00

LP, *Red Rubber Ball*

    Columbia CL 2544, mono, 1966...10.00 – 20.00

    Columbia CS 9344, stereo, 1966 ....15.00 – 30.00

LP, *James Darren (Album No. 1)*, Colpix CP-406, mono, 1960
   Black vinyl..20.00 – 40.00
   Green vinyl ....75.00 – 150.00

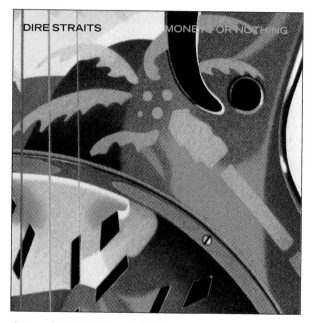

45, Money for Nothing/Love Over Gold (Live), Warner Bros. 7-28950, 1985
   Record only..2.00 – 4.00
   Picture sleeve only..2.00 – 4.00

LP, *Home Free*

    Columbia KC 31751, 1972, original..6.00 – 12.00

    Columbia PC 31751, 1970s, reissue with new prefix, no bar code

    ....4.00 – 8.00

    Columbia PC 31751, 1980s, reissue, with bar code ....3.00 – 6.00

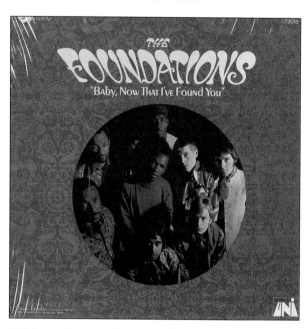

LP, *Baby, Now That I've Found You*, Uni 73016, 1968 ....15.00 – 30.00

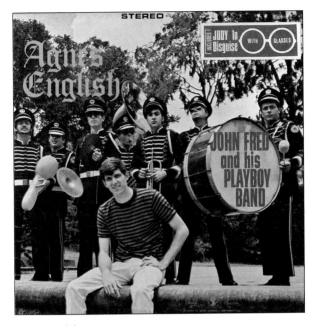

LP, *Agnes English*
> Paula LP-2197, mono, 1967...12.50 – 25.00
> Paula LPS-2197, stereo, 1967...10.00 – 20.00

LP, *Do the Freddie*

    Mercury MG 21026, mono, 1965 ....10.00 – 20.00
    Mercury SR 61026, stereo, 1965 ....12.50 – 25.00

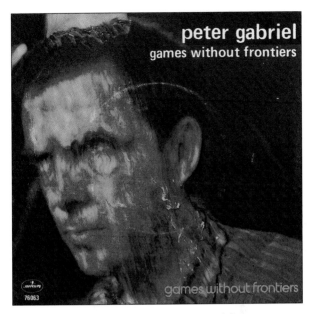

45, Games Without Frontiers/Lead a Normal Life, Mercury 76063, 1980
  Record only..2.00 – 4.00
  Picture sleeve only..6.00 – 12.00

45, Centerfold/Rage in the Cage, EMI America B-8102, 1981

Record only, gray label ....2.50 – 5.00

Record only, pink label ....1.50 – 3.00

Picture sleeve only...5.00 – 10.00

LP, *I'll Cry If I Want To*

    Mercury MG 20805, mono, 1963, with no large blurb advertising "It's My
Party" ....15.00 – 30.00

    Mercury SR 60805, stereo, 1963, with no large blurb advertising
"It's My Party" ....20.00 – 40.00

    (Other versions sell for less.)

LP. *Johnny Horton's Greatest Hits* (add 5.00 – 10.00 if bonus photo is enclosed)
    Columbia CL 1596, mono, 1961, red and black label with six white "eye"
    logos ....12.50 – 25.00
    Columbia CS 8396, stereo, 1961, red and black label with six white "eye"
    logos ....15.00 – 30.00
    (Other label variations go for less.)

LP, *Joan Jett,* Blackheart JJ 707, 1980, original ....25.00 – 50.00

LP, Robert Johnson – The Complete Recordings, Columbia C3 46222
(3-record set), 1990 ....25.00 – 50.00
NOTE: Any 78 rpm record on Vocalion, Perfect, Melotone or Conqueror by
Robert Johnson, in almost any condition, is worth over $1,000.00!

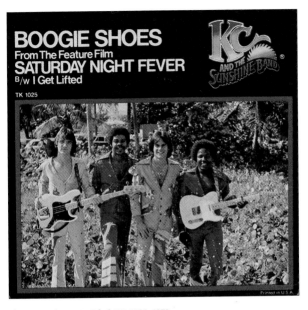

45, Boogie Shoes/I Get Lifted, T.K. 1025, 1978
  Record only..2.00 – 4.00
  Picture sleeve only..4.00 – 8.00

45, Good Girls Don't/Frustrated, Capitol 4771, 1979
  Record only..2.00 – 4.00
  Picture sleeve only ....3.00 – 6.00

LP, *To Sir With Love*
    Epic LN 24339, mono, 1967...12.50 – 25.00
    Epic BN 26339, stereo, 1967...15.00 – 30.00

LP, *Blues from Laurel Canyon*, London PS 545, 1969......................7.50 – 15.00

Don McLean

45, Vincent/Castles in the Air, United Artists 50887, 1972

    Record only..2.50 – 5.00

    Picture sleeve only...5.00 – 10.00

LP, The First Family, Cadence CLP 3060, 1962 ....5.00 – 10.00

LP, *Hair of the Dog*
A&M SP-3225, 1984, reissue...4.00 – 8.00
A&M SP-4511, 1975, original...5.00 – 10.00

45, Don't Hang Up/The Conservative, Cameo 231, 1962
  Record only...10.00 – 20.00
  Picture sleeve only..20.00 – 40.00

45, All Shook Up/That's When Your Heartaches Begin
    RCA Victor 47-6870, 1957, with or without horizontal line on label
    ....15.00 - 30.00
    RCA Victor 47-6870, 1957, picture sleeve only...........................45.00 - 90.00

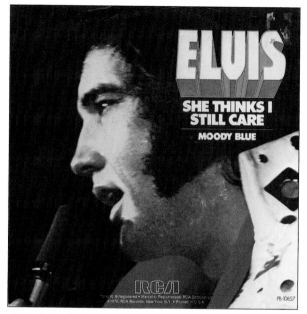

45, Moody Blue/She Thinks I Still Care

RCA PB-10857, 1976, black label...2.50 - 5.00

RCA PB-10857, 1976, picture sleeve only....................................5.00 - 10.00

RCA JB-10857, 1976, cream label, promotional, black vinyl .....10.00 – 20.00

RCA JB-10857, 1976, cream label, promotional, various colored vinyl
editions (not black) ....500.00 – 1,000.00

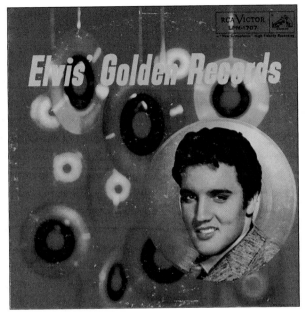

LP, *Elvis' Golden Records*

RCA Victor LPM-1707, mono, 1958, title on cover in light blue letters;
no song titles listed on front cover ....125.00 - 250.00

RCA Victor LPM-1707, mono, 1958, title on cover in light blue letters;
no song titles listed on front cover; "RE" on back cover ....75.00 - 150.00

NOTE: Later versions with different label designs, prefixes and numbers go for less.

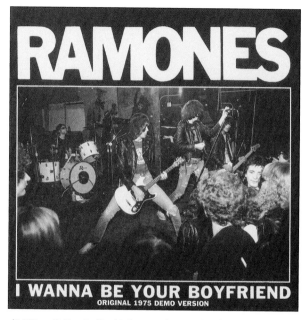

45, I Wanna Be Your Boyfriend/Judy Is a Punk, Norton 45-065, 1997,
  1975 demo versions
   Record only..1.00 – 2.00
   Picture sleeve only..1.00 – 2.00

45, Groovin'/Sueno, Atlantic 2401, 1967
  Record only..4.00 – 8.00
  Picture sleeve only...10.00 – 20.00

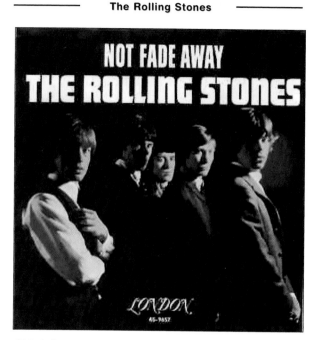

45, Not Fade Away/I Wanna Be Your Man, London 9657, 1964
  Record only; white, purple and blue label..................................20.00 - 40.00
  Record only; blue swirl label...4.00 - 8.00
  Picture sleeve only ....300.00 - 450.00

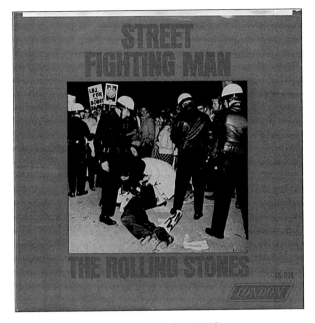

45, Street Fighting Man/No Expectations, London 909, 1968
    Record only ....10.00 - 20.00
    Picture sleeve only..8,000.00 – 10,000.00

45, Pretty Vacant/Sub-Mission

Record only, regular copy ....10.00 – 20.00

Record only, promotional copy with "Pretty Vacant" in stereo on one side,
mono on the other ....5.00 – 10.00

Picture sleeve only...5.00 – 10.00

45, Like to Get to Know You/Three Ways from Tomorrow, Mercury 72795, 1968
  Record only, orange and tan swirl label ....4.00 – 8.00
  Record only, red label, whiite "Mercury" in all capital letters at top
  ....5.00 – 10.00
  Picture sleeve only...5.00 – 10.00

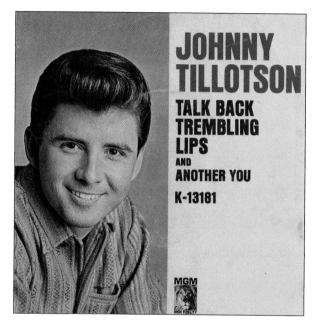

45, Talk Back Trembling Lips/Another You, MGM K13181, 1963
    Record only..6.00 – 12.00
    Picture sleeve only...10.00 – 20.00

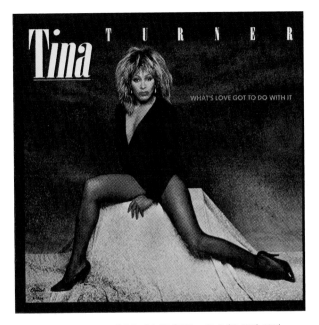

45, What's Love Got to Do with It/Rock 'n' Roll Widow, Capitol B-5354, 1984
  Record only...1.50 – 3.00
  Picture sleeve only..2.00 – 4.00

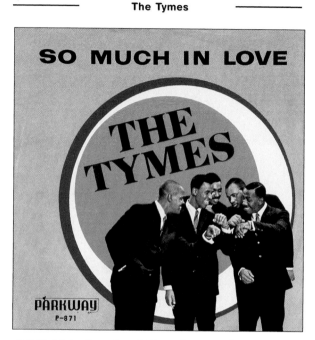

45, So Much in Love/Roscoe James McClain, Parkway 871, 1963
Record only, with title listed as "So in Love" ....12.50 – 25.00
Record only, with title listed as "So Much in Love".......................7.50 – 15.00
Picture sleeve only...15.00 – 30.00

LP, *The Magician's Birthday*
    Mercury SRM-1-652, 1972, red label..5.00 – 10.00
    Mercury SRM-1-652, 1974, Chicago skyline label.........................4.00 – 8.00

LP, Cruisin', Casablanca NBLP-7118, 1978 ....5.00 – 10.00

LP, *Journey to the Centre of the Earth*

   A&M SP-3156, 1980s, reissue ....4.00 – 8.00
   A&M SP-3621, 1974 ....6.00 – 12.00
   A&M QU-53621, 1974, quadraphonic ....12.50 – 25.00

LP, *Billy Ward and His Dominoes*

    Federal 295-94, mono, 10-inch LP, 1955 ....9,500.00 – 13,000.00

    Federal 548, mono, 12-inch LP, 1958..................................750.00 – 1,500.00

45, Tell Her No/Leave Me Be, Parrot 9723, 1965
  Record only...7.50 – 15.00
  Picture sleeve only...15.00 – 30.00